THE BOOK OF MONEY

THE BOOK OF MONEY

OK OF
NEY

Edited by
Klaus Heidensohn
with a foreword by
Harold Lever

McGraw-Hill Book Company
New York   St Louis   San Francisco
Toronto

Consultant Editor
Klaus Heidensohn

Senior Contributing Editors
Richard Jackman
Nicos Zafiris

Contributing Editors
Brian Morgan
Vicky Allsop
Brian Kettel
Sami Daniel
Ted Hyatt
Andrew Richardson
Allan Budd

A QED BOOK
© Copyright 1978 QED Limited.
All rights reserved. No part of this publication may
be reproduced, stored in a retrieval system, or
transmitted, in any form or by any means,
electronic, mechanical, photocopying, recording, or
otherwise, without the prior written permission of
the publisher.

Library of Congress Cataloging in Publication Data
Main entry under title:

The Book of money.

Includes index.
1. Money.   I. Heidensohn, Klaus.
HG255.B53 1979   332.4   79-3
ISBN 0-07-027862-8

Published in the United States by McGraw-Hill
Book Company, 1979

Colour origination in
Italy by Starf Photolito SRL., Rome
Printed in Hong Kong by Lee Fung Asco Ltd.

This book was designed and produced by
QED
32 Kingly Court, London W1

Project Director Edward Kinsey

Designer David Mallott

Illustrators Elaine Keenan Edwina Keene
Abdul Aziz Khan Martin Woodford David Staples
Nicholas Dakin

Editorial Director Michael Jackson

Art Director Alastair Campbell

Editorial David MacFadyen Jeremy Harwood
David Reynolds

Contributing Photographers and Artists Roger Pring
Walter Rawlings Jon Wyand Sally Launder
Nigel Osborne   Geoff Hunt

Editorial and Picture Research Maggie Colbeck
Pamela George Sarina Turner Anne-Marie Ehrlich

Paste-up Jean Kelly

Devised by Laurence Orbach

QED would like to thank the many individuals and organisations who have helped in the preparation of this book. Invaluable assistance was given by: Linda Edgerly of Chase Manhattan Bank Archives, New York; B.S. Hone of the Bank of England Information Division; Susan Watters of The World Bank, Washington DC; C.Craet of Samuel Montagu and Co.; Peter McGregor of the Anglo German Foundation for the Study of Industrial Society, London; P.F.P. Lodge, National Westminster Bank, Chelsea; Robin Pringle, The Banker magazine, London; M.C. Moore of UML Ltd., Port Sunlight, England; Alan Jeaps of the BBC Television Centre, London; The Kirkcaldy Museum, Scotland; James King of the Information Office, United Nations, London; For their help and expert information, thanks are due to: The International Monetary Fund, Washington DC; The Bank Education Service, London; The Tennessee Valley Authority, Knoxville, USA; BankAmerica Corporation; General Motors; Caisse Nationale de Agricole; Exxon Oil USA; Citicorp; Ford Motors; Mexican Embassy, London; Deutsche Bank, Frankfurt; Banque Nationale de Paris; Royal Dutch/Shell group; IBM; Ministere de Finance, Paris; Iranian Embassy, London; Banco do Brasil. The Index was prepared by Richard Kennedy and Bruce Leigh

Other invaluable assistance was given by: Geoff Whitehead; Mark van der Weyer; David Hardy; Moira Clinch; Robert Morley Harry Hillier; Heather Jackson; Joan Kavenagh; Linda Proud; Alastair Dougall; and Susan Kinsey.

CONTENTS

FOREWORD
by Harold Lever

Money is a fiction – an abstract construction of the mind –
though it can be given symbolic expression in a piece of gold,
a piece of paper or a book entry. The concept of money is one
of the great feats of man's imagination which has proved to be
as central to the development of economic life as the wheel
was for transport. Even in primitive societies, money was used
as a store of wealth and sometimes as a medium of exchange.
But the great break-through came later when money became
the instrument for measuring economic activity of all kinds.
It then became an indispensable tool of man as a gainfully
calculating being. Custom and habit, often with a religious or
mystical background, which had hitherto dominated economic
life, started to break down under the assault of gainful
calculation; man's activities became more and more ruled by
the principles of reckoning and economising. He started to live
uneasily and often illogically with a mixture of custom and
gainful calculation. Ruthlessness and dispassionate reckoning
were still tempered by habit, but money values and reckoning
became predominant in economic life and increasingly took over
from the traditional ways. The market economy had been born.

It was the invention of money and the resulting market
economy which enabled man to harness the pioneering
innovational effort in every field of enterprise which has led to
the modern world, with all its dangers and disfigurements but
with all its glories and achievements and with all its stimulation and
enlargement of human possibilities. Without money as the
basis for measuring and calculating economic activity, man
would not have readily known whether the time of an
invention had arrived, whether it cohered with the other
achievements of mankind needed to support it, or whether it
had to remain in the notebooks of a Leonardo da Vinci as just
another beautiful idea.

The material achievements of the market economy have been staggering in their size and range. But man has never become and never will become a completely gainful calculator; *homo economicus* is an abstraction not a real man – or more exactly, not the whole man. Money and economics therefore continue to express the aspects of logic and calculation of a personality, whose needs go wider. An economic life too heavily dominated by the calculations of the market place cannot completely satisfy such a personality. Indeed, many of our current economic predicaments can be seen as deriving from the struggle of modern man to find a more complete fulfilment of the enlarged and varied expectations that economic success has itself created.

An informed democratic society is the ideal instrument to enable modern man to use the achievements of rigorous economic thinking to emancipate himself from many of its deformities. We will need a copious democratic expression to discover the new needs and new possibilities of modern man and that will require a wider understanding of economic history and economic life. This is a valuable and courageous book because it sets out to meet the needs of a large audience in achieving that understanding.

Harold Lever

Harold Lever has been Economic Adviser to successive British Governments

Gold deposits, in the
Federal Reserve Bank,
New York.

1.

THE PURPOSE OF MONEY

Though it is only a token, with no real value of its own, money is accepted by everyone, everywhere; the coin, the banknote and the cheque can be translated into all the staple necessities of life, such as food, drink and shelter. This section traces the history of money through the ages. Starting with the principles of barter, it takes the story of money, and the institutions that have grown up with it, from the cowrie shell to the credit card and from the goldsmiths of the Middle Ages to the international banks of today.

THE STORY OF MONEY

It would be difficult to imagine the world without money. We have money in our pockets and money in the bank; we receive money in exchange for our work and notes and coins are accepted without question at the supermarket check-out.

Cheques are offered and accepted in payment for all kinds of commodities and services. Banks can be instructed at the stroke of a pen to move funds directly from one account to another so we can even be saved the inconvenience of writing and depositing cheques into a bank account. An example of this is the computer transfer system by which an employee's wages, say, can be paid directly.

Yet not all people throughout history have used money and many who did so used it only irregularly. Currencies have taken many different forms from exotic sea shells or barley to gold, silver and pieces of paper. There is nothing mysterious about the nature of money. Since its conception, money has simply been what was commonly offered or accepted for the buying and selling of commodities and services, and, of course, for the payment of debts.

Early Trade by Barter

A man who can produce all his own requirements has no need of money and even those who cannot be self-sufficient have found it quite possible to do without it. Our far-off ancestors, the hunters and gatherers, apparently exchanged surplus skins with wandering traders for the decorative beads they could not produce themselves.

Prehistoric farmers traded their surplus produce with the manufacturers of flint tools and weapons. Later, they exchanged the fruits of their labours for tools of bronze. The making of such tools was much too complicated a process for the farmer to master on a part-time basis.

Raw materials for production, or luxury items, often had to be brought from distant parts, so that trading was important even at those very early

Right: A peasant barters grain for his counter part's sheep and livestock. **For many centuries, barter – the notion of placing a value on goods and services and exchanging one for the other – was the staple of world trade. The system, however, was suited only to small communities, so, as societies grew, a single acceptable token of exchange became acutely necessary. In addition, barter was often extremely time-consuming and complex to operate. If, for instance, two peasants could not agree on the articles to trade, subsidiary transactions would often be needed.**

Above: Australian Aborigines in European dress with a painting designed for sale to tourists and *right* Aborigine children in school learning the principles of numbers through measuring height. **The Aborigines, until recently living within a primitive economic system, have had to adjust their way of life under the** impact of the advanced technological and economic society of the white man. For instance, they have had to learn how to use money and adapt to the needs of trade. Other primitive economics, too, have had to make the same adjustment. The Eskimo, for example, used to be a nomadic race; now many of them live in modern settlements.

stages of man's economic development.

In these early transactions no money changed hands, for commodities were simply bartered. Without money, the prehistoric farmer who wished to exchange a cow for hens, had first to find someone who wanted to acquire a cow and also had hens to spare, and was willing and able to trade an acceptable number of chickens for the cow.

If a cow normally exchanged for 20 hens and the farmer with the cow only wanted 10 hens, no deal would be possible unless the cow owner was prepared to accept a very bad bargain, or his trading partner could give him something else in addition. It was not possible to split the live cow into two. And so a great deal of time was wasted trying to match exactly the desires of would be traders, finding a 'double coincidence' of wants, particularly when commodities were not easily divisible.

Without money, specialization within a community could not go very far. In general, men were 'jacks' of most trades and relatively self-sufficient. Although a few specialist craftsmen existed, it was impossible for a barter system to accommodate a large number of different specializations and so economic development was constrained. Although barter worked reasonably at a local level of low economic development, it held back wider trade and production for the market.

The way of overcoming the problems of barter was to find a commonly accepted commodity which could be

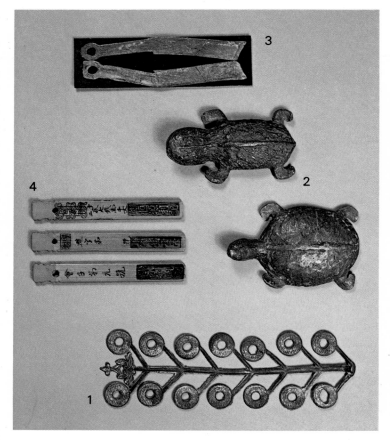

Exchange tokens. **A selection of the tokens used as money by peoples from all over the world. The main factor governing the choice of token was the way of life of the people concerned; hunting communities frequently used skins, for instance. But there were two important drawbacks, as the tokens were often cumbersome in size and often not accepted outside their area of origin.** *Left:* 1 **Pokoh Pitis (coin tree), Lower Siam; 2 Malayan tortoise and frog; 3 Knife money, China; 4 Chinese bamboo money.** *Above right:* **bell money from Zambia,** *below right:* **Chinese bridge money.** *Far right:* 1 **Tibetan machine presses and brick of tea; 2 Congolese cruciform copper ingot; 3 potuma – the spatula of a dolphin's jaw bone – used in Marshall Bennett Island, Pacific; 4 shell money, New Guinea; 5 Ba Bunda salt packet; 6 quartz pebbles, West Africa; 7 Shell beads, used as both ornament and money.**

used as money, or as a medium of exchange. The man selling his cow could simply accept money from the first person who wanted to give him a reasonable price for his animal. He could then spend the money or save it. Money also acted as a common standard of value or a unit of account.

Crowther, the economist, suggested that money 'was the invention perhaps

of some lazy genius who found himself oppressed by the task of calculating how many bushels of corn were equal to one tiger skin, if three bushels of corn were equal to five bananas, twenty bananas to one goat and twenty goats to one tiger skin.' Money provided a common denominator in which to value a wide variety of commodities.

But for money to serve its functions

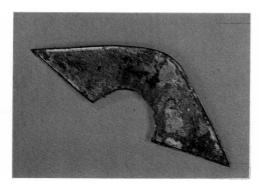

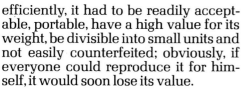

efficiently, it had to be readily acceptable, portable, have a high value for its weight, be divisible into small units and not easily counterfeited; obviously, if everyone could reproduce it for himself, it would soon lose its value.

Types of Primitive Money
It is not surprising that some very primitive communities resorted to the use of money as a convenient means of trade. Primitive money tended to reflect the livelihood of the community. Hunters used skins of wild animals, pastoral communities livestock, and farmers used grain. For example, barley was the first acceptable form of money in Mesopotamia while cattle served as money in ancient Rome.

Some primitive currencies were highly exotic. Cowrie shells were accepted on the west coast of Africa, and on the American continent, certain tribes used wampum, a beaded belt of sea shells. In the North American colonies of Virginia and Maryland, tobacco was legal tender during the seventeenth and eighteenth centuries. Cigarettes functioned as a medium of exchange in prisoner of war camps

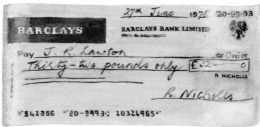

Left: From barter to credit card. **Barter was the earliest form of trade. Tokens were then introduced as the first money, but, in turn, were largely replaced by precious metals. It was not long before the first coins were struck, then came banknotes, cheques and, finally, the credit card.**

The Purpose of Money

during the Second World War as well as in the Black Markets of wartime and immediately post-war Europe.

Shortcomings of Primitive Money
All these primitive forms of money had serious shortcomings in one way or another. It was not very convenient to carry around sacks of barley, which were heavy in relation to their value, or to perpetually weigh measures of barley in payment for goods. A cow was impossible to divide into very small amounts and difficult to transport over long distances.

Although cowrie shells were light and impossible to counterfeit, they were useless as a widespread currency. Though they were rare in Africa, on the Indian seashores there were vast quantities available which made them worthless for worldwide trade. In an expanded market system, the scarce commodity which was highly prized and used as money in one locality was not necessarily acceptable to merchants from distant lands.

When early farmers were able to provide a sufficiently large surplus of food to support groups of specialist workers, such as smiths, glaziers, seal cutters, potters, scribes, shopkeepers and merchants, who produced goods not for their own needs, but for sale in the market, a convenient form of money was essential if the development of trade and industry were to continue.

It was at this time that precious metals began to replace more primitive forms of money. The growth of civilization and the complex trade patterns of the ancient world depended on a convenient and generally acceptable medium of exchange.

Because of the various limitations of the primitive forms of money, for about 4,000 years and until very recently in man's history, money has been made of a more or less precious metal. Gold was used in very early trade by merchants, and coins of silver, copper and even iron, came gradually into widespread acceptance. Silver ranked as the dominant basis of currency in most of the world before the gold discoveries in Australia and California in the nineteenth century. Until then, the use of gold was restricted to very rich merchants and kings.

In the ancient world precious metals were scarce and in permanent de-

World coinage. **Coins were the first form of ancient currency that would be instantly recognizable by the average man and woman. today. They were probably first introduced by the Sumerians to replace barley and their great advantage was that they could be of standard weight, size and value.**

Electrum nugget from Cyprus, from about 1100 BC.

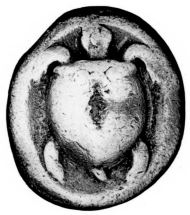

Aegina stater, perhaps 6th century BC.

Athenia tetradrachm. Struck in the 5th century BC, it is decorated with an owl – the symbol of the goddess Athena.

Athenian decadrachm, dating from about 460 BC.

A silver stater from Corinth, another leading Greek city-state. The stater dates from the 5th century BC.

Coin from Antioch, decorated with an anchor.

Gold coin, minted for the Roman emperor Maximus (AD235-238), showing the temple of Diana at Ephesus.

Small yap fei.

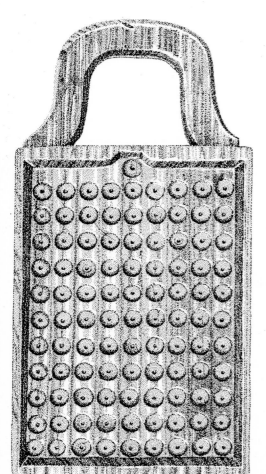

A coin board from a Hindu temple. It was used for counting coins of small denomination.

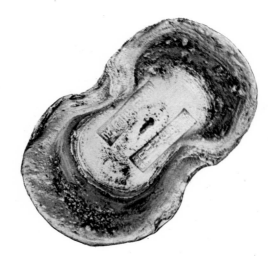

Sycee silver from China, with a value of 50 Tael.

A gold oban from Japan.

Left: Back to the token. **The two faces of a wooden nickel, issued as a token that the unemployed could exchange for food in the depression-hit USA of 1933. In that year, banks throughout the nation were forced to close their doors – some never to re-open.**
Below left: German coinage of 1939. **Hitler spent his way out of the German slump by launching a great arma-**ments programme, but **only maintained the stability of his currency by tight government control.**

Above: Official dye-punches, used to frank coins in an emergency. **These date from the First World War.**

Below: A US 20 dollar gold piece. **Like all currencies, the US dollar started life in coin form minted in gold; today, such coins are issued only to mark special occasions.**

Right: Shanghai dollars, clipped into pieces. **These fragments served as small change.**

mand for the manufacture of jewellery and other luxury goods. Gold was particularly desirable and unlike silver it did not tarnish. In addition, it had a far greater scarcity value. Metals did not easily wear out, were recognizable and generally known to be commodities which, because of their high and stable price, would be acceptable to most people. Their stable price arose from the fact that their value was not affected by changes in current production which were generally small. Also the metals were easily divisible into extremely small sums, and they functioned as money very effectively for a long time.

In the ancient world money was weighed. Silver was the medium of exchange and was weighed out at each transaction. Every merchant had to carry around a pair of highly sensitive scales to make sure he did not pay too much silver, or receive too little.

Some temples turned out silver bars stamped with a certification of weight. Although this saved the inconvenience of weighing silver for each transaction, the bars were of high value and only used by rich merchants. The small retailer found it a very great handicap to use scales or bars. It was the introduction of coinage, as small change, which corrected this.

The first coins
Although it is often said that a King of Lydia (Western Turkey) around 650 BC first had the idea of issuing what are now called coins, pieces of gold and silver of standard size and weight called electrum, there are indications that coins were used before. References in Hindu epics suggest that coins and a decimal system too, was used in India some hundreds of years earlier. Metal coins which replaced barley as legal tender were probably used earlier still by the Sumerians.

The Lydian coins were carefully weighed and had marks on the face so that there was no necessity to keep weighing them. People could accept them at their face value. The man in the street or the merchant could see what he was being offered. The use of coins spread very quickly throughout the ancient Mediterranean world for they helped to streamline trade enormously. Also their value was underpinned by their silver content.

The practice grew up of decorating

the coins and stamping them with pictures. A tortoise was depicted on some Lydian coins. Coins produced by the Greek cities, often showed heads of gods, although it became the custom, after Alexander the Great, to stamp the head of the sovereign on coins. Archaeologists have demonstrated that coin pouring and striking was a relatively quick and simple process. A man probably could make about 100 coins an hour.

£, d. and dinars
The first Roman coins were produced somewhere between 350-301 BC, and the influence of Roman coinage spread throughout the Empire. While under Roman control, mints were established in Britain and elsewhere which issued silver and bronze copies of the Roman silver denarii. The Roman influence has given the sign for the British pound, £, which represented the Latin, libra, meaning a pound of silver, from which the name of the Italian and Turkish lires were also derived. The denarii gave the sign which symbolized old British pennies and provided the name too, for the Arabian and Yugoslavian dinars.

Even before the collapse of the Roman Empire there was a reduction of trade, and until the early Middle Ages there was very little gold circulation because the amount of transactions in money was limited.

With the growth of the manorial system, whose typical unit was a small, quite self-contained rural community, most people were paid in kind. But there was some market activity and trade fairs flourished. Such transactions in money which did occur were carried out in silver. The new silver denarius developed by trading communities of Northern Europe was ideal for the purposes of the emerging merchant class.

The adoption of silver coinage in Western Europe was also helped by the increasing quantities of silver which were mined during the eighth and ninth centuries, used generally to

Top left: A medieval market and, *below*: the great fair in the market place at Leipzig in 1846. **Fairs and markets have a tradition stretching back thousands of years. With the origin of towns and cities in the Middle East came the birth of industry and the gradual growth of trade between town and country. This made the introduction of a universally-recognized form of currency essential.**

make poor copies of the old Roman coinage. One of the more long lasting small silver coins minted in the following centuries was the gros, introduced in France in the thirteenth century. The equivalents of these coins spread widely; Germany, for example, had the groschen, and England the groat. Not until the rise of the great northern Italian city states, was there any form of gold coinage in Europe.

In the late Middle Ages, international trade increased enormously. With larger commercial transactions becoming more frequent, merchants needed leather bags full of silver, which were too bulky for easy carrying.

To overcome this problem, Florence produced the golden florin in 1252 and during the next hundred years or so many nations adopted gold coinages alongside their silver ones. In England, gold florins were introduced in the fourteenth century to supplement the silver pennies. In the Netherlands the influence of the florin can be seen in the abbreviated sign 'fl' for the gilder.

A further large expansion in silver coinage took place with the discovery of silver in Bohemia in the sixteenth century. New coins, called thalers, were minted, which were the forerunners of other types of currency, including the dollar. In addition, the flow of precious metals from the new world in the sixteenth century increased the amounts available for coinage.

In England, silver shillings were introduced at the beginning of the sixteenth century with crowns and halfcrowns minted later. In 1661, the first golden guinea was issued.

Gold, silver and copper coins continued to be minted in most countries in the following centuries. Indeed, some coins such as the Maria Theresa thalers (dollars) are still minted in various places. In the Arab world, thalers are sometimes used in preference to local coins even though they are not legal tender.

Some low value coins were struck by entrepreneurs. This frequently occurred in Britain during the early stages of the Industrial Revolution when the state did not meet the demand for small coinage.

Businessmen were forced to mint coins themselves to pay factory workers. These coins were generally acceptable in local shops and ale houses. Eventually, they were outlawed when the state began to produce its own small coinage.

Shaving, clipping and sweating

Though convenient to use, coins created a whole range of criminal activities. The story goes that as early as 540 BC, Polycrates of Sornos cheated the Spartans with coins of simulated gold.

Early coins were not perfectly round and they could quite easily be shaved or clipped in order to acquire some precious metal, before passing them on.

To get over this problem, coins with milled edges were eventually produced, making it easier to see if they had been shaved or clipped.

Sweating and shaking a large number of coins in a bag to remove some valuable dust was another trick, and when this practice grew significantly, merchants refused to accept the coins at face value, and back came the scales. This meant that much of the usefulness of coins had been lost.

Kings and emperors could play a very profitable fraud. In order to raise money they could make some excuse for re-coinage and add in some cheaper base metal before re-minting.

In the Roman Empire the coinage was subject to steady debasement by this means. More coinage with the same output of goods led to inflation. In England, by the time of Queen Elizabeth I, debasement had been such that 1lb of money contained only about 4oz of silver. In 1558, the first year of her reign, Queen Elizabeth tried to prevent further debasement by refusing to issue coins bearing her imprint.

It was at this time that Sir Thomas Gresham, her adviser, put forward his famous dictum 'bad money drives out good'. Only the debased worn coinage would be kept in circulation and 'good' money with its higher silver content would be kept back. Queen Elizabeth insisted on recalling all the old coinage before a new issue was produced.

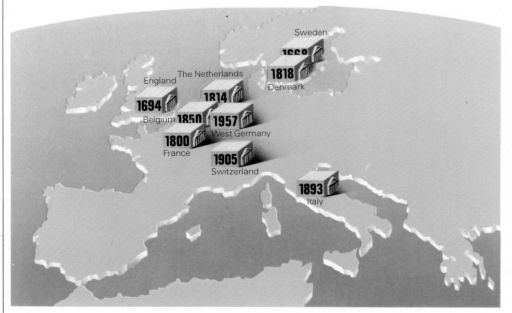

Above: Europe's central banks, with the dates they were founded. **Their prime role is to act as the government's agent in controlling the credit system. To this end, they usually have a monopoly on the issue.** of bank notes, serve as the government's banker, support the currency to ensure its stability, make loans to and take deposits from the commercial banks and the money market (though the Bank of England will only lend to discount houses), establish rates of interest, and make money and bullion transactions with the other central banks. One of the main reasons for their origin was to fulfil the function of what economists term the 'lender of last resort', that is, to lend money to commercial banks or discount houses that find they cannot temporarily balance their books.

Early bankers were all too often tempted to lend too much; this precipitated many bank runs and crashes. In addition, most private banks were then too small to finance the growth of trade and industry, or the government in time of war. The Bank of England, for example, was founded to help pay for William III's campaigns against France, as all other attempts to raise money for them had proved inadequate. From this, it grew to become the most influential central bank in the world. Central banks have thus always been closely linked and today these links are more necessary than ever before. The complexities of economic life mean, say, that no one central bank can stand alone if its currency is under attack. It not only has to co-operate with its fellows, but also with international institutions.

Perish credit! Unlike Europeans, many early Americans fiercely opposed the idea of a central bank, chiefly on the grounds that such a monopoly would be against the spirit of the constitution. The First Bank of the United States lasted from 1793 to 1811. The token (above) was minted as part of a vitriolic campaign against the second bank, which ended in victory when the federal government, under President Jackson, vetoed the renewal of its charter and withdrew all federal deposits. Even today, this legacy still lingers. The Federal reserve system is not centralised in the same way as European central banks. Instead, it has 22 regional branches of issue.

Banking in Babylon

It seems that banks existed in long-ago Babylon. Records of transactions were found on baked clay tablets which date back to 2500 BC at least.

Banks existed in Roman times and letters of credit were used even at this early date, not perhaps surprisingly given the difficulties of transporting heavy metallic currency from one end of the Empire to another.

In China, a similar form of letters of credit was known in the ninth century BC; so too were treasury notes inscribed 'to be circulated as cash'. China had a long subsequent history of the use of paper money in preference to coinage.

Left: During the 1920s in Turkey, stamps were perfectly acceptable in lieu of small change currency. **To make the stamps more durable, they were stuck in sheets to thin card, which was then perforated to match the stamps, which could then be detached according to the amount of change required.**

Below: Banknotes being printed and, *right:*

Russians exchanging new roubles for old at the time of the 1948 revaluation. **All governments take immense care to make their bank notes as forgery-proof as possible. The reason for the redesigning of Bank of England treasury notes after the Second World War was the knowledge that a vast stock of perfect German forgeries had never been discovered.**

Banks declined in Europe with the fall of the Roman Empire when trade became more hazardous and there were religious objections to making money from usury. The Rennaissance saw a revival of trade and the growth of banking houses in the Italian cities during the thirteenth, fourteenth and fifteenth centuries. These were the forerunners of modern commercial banks.

In other countries, however, banking developed much later. The Bank of Amsterdam was founded in 1609, but this was primarily concerned with coinage rather than paper money. The Swedish State Bank was the first European bank to issue notes, which were devised by the Swedish financier Johann Palmerstruck.

Another early issue of paper money was in 1690, by the Massachusetts Bay Company. A band of colonists from Massachusetts had attacked Quebec. When the attack failed, there was no money to pay the colonists and notes were printed because of the absence of sufficient coin, and the difficulties of raising money by taxation.

Good as gold

The first banks in England were set up by the London goldsmiths in the mid-seventeenth century. These craftsmen who worked with such a valuable raw material had very secure vaults in which to store gold. It was profitable to allow others to use these facilities for storing valuables.

A goldsmiths' receipt was given for each item deposited, and on presentation of this ticket the valuables would be handed over. It was not long before these receipts were themselves used as a means of payment. If people knew the goldsmith to be reliable, instead of going to the very risky and cumbersome business of transferring gold, all that was needed was to transfer the receipts which promised to pay so much gold on demand.

These goldsmiths' receipts were the forerunners of modern bank notes. Pieces of paper circulated as money, performing money's functions. In England, the first recorded instance of this was a payment by Samuel Pepys to his father in 1668. Also, before the end of the seventeenth century the use of signed orders to goldsmiths to hand over certain sums of gold to another person named on the order

History in banknotes.
These two notes – Austro-Hungarian (above) **and Russian** (right) **reflect the collapse of the great dynastic European empires that took place in the aftermath of the First World War. On the Austro-Hungarian note, the Hapsburg Eagle, symbol of the old Empire, has been overprinted in acknowledgement of the founding of the German-Austrian Republic on 12 November, 1918. Hungary too, became a republic four days later. The Russian 100-rouble note, bearing the Imperial Eagle and the monogram of Nicholas II, last of the Tzars, was declared worthless by the Bolsheviks**

Above: Great moments in the history of mankind – and a morbid fear of forgery – are implicit in these old banknotes. **Five cover the period of the American War of Independence and the birth of the United States; the French note was issued shortly after the French Revolution, while the miners' note, redeemable in old dust, recalls the Californian gold rush of 1849.**

began. These were the forerunners of modern cheques.

Other forms of paper which can be said to function as money are bills of exchange, which were first developed by merchants to facilitate trade. The bill was a written undertaking by a debtor to pay his creditor for goods at some future date, say three months ahead, like a post-dated cheque.

In Italy, around 1600, debtors agreed to pay the person who presented the bill rather than the person originally named on it, and the bills became transferable as negotiable securities. Creditors did not have to wait for the bills to mature, as they could sell them at some discount and have their money immediately.

The various forms of paper which can be said to function as money were particularly convenient where large sums were involved and cheques and bills of exchange gave increased security in transit. They were much less risky to handle than large quantities of gold.

It was not long before the goldsmiths realised that there was money to be made from banking. They could lend out some of the gold deposited with them at interest because not all of the gold in their stores was withdrawn at any one time.

These withdrawals usually occurred if businessmen were undertaking distant transactions where goldsmiths' receipts were not acceptable. Banks began the practice of lending out the promises to pay in cash in excess of gold that they had in hand.

Panic at the bank

In such a situation it is said that money is only fractionally backed by gold. But bankers were often unable to resist the temptation of lending out too much and the history of banking in many countries contains horrendous stories of crises and panic runs.

A run on one bank would precipitate runs on others, each man clamouring to secure his own gold. Many would be left holding worthless bits of paper, losing all their money, and it was only gradually that sound banking practice evolved.

Not all banks originated from goldsmiths. Many early banks were land banks. The first official paper money issued in Russia in 1769 by Catherine the Great was backed by land rather

than gold. The Banque Royale of France in the eighteenth century provides a spectacular example of how paper money was linked with land – and the consequences of unsound banking practice.

The Scottish emigré John Law set up the Banque Royale in 1716, largely to provide finance for the Regent, the Duc D'Orleans. His attempts to bolster the strength of the bank by selling stock in the Mississippi Company which owned land in Louisiana brought one of the most outstanding early bank collapses. Fifteen people were crushed to death while attempting to withdraw their money from the bank in Paris.

The impression left by this banking disaster lasted until the French revolution in 1789 when the system was reinforced by the issue of notes backed by the land of the church. The notes, known as assignats, were issued in such large quantities that they soon became worthless. French banking remained primitive until the nineteenth century and government stimulus was needed to encourage banking.

Banking in other countries has developed in a variety of ways. In Britain, there were government restrictions on joint stock banks, while in the US, banks were restricted to individual states. Such banks as developed were generally set up by wealthy businessmen. In Britain, provincial banks had no common origin. Many were established by local businessmen to cater for the needs of their communities. By 1760, private banks were commonplace throughout the country.

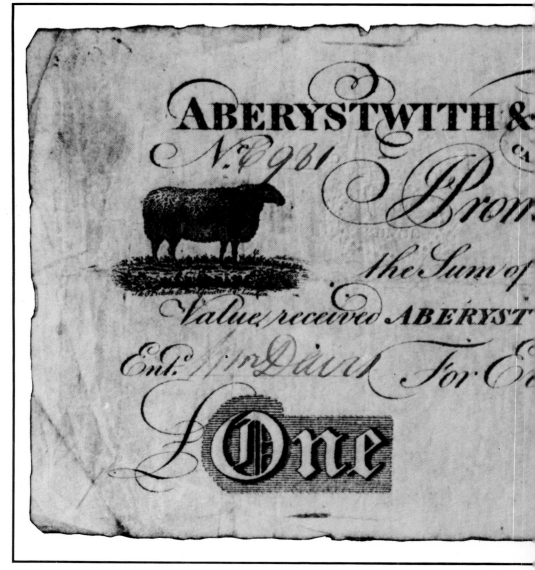

Banknotes for the illiterate

In Wales, drovers at Llandovery set up an institution known as the Bank of the Black Ox, and at Aberystwyth there was the Bank of the Black Sheep. It produced its own £1 note which bore the picture of a black sheep, whilst the ten shilling note had one black lamb, apparently as an aid to drovers who could not read.

Some of these private banks issued their own bank notes until the end of the nineteenth century. But as in other countries, they were very small concerns and not able fully to meet the needs of an industrialized society.

In the US, banks had various levels of reserves. This, and the distance from the bank issuing the notes produced a most complicated range of discounts at which the notes circulated. There were even periodicals advising the public how much notes, bearing the same face value but issued by different banks, were worth.

There was a variety of needs which small private banks could not fulfil and this led to the development of central banks. Although the Bank of England was not the first to be established as a central bank, its development and practice shaped the majority of central banking practices.

As Galbraith described it: 'It is, in all respects, to money as St. Peter's is to the faithful'. The Bank of England was set up in 1694 by a group of merchants headed by William Patterson, to help provide money to pay for the war with France, because public revenues were insufficient. All sorts of measures had been tried previously including a State lottery, but none were successful.

The capital of the Bank of England was £1.2m. and this was lent to the State. In return, the Bank received certain privileges in the issuing of bank notes. By 1770 it had become almost the only source of bank notes in London, while other banks in the metropolis became cash depositories. When these banks made loans it was deposits and not note circulation that expanded.

It was not until 1914 that the Bank of England became regarded as a true central bank, and accepted as such by other banks. It had by then become the holder of the country's gold reserves and the ultimate support for the country's financial structure in times of difficulty. The Bank of England was nationalized in 1947.

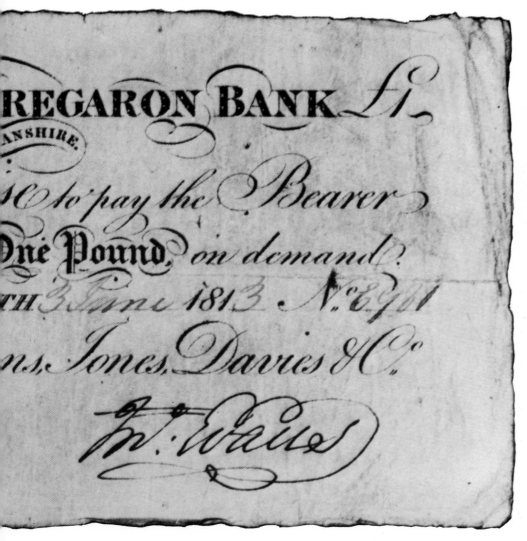

Worth its weight in wool?

Paper money was perfectly acceptable to the ancient Chinese, but in the Western world, until a century or two ago, it was generally looked on askance, as a measure to be taken in times of national emergency at best, and a vehicle for profiteering and inflation at worst. Money should be seen, be felt; gold and silver coins were worth exactly their face value in precious metal and in terms of goods.

By the late eighteenth century, however, Britain was in the throes of a money crisis caused partly by the huge expenses of the Napoleonic Wars, and partly by the mushroom growth of the Industrial Revolution. With insufficient coin to meet demand, paper money proliferated, each bank throughout the country issuing its own notes, with very little effort at central control. One of the most colourful of these banks was the Aberystwyth and Tregaron Bank that served a sheep-rearing community in Wales. The directors hit on the idea of using the symbol most familiar to their clients – the sheep. Thus, the ten-shilling note depicted a lamb, the one pound note a single sheep, the two pound note two sheep, and so on. All the sheep were black, and the bank rapidly became known as the Bank of the Black Sheep.

Such a state of affairs could not be allowed to continue, and by 1884, legislation had put an end to Black Sheep banknotes, and to the many other 'pirate' issues throughout the country. Today, Bank of England notes are the only legal notes in England and Wales, though Scottish banks sturdily continue to issue their own.

In an upsurge of Welsh nationalism in the 1960s, the black sheep made a reappearance on prommissory notes issued by Prif Trysorfa Cymru. Unfortunately, the Board of Trade discovered that in Welsh, this meant Chief Treasury for Wales, and the issuers were made to change their names to the Black Sheep Company of Wales.

In the United States, during the eighteenth and nineteenth centuries, a similar situation occuured in which hundreds of different banks issued their own notes. Communications over the continent were so difficult, however, that no one knew whether a particular bank had funds to cover its notes or not, and many went out of business. Their notes, some of which were beautifully engraved, became known as 'broken' notes.

The influence of the Bank of England is seen by the establishment of other central banks such as the Banque de France. The US had two attempts at setting up central banks at the end of the eighteenth century and again in 1816. When the last charter expired in 1836, the US managed without a central bank until the Federal Reserve Act of 1913. Hong Kong still has no central bank.

Trading with paper promises

Without the invention of bank notes, there would not have been enough precious metal to finance the huge expansion of output and trade both within and between nations which occurred from the late eighteenth century onwards. Today the major part of any industrialized nation's money stock is made up of bank deposits.

Even the substantial finds of gold in the nineteenth century were not sufficient to finance the unprecendented growth of trade. Countries which adhered to the gold standard, a system whereby a country's central bank is obliged to give gold for any of its own currency presented to it, found that their limited stocks of gold acted as a drag on the growth of the money supply in periods when productive capacity was increasing very rapidly and money was needed to lubricate trade and industry.

The advent of fractional reserves and the use of book and paper money greatly economized on scarce gold reserves. The gold standard was particularly important in regulating international transactions. Each currency was convertible into gold at a fixed rate and international debts were met in gold.

If a country had a deficit in its international trade there would be an outflow of gold. As the country's own currency was convertible into gold this led to a reduction in the paper money backed by gold. This was supposed to reduce prices, make exports cheaper and hopefully expand sales and reduce the demand for imported goods. In this way, a reduction in the deficit in international trade could be achieved.

Countries have been forced to abandon the gold standard, and although gold is still important in international trade and finance, it has largely been abandoned as an internal currency.

Gold is a dense, unalterable, inimitable, bright yellow metal that apart from its use as a radiation barrier in outer space, and its special applications in medical and dental contexts, is of little practical value. But it is also rare; in the whole history of the world, no more than 100,000 tons has ever been mined, and most of this never disappears. Apart from a small amount in ancient burials, so far undiscovered, most of the world's gold is still with us.

About 40 per cent of it is held by world monetary authorities, of which the most important is the Federal Reserve Bank, whose main depository is at Fort Knox, Kentucky. At one time, it was the custom if the US were making a loan to, say, France, then the amount of gold representing the sum borrowed

would be physically shipped to the Bank of France. Then, due to the risks incurred in transport, it seemed a better idea to put the gold on trolleys and move it to the 'France Room' within the vaults. Even this seemed a waste of labour, so nowadays it is simply a matter of bookkeeping. A portion of the gold in the vaults has been 'borrowed' by France, but it never actually moves at all. A further 20 per cent of the world's gold is held by other central banks and governments; the remainder is in private hands, in the form of jewellery, coin or ingots.

Gold has two prices; the official price – S35 per troy ounce – at which international debts are settled, and the unofficial price, used by jewellers, dealers and speculators. This fluctuates considerably and

almost daily, depending on the amount currently on the market. For years it has stood far above the official price, usually somewhere in the region of S180 an ounce.

One of the most curious features of this extraordinary metal is the fact of its appeal to all peoples – many of whom had no contact with the outside world – at all periods of history. It inspired awe; hence its frequent appearances in religion and folklore. To the Egyptians and the pre-conquest people of South America it was the metal of the sun, and therefore sacred. The ancient Hebrews worshipped a Golden Calf; Jason sought the Golden Fleece. This last legend, incidentally, is thought to be based on a historical gold-seeking expedition in

Above and left: Royal Gold. **Since the earliest beginnings of civilization, gold was the metal and the colour that signified spiritual purity and regal grandeur. The solid gold mask covered the face of the boy king Tutankhamun when he** was buried at Thebes in 1353 BC, and the armlet, of gold, carnelian and lapis lazuli, is older still. It belonged to Ah-hotpe, a Queen of Egypt who died in 1540 BC. By such standards, the gold cup, is relatively modern being made about 1380.

Left and below: Golden lads and lasses. **Gold strikes in New South Wales and Victoria during the 1850s trebled Australia's population in 10 years. Among the many thousands of gold-hungry immigrants was at least one artist, who depicted his fellow diggers in colourful, if unlikely costume. The Busby Berkely movie,** *Gold-diggers of 1933,* **points up a combination the world has long been attracted by – beautiful girls and gold. But as so often, it was Ian Fleming who devised the ultimate in the combination. In his film** *Goldfinger,* **one of James Bond's girl-friends, is doused from head to foot in gold paint by the villain**

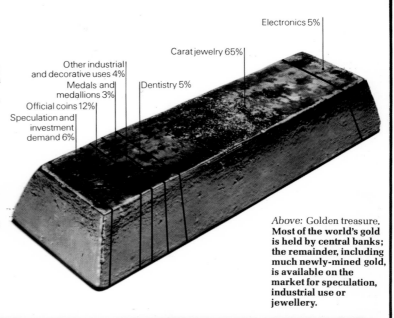

Electronics 5%

Carat jewelry 65%

Other industrial and decorative uses 4%

Medals and medallions 3%

Dentistry 5%

Official coins 12%

Speculation and investment demand 6%

Above: Golden treasure. **Most of the world's gold is held by central banks; the remainder, including much newly-mined gold, is available on the market for speculation, industrial use or jewellery.**

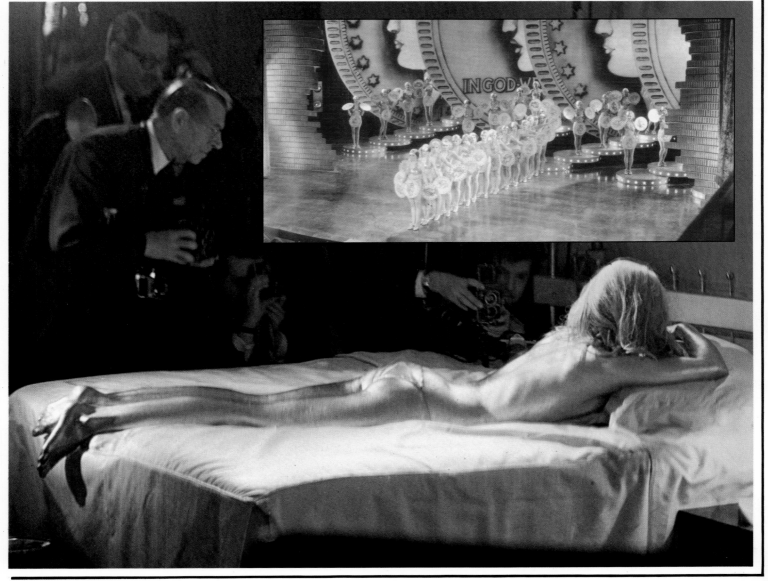

The magic of gold **Today, gold is no longer in use as every-day currency, but it still has a vital role to play in under-pinning the international monetary system.** Fort Knox currency vault, (*left*) **was built by the US government in 1936 as the nation's chief bullion depositry. Its underground vaults, proof against even the blast of an atomic bomb, house gold deposits valued at more than $10,000,000,000. Gold is also held in private hands;** the vaults of Samuel Montagu Brokers (*insert*) **are among the many in the City of London.**

DO NOT PARK
IN
TURNING AREA

Right An aerial view of a South African gold mine *far right* pouring the molten gold into ingots and *below* miners at work at the gold face **South Africa possesses one of the largest reserves of gold deposits in the world – a major contribution to its economic prosperity. Some 60% of all gold mined is held by central banks and governments to back their various currencies. However, it is no longer possible for the man in the street to go to the Bank of England, say, and demand gold in exchange for his currency, as it was in the days before the abandonment of the Gold Standard.**

1200 BC to what is now Armenia; there, gold was washed out of the river sands with the aid of sheepskins. Similar methods were used much earlier still by the ancient Egyptians.

Most countries have had their gold strikes at one time or another. The Romans mined gold in Wales, and a little is still found there; Queen Elizabeth II's wedding ring is made of Welsh gold. The chief sources, however, until the discovery of the New World, were the lands of the Aegean, India, Saxony and Spain. Even so, the amounts produced annually remained relatively small.

The golden flood that followed the discovery of the Americas surpassed anything the world had ever seen before. Mines, palaces, temples and

graves yielded gold in such quantities that it upset the political and economic balance of Europe. Between 1492 and 1600, eight million ounces – 35 per cent of world production – came from South America, which continued to be the major source until the Californian and Australian strikes were made in the mid-nineteenth century.

These induced a kind of world madness. Everywhere, men abandoned jobs, homes and families and rushed to the goldfields. Spectacular finds were made, especially in Australia, where nuggets up to 200 lb weight were discovered just beneath the surface of the soil, and a few spectacular fortunes; most of the miners, however, returned as poor as when they left.

The last great strikes were in the Klondike and in the Witwatersrand, South Africa, in the 1880s and 90s. In the first, the miners suffered almost unbelievable privations of cold and hunger, while the Rand discoveries were made by a wandering diamond prospector who later sold his claim for £10 and disappeared from history.

Though mining is now mostly, in the hands of great combines, and economists are beginning to wonder whether gold, compared with oil or land, has any real effect on the world's economy, the magic still remains. No diamond or precious stone has the same appeal or exercises the same nostalgic pull of romance and adventure. Gold has a beauty far beyond its simple intrinsic value.

The world's largest store of gold is housed in the vaults of the Federal Reserve Bank, New York **The bank handles, holds and transacts more business in gold than any other bank in the world.** Its main customers are nations, large corporations and some private individuals who wish to finance economic and business transactions. **Security is naturally immense; the alarm system is said to be sensitive enough to detect a fly.**

A security guard opens the entrance to the vaults *(above)*, while *(below)* members of the staff stand on a stack of gold blocks **Their protective shoes are designed to protect both them and the gold.**
An employee stacks gold bars in one of the store rooms *(above right)* and *(below and far right)* stock-taking and the weighing of currency is taking place. **These two stages are vital, for every grain of gold that goes into the bank must be accounted for.**

BANKS AND BANKING

Banks are the storekeepers and guardians of money whose role it is to ensure that the lifeblood of commerce continues to flow. Less grandly. banks exist to make a profit for their owners by providing services for their customers. Chief among those services is security – a place where the customer's money is safe.

This kind of security was first offered by the medieval goldsmiths who were, in a sense, the fathers of modern banking. The public held them in such trust that the receipts they issued against valuables deposited with them became negotiable in themselves and frequently accepted in lieu of money or gold. As time went on, and the goldsmith's establishments evolved into banks, it became apparent that only a small proportion of the notes were being returned in demand for gold. People were quite happy to leave the precious metal safely in the vaults and deal in the promissory notes instead. It quickly occurred to the early bankers, that it would be a good idea to issue still more notes to the limit of the gold they held and even beyond, depending on the increased flow of business to keep them solvent. This would have been a risky affair had it not been for the confidence in which they were held by the public. Such confidence, however, is the very keystone of banking.

Another major service the banks provide is the means of making payments – today, this is largely carried out through the cheque system, a convenience that has to be paid for by the customers. Of course, it is also possible to pay in cash – that is, in bank notes and

Left: Colourful 19th-century banknotes printed by state banks in Georgia, USA. **Today, however, the issue of banknotes is either a government monopoly or strictly controlled by finance ministries. In the USA, this came about with the National Bank Act of 1863.**

small coins. In countries where the banking system is not fully developed, this is still the principle method used to settle even large transactions. Even in Britain, with its long-established banking system, about 94 per cent of all payments – and there are about 600 made every second – are settled in cash. To put all payments through the cheque system, or through computers and credit cards, would be prohibitively expensive, though indeed, the provision of notes and coins also costs something.

For large payments, cheques are clearly more economical, as well as being more secure. In Britain in 1976, private individuals with bank accounts used cheques for some 26 per cent of their regular payments and cash for 44 per cent. The remainder were settled through standing orders or direct debit. Non-cash methods of making payments are now being greatly encouraged in countries such as France, that have

begun to insist that regular monthly salaries should be paid to employees through bank accounts. In the modern world, every country must have some system for making payments. In the United States and the United Kingdom, the system costs about one per cent of GNP in terms of real resources, indicating that banking has become an important industry in its own right. It is vital that it should be as efficient as possible. If banks did not exist, the costs of payments systems would be very much higher.

The moneylenders

Apart from security and convenience in payments, the banks lend money; just as bakers sell bread, so banks sell money. They lend it not only to individuals but to companies and even governments. In most countries, banks are the main source of external finance for companies, all of which need finance, and

Below Deposits and loans in the UK. **By far the greatest amount deposited in banks comes from the personal sector, in the form of either deposit or current accounts. Second comes industry and commerce, third, financial institutions, and, finally, government. The loans banks make fall into three types – short, medium and long-term. Industry and commerce take the biggest share.**

Below: The National Westminster Bank building in the City of London. **The earliest modern bankers were the goldsmiths of the Middle Ages and the first banks developed from their activities. By the 16th century, some banking houses had become as important to the economy of the time as are the banks of today. Charles V, ruler of an empire covering Spain, Holland and much of central Europe, depended on loans from the Fuggers, a banking family in Augsburg.**

Bank deposits come from

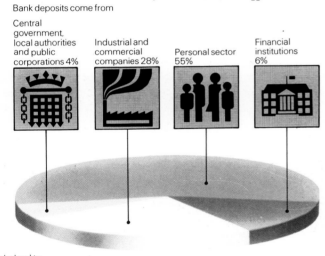

Central government, local authorities and public corporations 4%

Industrial and commercial companies 28%

Personal sector 55%

Financial institutions 6%

Banks lend to

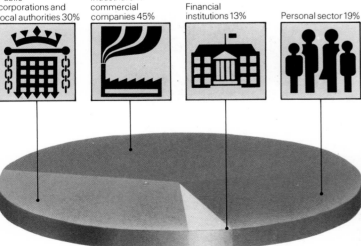

Central government, Public corporations and local authorities 30%

Industrial and commercial companies 45%

Financial institutions 13%

Personal sector 19%

Customer services. **Fierce competition between modern banks to attract customers has led to the introduction of an ever-increasing range of personal services. Chief amongst these is the provision of loans of various types, from which banks make the major part of their profit. The traditional and most frequently used loan is the overdraft. The chief advantage of this is that interest is paid only on the daily balance outstanding; thus, as the overdraft is reduced, the amount paid in interest goes down. The disadvantage is that the rate of interest can rise suddenly when governments decide to curb consumer expansion by making it** harder to borrow. **Many banks therefore advise their customers to take out a fixed-interest loan if repayments have to be spaced over a long period. The disadvantage here is that, once agreed, the installment period frequently cannot be varied so the amount of interest the borrower has to pay may well be higher than on an overdraft.** Other services include night safes *(left)* **so that shopkeepers, for instance, can deposit their takings after banking hours;** automatic cash dispensers *(above left)* **which provide a 24-hour service for customers;** displays of share prices *(above right)* – and even drive-in banks *(right).* **In addition, apart from the** obvious issue of a cheque book, **banks provide their depositors with credit cards, foreign currency, travellers's cheques, savings schemes, life insurance, hire purchase, standing orders – so that bills are paid regularly by direct debit – and advice on taxation and investment, as well as many other services. Nevertheless, banks have still not persuaded the majorority of their personal customers to switch from paying their bills with cash and there is also continuing resistance to the idea of paying wages by cheque or by direct computer transfer from the employer's bank to the bank of the employee.**

Above: An aerial view of the financial sector of Sydney, Australia. **During the great Australian mineral boom of the late 1960s and early 1970s, banks there played a vital part in the raising of loans to finance discovery, exploration and exploitation of the deposits. Later, the collapse of the boom illustrated one of the chief dangers bankers have to face.**

fast growing ones more than others. In general, they obtain it in two ways; by raising equity capital – that is, by persuading people to invest their money directly in the risks and possible profits of the undertaking, or by borrowing.

Traditionally, commercial banks in many countries tried to keep their lending to the short term, whether to companies or to individuals. In the case of companies, this meant lending them working capital to purchase raw materials, rather than lending them money to finance long-term projects. Merchant and investment banks also helped companies to raise funds from the general public in the form of equity issues. In addition, they would put their own name behind that of the company, so guaranteeing that, should they have over estimated the public's response, they would provide the money themselves.

In recent years however, there have been many changes in the traditional demarcation lines between different types of banks. Commercial banks make both medium and long-term loans and often have subsidiaries that provide merchant banking facilities as well. Nevertheless, the main function of banks remains the same – that of channelling funds from those sectors of the economy that have a surplus to those that wish to borrow. In this, they enable the country to economise on the use of cash, to mobilise its latent productive resources and help to keep its business activity ticking over.

Service to the customer

Banks also provide a wide range of supporting services. These usually include deposit accounts, on which customers can obtain a small rate of interest, 'time' accounts which offer better rates on larger sums left for longer periods, and many different methods of advancing money – practices differ considerably from one country to another.

In some countries, the overdraft is still very popular with bankers and customers alike – the great advantage being that the customer pays interest only on the daily outstanding overdrawn balance in his account. This means that if he finds himself in credit, he does not have to go on paying interest as he would in the case of a loan that must be repaid in fixed instalments.

In addition, banks offer a wide range of ancillary services; foreign currencies

The day the bank went bust

By the end of June 1974, the oil prices forced by OPEC were biting hard. During the previous year, foreign exchange markets had been fluctuating wildly, tempting a number of banks throughout the world to gamble on the rapid rise and fall of currencies. Many more were hard hit; the first to close its doors was the Herstatt bank of Cologne, whose assets were frozen by the West German authorities when losses totalling some $60 million were discovered. Similar losses were incurred by the Union Bank of Switzerland, the Franklin National Bank of New York and the West Deutsche Landesbank.

The situation was reminiscent of the early days of the 1929 crash when the closure of one bank led to panic runs on others, and further, widespread closures followed. By 1974, however, the central bank system was well established. The Herstatt bank was bailed out by the West German central bank, public confidence was restored, and what might have been a serious financial crisis was avoided.

Top left: The Herstatt Bank, Cologne, faced with a deficit of $60 million, ceased trading on 27th June 1974. Here, the police try to reassure anxious investors with the news that they may make withdrawals – but of no larger sums than they would usually take out for normal weekly expenditure.

Below left: Herr Iwan Herstatt, Director of the Herstatt Bank, is questioned on television about the events leading up to the bank's closure, which caused considerable anxiety throughout the Western financial world.

Left: The Bank's Chief Foreign Exchange Dealer leaves the Worker's Court, Cologne after the inquiry into the Bank's affairs. The crisis had been caused by speculation in world foreign exchange markets.

Left: the Bank of New York *centre:* the Chemical Bank New York and *below:* the Dime Savings Bank. **In theory, banks compete to attract customers by offering better interest rates or reduced bank charges to depositors. In practice, however, there is agreement on the amount of competition that is commercially feasible.**

Below: The leading banks in the world, with their assets at the end of 1977. **Deposits make up by far the largest part of the total; the BankAmerica Corporation, for example had $66,405 million on deposit.**

and travellers' cheques; cheque and credit cards; budget schemes and savings accounts; bridging loans for house purchase; personal loans, hire purchase and insurance services. They also provide the customer with advice on such matters as income tax, executor and trustee affairs and investments, and will buy or sell stocks and shares.

Banking for profit

The purpose of all these services from the bank shareholders' point of view, is to attract deposits either from individuals or companies, to provide funds for lending or investing. It is the interest that banks gain from customers on the money they borrow that is the main source of their earnings. Of course, they also make charges to customers for other services, such as a handling fee for cheques drawn or paid into accounts whose balance is below a certain amount. But the profit obtained from such sources is minute compared with

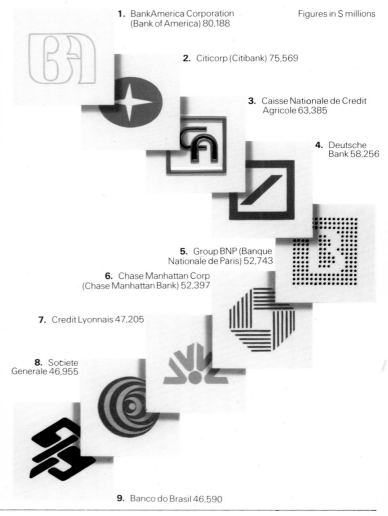

1. BankAmerica Corporation (Bank of America) 80,188   Figures in $ millions

2. Citicorp (Citibank) 75,569

3. Caisse Nationale de Credit Agricole 63,385

4. Deutsche Bank 58,256

5. Group BNP (Banque Nationale de Paris) 52,743

6. Chase Manhattan Corp (Chase Manhattan Bank) 52,397

7. Credit Lyonnais 47,205

8. Societe Generale 46,955

9. Banco do Brasil 46,590

the income banks earn from loans.

Like every other business, banks have their expenses, of which the major one is salaries. In most countries, bankers' salaries have risen very rapidly in recent years, encouraging banks to instal computers and other labour saving machines. Banks must also pay interest on time and savings deposits, and on money they buy from the money markets. Therefore, the interest they earn on their advances and investments has to be sufficient to finance both their payments of interest and their operating costs. They must also be able to cover bad debts and depreciation on fixed-interest investments. What remains, is profit.

Controls on lending

The bank's ability to extend loans and make investments is limited by the resources – mostly deposits – at its disposal at any one moment, and is further limited by the fact that not all deposits can be prudently lent out again. Bankers know from centuries of experience that they must retain a portion of deposits in liquid form – that is, in cash, or in other assets that can be very quickly turned into cash if the need arises. Such assets might be short term loans to other banks, balances kept with a central bank, or government treasury bills. A third barrier to extending loans is that put up by government regulations of various kinds. In most countries, for example, banks are required to keep a certain proportion of their deposits in particular assets specified by the government.

The concept of 'ratios' is therefore very important. A banker must always keep a close watch on his lending ratio – the proportion of advances to deposits – his cash and liquid assets ratios – the proportion of cash and other liquid assets to deposits, and his reserve asset ratio. That is, whether his bank is within official limits and has sufficient reserves available to finance further lending.

Bankers are constrained too by other considerations, such as maintaining a balance between short, medium and long-term loans; the balance varies from bank to bank depending on deposit structures. Above all, there is the need to keep bad debts to a minimum. When banks collapse, as many small British banks did during the crisis of 1973-75, it is usually due to bad investments, or an effort to get rich quick, or because they have borrowed short and long.

The role of the central bank

Central banks frequently operate, and sometimes decide, the fiscal policies of nations. Among their chief responsibilities are those of watching over the health and stability of their commercial banking systems, and of making sure that they maintain adequate capital resources. In most countries, they are also deeply involved in external matters, such as the exchange rate policy and relations with other central banks. But so long as the world finance is in equilibrium, the main function of central banks is to advise their governments on monetary policy and help them implement it.

The need for competition between banks

Banks compete with each other by offering more attractive rates of interest than their rivals, or by lowering their charges on advances to customers – at least in theory. In fact, in many countries,

Right: The Bank of Credit and Commerce International, London, largely backed by Arab funds. **In recent years, the vast profits made by Middle Eastern states from the sale of oil have been a constant factor in the banking and investment scenes.**

banks have instituted all kinds of formal and informal agreements that tend to limit competition – especially in interest rates. Services offered to personal account holders by different banks are also very similar. All the same, it is impossible to conclude that the system is not competitive, and still less that any alternative system – say, one with complete governmental control – would serve the customer better.

In order to continue to make profits for its shareholders, the first duty of any business is to survive. However, experience has suggested that totally unregulated banking leads to periodic crises, as happened repeatedly during the nineteenth century. It is possible for banks to attract business away from each other by underwriting dubious investments, or by offering higher interest rates to depositors. But this leads all too often to a crisis of confidence that affects all the banks and, on the whole, it seems better that they should abjure

Above: The Bank of England. **Affectionately nicknamed 'the old lady of Threadneedle Street,' the bank was founded by a group of London merchants in 1694. It was nationalised officially in 1946, though it for long had been the central bank of the UK. As such, it implements much of the government's economic and financial policy.**

Left: The 'big three' banks – The Bank of China, the Hong Kong and Shanghai Banking Corporation and the Chartered Bank – in Hong Kong, the leading financial centre of the Orient. **Hong Kong has more banks per square mile than almost any other place in the world. Because funds there are readily available and interest rates are relatively low, the city is a major source of 'cheap money' for multinational companies.**

some forms of competition. Having done so, however, it becomes equally impossible for bankers to prove they are competitive as it is for customers to prove that they are not.

Banks for all customers

To discover whether the banks offer an adequate service to all their customers it is again necessary to look at the degree of competition they have in the different markets they serve. So far as large companies are concerned, there is no doubt that competition between banks is extremely active. As well as domestic banks, all major cities contain a large number of foreign establishments, all willing and eager to provide large companies with a wide variety of servics, and it really is the companies' own fault if they do not get a good deal from one of them.

At first glance, it may seem that by comparison, the personal customer is offered rather a poor choice. Until recently, this was indeed the case then, in the last decade or so, a whole new range of facilities appeared – savings banks, co-operative banks, mutual banks – all presenting a brisk challenge to the old commercial houses. Germany, for example, has some 6200 independent credit insititutions, of which only 279 are commercial banks. The remainder are specialist banks of one kind or another – mortgage banks, savings banks, co-operative banks and instalment credit institutions. Germany at least is not suffering from any lack of competition in its personal banking services.

International banking

Since the Second World War, banking philosophy and practice has concentrated more and more upon internationalization and the cross-country interpenetration of banking systems.

One aspect of this is the rapid growth of the international pool of short-term, footloose funds known as the Eurocurrency market, the size of which was estimated in 1978, by the Bank for International Settlements, at about $400 billions. Broadly speaking, it is made up of ordinary bank deposits held by companies, financial institutions and governments with banks outside their own countries. The centre of the Euro-dollar market, and of many other currency markets, is in London, a vast, international banking system that ex-

Above: The Amsterdam branch of the US-owned First National City Bank. **Until fairly recently, US commercial banks were alone in being active in both the domestic and international fields. Now, they have been joined by many other banks, chiefly from Europe and Japan.**

Right: The Seaman's Bank in Wall Street, the financial centre of the USA. **Wall Street was the scene of the great crash of 1929 into which an over-adventurous banking policy made a major contribution.**

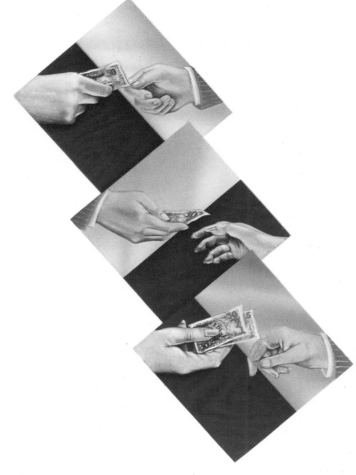

pands at the rate of about $70 billions a year.

From an institutional point of view, this system is dominated to an increasing extent by the leading banks of the United States, Europe and Japan. A further 400–500 banks also take an active part in international banking business, helping to keep the market competitive, but the big banks have most of the advantages. Their stability is beyond question, since their governments could not let them fail. They also have branches all over the world, they have firm contacts with the major borrowers, corporate or governmental; and they can raise the billion-dollar loans that the major borrowers require.

The huge jump in the size of loans, caused by the ever-growing financing needs of governments and companies, as well as by crises such as the payments deficits arising out of the oil price increase in 1973-74, has revolutionised the structure of international banking.

Only a couple of decades ago, banking was still to a large extent specialised, in the sense that different banks concen-

Above: The Jersey base of Hambros Executor and Trustee Company Ltd. **Because taxes in the Channel Islands are far lower than in mainland Britain, many companies are registered there. Liechtenstein and the Cayman Islands are among the world's other 'tax havens.'**

trated on different aspects of banking. In Britain, the clearing banks confined themselves largely to servicing their domestic clients, while foreign business was handled by the British overseas banks. French banking was divided in a similar way. Only in the United States, was overseas banking conducted from the start by the large commercial banks – partly bcause US banking regulations prevented them from expanding as fast as they wanted at home.

In those days, international banking was mostly concerned with trade finance – the movement of raw materials, semi-manufactured and manufactured goods between countries, their passage being assured by bills of exchange and other traditional banking techniques that had remained unchanged since the nineteenth century. Trade is still important, and banks still use bills of exchange, but the really big business lies elsewhere. International lending is now far more involved with making direct loans to big corporations and to governments than with financing specific trade transactions. Only the

How banks use their funds. 1 **Money is deposited in either a current or deposit account, the bank paying interest on the latter.** 2 **The bank then loans to borrowers who repay the loan either in a lump sum or in stages – plus the bank's interest shares** 3 .

largest banks can handle business like this, which is why most of the old overseas banks have been taken over by large combines, or have formed mergers between themselves.

The survivors

One famous group of banks, though small as individuals, has managed to survive in this new banking era. These are the old-established merchant banks, such as Rothschild, Hambro and Hill Samuel, whose solid expertise, gained over centuries, still assures them of a place in the modern world. Their contacts are impeccable, they can move faster than bigger and more bureaucratic organisations and their advice is pure gold. In the international field, they specialise in export credits and long-term Eurobond business, where borrowers raise fixed rate money from the public, as well as from banks. In addition, they manage large investment portfolios on behalf of international clients. Though none figures in the list of the top world banks, the merchant banks continue to flourish among the huge, faceless combines.

Banking and world development

Every year, to an ever-growing extent, economic development is coming to depend upon loans advanced by the international banks. Oil rigs in the North Sea and in Alaska, the search for minerals in the Amazon Basin, the building of petrochemical plants and new towns in the Middle East, and of atomic power stations, new industries and harbour installations throughout the world, are all financed by banks.

The reason why so many countries, including most socialist ones, have turned to the international banks to help them maintain growth, is partly due to the old-fashioned source of equity capital drying up in an inflationary age, and partly because taxpayers in the rich countries are not prepared to increase their contributions to the World Bank or to Direct Aid. Another reason, of course, is that many of these projects are highly profitable and it is well worth the bankers' trouble to seek them out. But there are heavy risks. The banks can never be quite sure whether all the countries they have advanced money to will be able to repay their loans, and there is always the chance that the whole banking structure might come crashing down if too many borrowers defaulted.

Whether profit motivated or not, it must be remembered that the contribution the banks are making to world development, and especially to the development of emerging countries, is a very real one. At a time when growth has practically ceased in the advanced nations, it is perhaps only the banks who can afford to take the risks.

Right: An oil rig in action in the North Sea. **The burden of the huge financial investment needed to exploit these resources was largely shouldered by the international banks. Their involvement is worldwide, stretching from Alaska to the Amazon Basin to the Middle East.**

Otavolo Indians,
Ecuador, trade beads at a
stall in a street market.

2.

MONEY AND THE CREATION OF WEALTH

Money is the essential sinew of world wealth. Without it – and the economic systems and financial organizations that have grown up around it – the wheels of industry would grind to a halt, trade would cease and society as we know it would crumble. Mankind would return to a primitive battle for day-to-day survival, dependent on what each individual, or groups of individuals, could grow or produce. This section explains such questions as the nature of economic wealth, how economic policy has developed from the days when every nation's sole aim was to enrich itself at the expense of its competitors, and the role that money plays in trade, the production of goods and in the world market place.

THE MOBILIZATION OF RESOURCES

One of the most significant works in economics is Adam Smith's *An Inquiry into the Nature and Causes of the Wealth of Nations*, published in 1776. The questions it deals with are truly fundamental; what is the nature of economic wealth? Why are some nations wealthy and others poor? How is the wealth of a society related to its economic organization?

To Adam Smith, a nation was wealthy if it provided for the economic wants of its people. Until his time, it was thought that just as a man was wealthy if he had a lot of money, so a nation was wealthy if it possessed a large stock of gold. This view, known as mercantilism, led nations to increase their wealth by exporting goods in exchange for gold. World economic policy was simply a matter of each nation striving to enrich itself at another's expense.

To Smith, the wealth of nations depended not on the gold they held but on the goods and services they produced – a concept that has now become more familiar under the name of Gross National Product (GNP). But what determines how much a country can produce? Its main resource, according to Smith, is the labour of its people. People create economic wealth as they work. Smith, in fact, thought wealth was created only by labour, and that the value of a product was determined entirely by the amount of labour time that went into its production.

Trade and Living Standards

But, if all wealth is created by labour, how is it that some countries are wealthy and others poor? Some nations might have natural advantages – a more fertile soil, or a better climate perhaps.

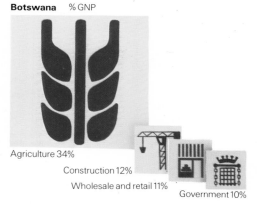

The Netherlands   % Exports

Manufacturing 56%
Chemicals 28%
Agriculture 9%
Mining and quarrying 7%

Botswana   % GNP

Agriculture 34%
Construction 12%
Wholesale and retail 11%
Government 10%

Rich and poor. The contrast between developed countries and the emergent nations is clearly set out in this comparison between the Netherlands and Botswana. The Netherlands has a long history of prosperity. Its chief earnings come from its role as a communications centre and its manufacturing industry, which contributes 56% of its export potential *(above).* **Per capita income is about $2,500 a year. Botswana, on the other hand, is a poor country, which, despite mineral discoveries in recent years, depends largely on agriculture to make a living; 34% of the Gross National Product comes from farming. Per capita annual income is about $100.**

But even more important is the ability of a community, or of a nation, to enrich itself through trade. In a subsistence peasant economy, each family tries to grow enough food to feed itself. Typically, this means endless toil, a monotonous diet and a low standard of living, forever vulnerable to poor harvests or other natural hazards. However, if the economy is opened up to trade, people can instead specialize in the production of goods for which their land, or abilities, are best suited, sell their surplus, and raise their living standard by buying goods from the outside world.

Through trade, everybody can be better off. Take, for example, the case of two farmers, each of whom devotes half his land to growing wheat and the other half to vines. One farmer has land on which wheat flourishes, but vines grow only with difficulty. He produces 300 bushels of wheat and 100 litres of wine. The other, working on different soil, produces 100 bushels of wheat and 300 litres of wine. The first farmer will be well-fed but sober, the second hungry and drunk. But if they entered into a trading agreement, the first could give all his land to wheat, so producing 600 bushels, while the second, growing only vines, could make 600 litres of wine. They could then exchange 300 bushels of wheat for 300 litres of wine, and both have sufficient to eat and drink. The standard of living of both farmers has increased as a result of trade and specialization. In simple terms, this demonstrates the basis of the argument that people and nations should be permitted to trade freely with one another, unhampered by controls and regulations. This is the doctrine of 'laissez faire', that asserts it is free trade that allows the

Planning 'The Wealth of Nations'

Adam Smith, the great Scottish political economist and philosopher, was born in Kirkcaldy, Fife, in June 1723; his father, a customs official, died some months before his birth. He was educated at Glasgow University and Balliol, Oxford, but soon abandoned the English university as having little to offer him in the pursuit of what was to be his life's work. He returned to Scotland, and in 1748, embarked on a series of public lectures in Edinburgh whose chief theme was 'the obvious and simple system of natural liberty'–a theme which laid the foundations of his later, monumental work, *An Inquiry into the Nature and Causes of the Wealth of Nations.*

During the early 1750s, Smith joined the faculty of Glasgow University, first as Professor of Logic, and later, Professor of Moral Philosophy. By this time, his views on ethics, economics, politics and jurisprudence were commanding world-wide attention; however, in 1763, he surrendered his chair to become mentor to the young Duke of Buccleuch, then about to embark on the Grand Tour. During his sojourn abroad, Smith met many of the savants of his day, but after two years, he returned once more to Kirkaldy to begin work on *The Wealth of Nations,* published finally in 1776. Two years later, he gained an appointment to the customs service, a post he held until he died in 1790. Shortly before his death, he destroyed most of his papers, but from the fragments remaining, it would seem that he had been planning two further major works, one on law and the other on science and the arts.

But it was the great canvas of *The Wealth of Nations* that had such a profound effect on his contemporaries and, at the same time, assured him of a place among the immortals. Summarizing so great a work is almost impossible, but briefly, the cornerstones of his thesis were these:

The annual labour of every nation is the fund which originally supplies it with all the necessaries and conveniences of life.

'The state should not seek to control or restrain individual activity or employment. Following on this 'the obvious and simple system of natural liberty establishes itself of its own accord. Every man, so long as he does not violate the laws of justice, is left perfectly free to pursue his own interest his own way, and to bring both his industry and his capital into competition with those of any other man, or order of men. The sovereign is completely discharged from the duty…of superintending the industry of private people, and of directing it towards the employments most suitable to the interests of society.'

In the natural course of things, the capital of every growing society should be directed first to agriculture, second to manufacture and only third to foreign commerce. Colonies could benefit only a few; the country as a whole could only lose by overseeing them. (On the other hand, he foresaw a Commonwealth system in which the colonies would evolve, together with the mother country, into a free-trading group of independent partners who were 'faithful, independent and generous allies.')

The division, or specialization of labour, is vital to economic progress; the role of money is in assessing the relative values of specializations. Apart from this, and the purchase of goods, so occasioning further labour, money serves little purpose at all.

'Every frugal man is a public benefactor,' for any form of private saving, since consumption has been rejected, is an investment on behalf of society as a whole.

Some of Smith's arguments are difficult to follow, he digresses frequently and his writing is occasionally tortuous. But *The Wealth of Nations* was the first noble attempt to show the interdependence of all facets of economic life, and through it to reveal political economy as a discipline in its own right.

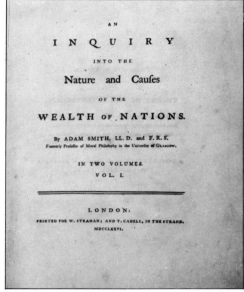

Born in Kirkcaldy *(above right)* **and part educated at Balliol college, Oxford** *(below),* **Adam Smith was one of the 18th century's leading economic thinkers. His**

The Wealth of Nations' *(right)* **was one of the first attempts to set out all the facets of economic life and combine them into a unified whole.**

greatest growth in people's standards of living.

The Meaning of Money
Trade itself uses economic resources. Goods must be transported and distributed, creating specialist traders such as dealers, wholesalers and retailers. Because these people do not produce goods their work is sometimes thought to be unnecessary – even parasitic. In fact, their work makes an important contribution to the wealth of a nation, as does that of the banker. Just as exchange may create a need for specialist traders, so it also requires a means of payment. Money allows resources to realize their potential through the mechanism of exchange.

Among other factors that contribute to economic wealth are capital accumulation and the division of labour. Capital in one sense means goods that are produced not to be consumed, but to be used in production of other goods. Capital goods do not contribute directly to the standard of living, but indirectly through increasing the productivity of labour. Capital goods exist in all types of economic organization. For example, a subsistence farmer may well own agricultural tools and buildings. But beyond the requirements of his work and living, it is quite pointless for him to accumulate capital.

By contrast, in a developed economy, capital accumulation providing mechanization and the division of labour is highly beneficial. The idea is that, by breaking up a process of production into a number of stages, each stage can be operated with much greater efficiency using specialized labour equipped with equally specialized tools. Through specialist production a very much larger amount of goods can be produced with a given labour force.

Specialization requires a new form of economic organization: the large industrial firm. With small-scale production, each man is his own master and makes his own decisions. In the large firm, the managers of the firm employ workers to do specific tasks over which the workers have little control. The managers may be responsible to the firm's owners, or to the state, or even to a workers' council, but in every case it is the managers who determine the workers' tasks. In return, workers receive wages which they can spend on whatever goods and services they can

Production possibility. A simple economic model illustrates the theory of production possibility. In a society with two main products – bread and wine – the quantities of each of the two products the society can produce, given the physical resources at its disposal, is charted. If A amount of bread is produced, then A is the optimum figure for wine production. If bread production rises to B, then wine falls proportionately. The curve produced is known as the production possibility factor. It indicates the maximum quantity that can be produced, depending on the allocation of resources.

Bread

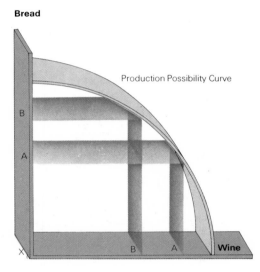

Production Possibility Curve

afford. Again, it is the existence of money and exchange which makes large-scale production and economic growth possible.

The 'Invisible Hand'
Apart from the creation of wealth and the roles of capital accumulation and money in an economy, it is also necessary to consider how goods are produced to match people's wants. Adam Smith argued that a system of prices and free markets would lead the economy 'by an Invisible Hand' to produce goods which best matched people's preferences. If people wanted more of a certain article, its price would rise and its production become more profitable. Production would therefore increase in response to the increased opportunities for profit. If the costs of producing the article fell, competition among producers would cause a decrease in its price, and consumers would respond by buying more of it.

One aspect of the economic process is the creation of goods to satisfy consumers' desires; such desires are generally thought of as being either unlimited, or in excess of what can be

satisfied from available resources. Therefore, the resources available for production are not limitless, and we must choose the ends to which they are put. The process of production itself involves the combination of many different factors. Raw materials enter into production processes and may emerge as intermediate goods, which are then reprocessed until final consumption goods are created for either industrial or domestic consumers. At each stage, the producer is faced with decisions as to how best to mix the factors of production available to him – how best to combine his 'capital', raw materials, machinery and labour, so as to achieve his product at the lowest cost.

In theory, then, economies have many options when allocating resources to produce goods. These options always permit certain types of production to expand to meet demand, though only at the expense of other goods being produced. This is true so long as the labour supply remains constant, the exploitation of raw materials continues on an even level, and there is no sudden and startling technological advance. Within this theoretical framework, it is possible to chart the impact of choosing from unlimited alternatives for allocating available resources. But, of course, in time many changes occur which shift this 'Production Possibility Frontier', as it is called, far beyond the simple transactions of the wheat producer and the wine producer.

The World of Walras
In an economy where thousands of goods are being produced, the same conditions – scarcity, choice and cost, the law of diminishing returns – will prevail, but at the same time it is necessary to consider how each individual in this far more complex world, will make and carry out his production and consumption plans. In an economy involving only two products, wheat and wine, moving outward to the Production Possibility Frontier seems plausible – but can the same balance be achieved in a society where literally millions of goods are produced? This problem was approached at the end of the 19th century by the Swiss economist Léon Walras, who demonstrated that even in a modern, complex economy, general equilibrium would be reached.

In an ideal world, according to Walras, each individual devises for himself a consumption plan and a production plan. Some people plan to supply labour, and others will have already supplied it to produce goods which now figure in their plans. In return for their labour, everyone will be planning to consume some of the various commodities available.

Seeking an equilibrium

At the beginning of the week, in Walras' world, everyone gathers in the market-place to pool their various consumption and production plans. An auctioneer calls out a complete list of exchange rates (or relative prices) between each pair of commodities, and observes the results in terms of the bids he receives from the people in the market place. For instance, he might call an exchange rate of two loaves of bread and one bottle of wine and discover that more bread was being offered for wine than there were offers of wine for bread. If so, he has to alter the exchange rate, perhaps to three loaves for one bottle. In other words, the auctioneer seeks for a general equilibrium that will please everyone. This process of moving towards a set of exchange rates in which each trade is satisfied is known as 'tatonnement.'

It is, of course, not necessary for the auctioneer to call out the exchange rates in terms of every pair of goods – he can take one item as a standard measure and call out the price of every other product in terms of that single chosen commodity, which is called a 'numeraire'. In this way, every product might be measured against the standard loaf of bread – a bottle of wine exchanges for three loaves. Therefore, the auctioneer has no need to call the exchange rate of ten bottles of wine for one sack of coal. The numeraire commodity is now acting as money in one of its functions – that of a unit of account. Each transactor can state his plans in terms of their value in the unit of account, and the task of the auctioneer becomes much simpler as the number of prices he has to call is reduced.

Trading in the Walrasian world occurs only when the general equilibrium list of prices is called. 'False' trading (at prices above or below the equilibrium levels), cannot therefore occur; the auctioneer gathers all the information necessary about the plans of the individuals and uses it in the tatonnement process.

Below: Léon Walras (1834-1910), author of the classic 'Elements of Pure Economics'. **In this book he set forward his idea of the perfect economic society.**

In this imaginary world, the problem of allocating labour services and consumption over time is not significant, since it is a world in which both markets and employment are assured. By its nature, production takes time – time for an entrepreneur to hire labour, to rent or buy machinery and raw materials and to supply his output. But if he lived in a world of certainty, these contracts would all be made at the beginning of the production process with no risk of default, or of not being able to satisfy the contracts. All decisions that an entrepreneur might, in the real world be making in sequence, as production advances, are made here at the beginning, and the process goes forward without a hitch. The same is true for the consumption process. In this world too, money ceases to be of any importance except, perhaps, to be retained as a unit of account, since all the contracts stretching between so many people and firms are certain and will be met by goods. In effect, time has ceased to be relevant to trading.

This Walrasian model is a useful starting point in understanding the role of money in a modern economy. It high-

lights the problem of co-ordinating the plans of different consumers and producers in determining how much of the various goods and services are supplied at prices which ensure that these commodities are sold. Also, that the amounts sold are those that people wish to, and are able to, buy at these equilibrium prices. These exchanges are carried out through a hypothetical process in which trading plans are co-ordinated, without cost, by a central authority – the auctioneer – whose function is to determine the exchange rates that will permit individuals to engage in a series of mutually beneficial transactions.

The introduction of the numeraire as a unit of account makes it simpler to express exchange rates or relative prices. But in this process, the choice of the numeraire commodity is an arbitrary one. Any one commodity would do: instead of choosing loaves of bread, we could just as easily have chosen bottles of wine or sacks of coal. Thus this view of exchange does not assign to any particular commodity the role of a unit of payment. Since any article may be traded directly for another, all commodities are perfect substitutes as means of payment.

Time and money

The only role that the time factor plays in this Walrasian world of certainty, is when exchange ratios are fixed at the very outset of the commercial process. Again, there is no need for money. Instead, there are claims over future goods which, in a certain world, will be delivered without default.

The distinctive features and functions of money begin to appear only when we leave this simplified system, and consider a more realistic situation where transactions do have costs; where uncertainty exists, especially about the future, and where the attempt to reduce uncertainty by obtaining information also has costs. These features of money become particularly apparent when the view of the economy changes from one market, in which all commodities are universally acceptable as means of payment, to one containing a large number of markets.

In the market place

In economics, the term 'market' does not simply mean an area where buyers and sellers meet to buy and sell produce.

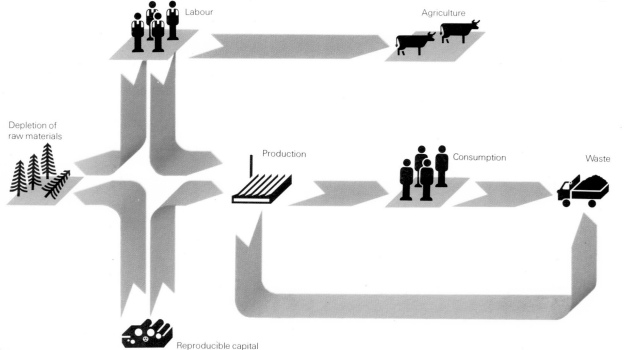

Labour

Agriculture

Depletion of raw materials

Production

Consumption

Waste

Reproducible capital

Above: Indian labourers threshing rice in a paddy field in Goa. **This type of farming, labour intensive but technologically backward, is a pattern which almost all underdeveloped nations are trying to change. The chief reason is that, though many are employed, not enough is produced.**
Left: The complex factors involved in production. **The elements – labour, raw materials, and reproducible capital – are all essential, whether the production is industrial or agricultural. The end products are consumption, together with a percentage of waste. Thus, a thriving consumer market is essential for a healthy economy, and, to economic planners, consumer reaction to price is an indication of how much should be produced, of what, and at what cost.**

Above: A combine harvester working on a farm in Lincolnshire. **Britain has one of the most capital intensive farming industries in the world, with a high level of production and a correspondingly reduced work force.**

Rather, it implies a device that enables buyers and sellers of a product or service to negotiate and agree the terms on which the particular commodity will be sold. It is too, a device for identifying sellers or buyers, so reducing the cost of searching for information on exchange opportunities. In this sense, therefore, it is an institution through which goods are exchanged. When an economist speaks of a market, he means the market for a particular commodity, usually at the level of the economy; examples might be the market for wheat, the market for books, the labour market or the market for second-hand cars.

In considering an economy in which thousands of products are being produced for millions of consumers, the problem of co-ordinating the various plans for buying and selling becomes immense. How can producers tell what quantity of any commodity they should produce? Or, indeed, whether they are producing exactly the product that

consumers want? Somehow, information has to flow between the production and consumption sectors of the economy. The market is one mechanism that ensures that such information is regularly issued and up to date.

Take the example of the competitive market in which the production of a single commodity has so many competing producers that no one among them has, by himself, the ability to influence the price at which the commodity is sold. Each producer must enter into contracts to buy materials and machinery, hire labour and offer contracts to sell his output. The higher the price he can obtain per unit of his output, the more he will be prepared to supply. The same would also be true of his competitors in the market who would also be willing to offer more if the price were higher. On the other hand, consumers have to decide how much of this commodity to purchase; they

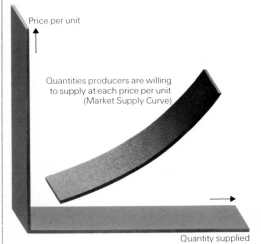

Price per unit

Quantities producers are willing
to supply at each price per unit
(Market Supply Curve)

Quantity supplied

Supply and demand. In a competitive market, one of the most important elements are the twin factors of supply and demand. If demand is left out of account, the price per unit would rise with the quantity supplied. This is known as the Market Supply

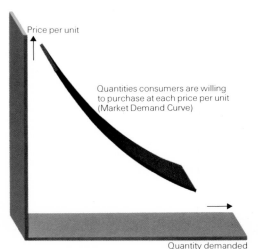

Price per unit

Quantities consumers are willing
to purchase at each price per unit
(Market Demand Curve)

Quantity demanded

Curve. However, consumers are usually willing to purchase more if the price comes down – the Market Demand Curve. By analysing the two factors, the unit price at which supply and demand are in balance is established.

would be willing to buy more if the prices were reduced.

Information from price changes

If in the market, where consumers and producers confront each other, there is only one unit price at which the willingness of producers to supply is matched by the willingness of consumers to demand, then the market is in equilibrium. Suppose, however, that producers had decided to put more goods on sale than consumers would be willing to buy at the price being charged. This means that there is excess supply in the market. Producers will find that stocks are building up in their warehouses, and that shops are not reordering. The market is no longer in equilibrium, and this information is quickly passed to the production sector. It reacts by reducing the unit price, thereby sending a signal to the consumption sector that conditions in the market are changing. As the price falls, so consumers will be prepared to buy more and producers to supply less – as a result the excess supply is reduced until once more the market achieves equilibrium.

In this way, prices act as signals, allowing information to flow, so co-ordinating the plans of producers and consumers. Each individual producer and consumer urgently needs information concerning the availability of all products and the exchange rates between them. The consumer can only decide how to allocate his total expenditure amongst the goods he wants if he has that information. Prices provide this, and price changes are the signals he reacts to in deciding how to choose the particular bundle of goods that best

meets his requirements. Producers also need information regarding availability of materials, labour and machinery. Again, the availability of price information from the relevant markets enables them to choose the appropriate 'mix' of resources which minimizes the cost of producing at any level of output. Of equal importance, the pattern of price changes over time helps producers to decide which range of goods they should be manufacturing in the future.

The workings of markets in the economy permits the co-ordination of production and consumption decisions through the reactions of consumers and producers to price signals. The flow of resources from one line of production to another, as a response to the information transmitted by price changes in various markets, is the mechanism that enables this co-ordination to take place. Resources are reallocated as a result of the information transmitted by the markets. This process is known as the price mechanism, or the market mechanism.

Disruption in the market

The market mechanism does not invariably work smoothly, however, since "shocks" can occur which cause the plans of sellers and buyers to move sharply out of balance. One case where the flow of information to consumers can cause massive imbalance, is the threat of a shortage of a particular product. Suppose, for example, that bakers call a strike; immediately the information to consumers is that far less bread will be available in the shops. Within the context of the competitive market, it could be expected that the demand would remain constant but the

price would rise because of the reduced supply. However, experience shows that the price of a loaf does not rise when some event occurs to disrupt production. Any shop that did put up its prices under such circumstances would become intensely unpopular, and in the long run, would lose trade.

What generally happens is that people react to the shortage with "panic buying" – that is, they will purchase far more than they could possibly use. To buy bread, they are prepared to stand for hours in long queues – and to send other members of the family out to queue at other shops in the district. At the same time, the shops take action by limiting each customer to only one loaf; or by serving only regular customers; or by working on the principle of first come first served. Economists call this 'allocation by sellers' preferences'. Nevertheless, in real terms, the price of the loaf has not remained constant, for to the normal price there must be added the cost of the time spent in queues and that of the stress and strain that goes with it – depending, of course, on the value of each individual's time, and on the degree of stress that queuing might impose upon him – or, more likely, her.

Side-issues of war

Similar problems of excess demand occur in wartime whenever the production of consumer goods is severely disrupted; they occur, too, in planned economies where consumer goods may appear low on the planners' list of priorities. Illegal 'black markets' arise, though oddly enough, they may still be governed by the signalling mechanism and rationing by price. People who have illicit supplies of a commodity

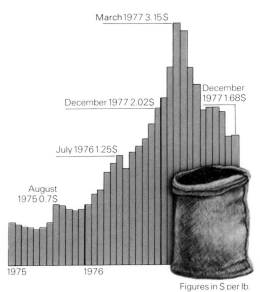

March 1977 3.15$

December 1977 2.02$

December 1977 1.68$

July 1976 1.25$

August 1975 0.7$

1975   1976

Figures in $ per lb.

Countries which are largely dependent on a single product for economic prosperity can fall victim to market forces, as this diagram illustrates. In July 1975, a world coffee shortage, brought about by a frost in Brazil combined with drought and disturbances in other coffee-producing countries, led to a fantastic price increase. Prices soared from 50 cents a pound to 3.20 dollars by April 1977; However, by mid-1977, prices had begun to fall, and in an effort to maintain them, Brazil first withheld coffee from the market and then, with Columbia, organised the Manuas Agreement, that set $3.20 per pound as the minimum selling price. Other coffee-producing nations were asked to join in. However, the coffee growers were unable to emulate the oil-producing nation's success in controlling the price of their product, largely because consumers refused to buy.

for which demand cannot be satisfied at the open market price, offer their goods at higher rates and so soak up some of the excess demand. Naturally, they risk severe penalties, but they balance that risk with the benefits of sale at inflated prices.

Similar black markets arise when commodities – such as heroin, marijuana, or alcoholic drinks during Prohibition in the US – are illegal. Though the law has made open market dealings in these goods impossible, the general rules of supply and demand prevail and the price of goods sold in the black market will reflect the extra risks involved.

The monopoly game

Setting minimum prices can also distort the workings of the market. For example, one firm might control the majority of the market output of a commodity, and so have monopoly power which it could use to raise the price above the competitive equilibrium. An international example of this was seen

Above: Queueing for bread outside a London bakers during a bread strike. Here, the action of a small, but vital, group of bakery workers led to disruption in the market and hence to "panic buying", which also affected the price of flour. The result was the imposition of a rationing system by the retailers, defined by economists as allocation by sellers' preferences.

Left: Russians queue for alcohol, served directly from a tanker. **In a Communist economy, such scarcities occur through state action, never through the actions of individuals. As the state controls the entire market, it is impossible for anyone to profit from shortages.**

recently when Brazil held back large amounts of raw coffee from the market and so forced up the price. Even more far-reaching were the activities of OPEC who, in 1973 and 1974, used their control over vast oil resources to force dramatic rises in the price of crude oil. Though such distortions reflect the influence of imperfections in the system, in pure economic terms, the general rules of the competitive market still apply.

The function of money

It is in the context of organized markets that the functions of money can be best analyzed. We do not buy books by giving up cigarettes, beer or by offering labour. Nor do we normally receive payment in such goods. The costs to each individual in terms of time and effort to engage in such transactions would be prohibitive. However, for the

sake of argument, these costs consist of two elements, those of bargaining and search, which can be viewed as being independent of the quantities exchanged, and are incurred every time an exchange takes place. Other costs to such an exchange reflect the inconvenience, storage and transport involved which vary enormously with the quantities traded. All these costs will obviously be much reduced when transactions are carried out in markets where products can be exchanged through an accepted medium, which makes the search for mutually beneficial trading less costly. By lowering transaction costs, it releases wealth, time and energy for other purposes. Traders no longer need to search for the double, or multiple, coincidence of wants necessitated by barter, as they can sell their goods for the agreed medium of exchange and use their

receipts of that medium elsewhere for their purchases.

Once a sale has been made, the seller will still need to know something about the value and characteristics of the item offered in exchange – or, if payment is deferred, something about the honesty, reliability and credit worthiness of the purchaser. As the Bank of England economist, Charles Goodhart, puts it: "so uncertainty, a condition which would also seem to imply the existence of transactions' cost, is a necessary condition for a monetary system, defined as one which generally uses some specialized means of payment to implement exchanges".

It is therefore obvious that a complex market economy needs money and to function efficiently, "money" can be seen as one of the inevitable results of the development of such an economy.

Above: The 'black market' in the ruins of Berlin immediately after the Second World War. **Such markets exist whenever there is excessive, almost uncontrollable, demand for the few goods available – in this case, butter, flour and eggs, among many others.**

Right: Ticket touts selling football tickets at vastly inflated prices outside Wembley Stadium, London. **Touting is a classic case of the laws of supply and demand in operation. The price is determined solely by shortage and the willingness of people to buy.**

A medieval market,
based on a stained glass
window, Tournai
Cathedral.

3.

ECONOMIC SYSTEMS

The universal acceptance of money as a common means of exchange was the beginning of a long, evolutionary progress, in which various economic systems emerged, at times co-existed, survived and disappeared, as their usefulness came to an end. In the societies of early times, economic life, based as it was largely on the family or the tribe, was relatively simple. But, as life became more complex, so did the nature of the world economy and the systems used in its operation. Over the centuries came such developments as the birth of the market, industry, capitalism and Communism. Some of these changes have been the inevitable result of technological and economic progress; others, however, have been a deliberate choice.

SOCIETY AND ECONOMICS

Economic systems change over time. They also coexist at the same time. The contemporary industrial capitalist economic system is not the only one in the world but it is the outcome of a long evolutionary process. Some of the developments in economic institutions are inevitable because they are dictated by technical and economic progress. Others are more a question of choice for the particular society. So, different societies can have different institutions either because they are at different levels of development or because they have made different choices, or for both these reasons. (In fact, many would say that the choice of system open to a society is critically constrained by its level of development.)

During the early part of the history of mankind economic life was, of course, much simpler than it is now. Man was basically a food collector and hunting was the main economic activity. Tools and weapons were elementary and so was economic organization. Men did the hunting and fishing whereas women bore and raised children. Agriculture emerged much later to increase somewhat the complexity of man's economic life, although the organization still remained simple. The basic unit was the self-contained tribal family or community with a low degree of specialization and division of labour among its members. The system was hierarchical but relations between members of the community were generally determined by custom. It restricted the influence of the chief at the top. Self-sufficiency, low specialization and rule by custom were the main socio-economic characteristics of the primitive community. It is still thought to exist in some isolated jungle areas.

Soldiers and slaves

Occasionally the customs were disrupted. The community would find itself at war. Emergencies originating externally required adjustments to the community's organization. The basic adjustment was the partial abandonment of customary rule in favour of some form of military despotism and simple command. Fear made this acceptable until the emergency passed or until new customs developed to deal with changed circumstances. The alternation between custom and command was another feature of the traditional economy and society although it is not uncommon at higher levels of development as well.

At times it was possible for the traditional society to increase its consumption through plunder which enabled it also to support its armed forces at war. At some stage, however, it was found necessary to support at least a nucleus of an armed force on a regular basis and a specialist military class emerged. To maintain it, the rest of the community had to produce a surplus over and above its own requirements or plunder had to be regularized. That was achieved in some cases through the enslavement of captives. The surplus of

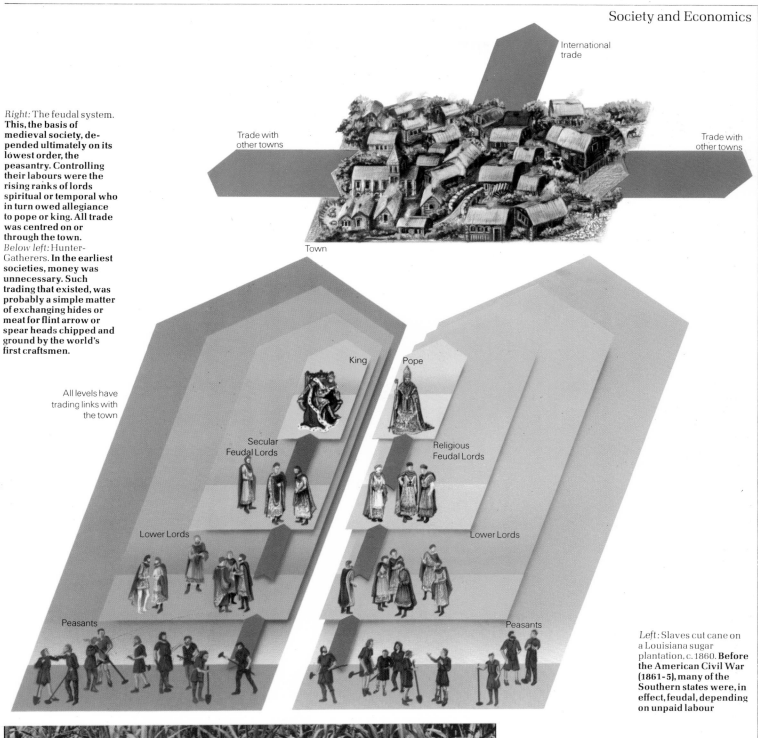

Right: The feudal system. **This, the basis of medieval society, depended ultimately on its lowest order, the peasantry. Controlling their labours were the rising ranks of lords spiritual or temporal who in turn owed allegiance to pope or king. All trade was centred on or through the town.**

Below left: Hunter-Gatherers. **In the earliest societies, money was unnecessary. Such trading that existed, was probably a simple matter of exchanging hides or meat for flint arrow or spear heads chipped and ground by the world's first craftsmen.**

International trade

Trade with other towns

Trade with other towns

Town

All levels have trading links with the town

King

Pope

Secular Feudal Lords

Religious Feudal Lords

Lower Lords

Lower Lords

Peasants

Peasants

Left: Slaves cut cane on a Louisiana sugar plantation, c. 1860. **Before the American Civil War (1861-5), many of the Southern states were, in effect, feudal, depending on unpaid labour**

the work of the slaves above their basic subsistence could not only support the army but also raise the standard of living of the community. For many centuries and until relatively recent times slaves were to remain an economically important class. In ancient Greece or Rome as much as 70 per cent of the population may have been slaves at certain times.

The feudal pyramid

A surplus could also be extracted, however, by the chiefs from the non-slave community either for the benefit of the community or for their own use. That was the basic pattern that characterized the whole range of feudal institutions. In the basic feudal unit, the manor, feudal lords with their armies and servants were supported by contributions from their subjects. These were given initially in agricultural produce, labour or military services but money also came to be used. In exchange the community enjoyed the lord's protection, together with a hereditary right of use of a piece of land,

the feudum, granted by the lord. The feudal peasant (serf) was, unlike a slave, not a piece of property. He could not be sold or separated from his land or his family. Feudal rights, however, could be transferred from one lord to another. The lord himself in turn paid contributions and owed allegiance to a higher lord whose protection he enjoyed. There was then a pyramid-like structure in which lower feudal lords generally stood in the same relation to higher ones as their own subjects to

themselves. At the very top stood the central lord, the king. But authority was not always easy to enforce. Distance made it hard for higher-order lords to make effective their claims on subjects for contributions on which the maintenance of their armies and servants depended. The feudal hierarchy was often a loose one.

Feudal society was also based on custom but this often shaded into command. Military, civilian and often religious leaders generally coincided

Left: Country market in Grenada. **The earliest market traders were usually the producers themselves – farmers and craftsmen – who brought the results of their labours to a centre determined by custom to barter or sell. The middlemen, the merchants and shopkeepers, were a much later development, and essential to the growth of trade, for they had the ability to settle the prices of commodities, one against another. But in some parts of the world, the old style trading continues.**

and the kings of the feudal states were mostly former chiefs of primitive tribes that had invaded the area. The lords administered the system of justice through the custom of the manor and naturally were often prone to interpret it in their own favour, but a system of rights did exist based on tradition.

In comparison with the traditional economy the feudal economy, although still predominantly self-sufficient, did involve more exchange. To that extent the role of money also grew during the feudal era, opening the way to modern economic institutions. But the development took place somewhat unevenly in the course of history.

In antiquity, and during the Middle Ages, there was a very developed commercial economy around the Mediterranean which did not extend to the European hinterland and rather existed in parallel with the traditional and the feudal economy. Indeed, around all densely inhabited coastal areas trade was plentiful – the ease of water trans-

port was the key to commercial vitality. It is only in the last few centuries that the mercantile economy finally triumphed in inland areas. So the economic history of the world cannot be neatly divided into chronological periods.

The first markets
The crucial development has been that of the market. Market exchange presupposes some specialization and division of labour but the two are not identically related. The traditional

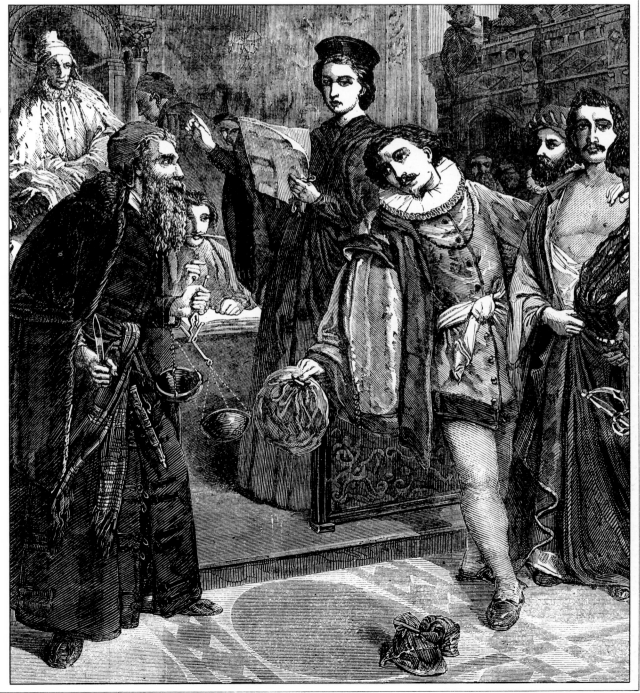

Right: The Merchant of Venice. **By the end of the 15th century, the merchants of northern Italy had grown so powerful that they were able to set up independent states such as Florence and Venice. They were ruled by merchant princes who controlled Mediterranean trade as the Hanseatic League commanded that of northern Europe. Tales of the merchants' lavish and opulent mode of living circulated even to far-off England, where they inspired Shakespeare to write his play.**

The wealth of the 'Hansa'

Map labels: Bergen, Oslo, Revel, Narva, Visby, Novgorod, Riga, Hull, Kiel, Rostock, Danzig, Konigsberg, Boston, Hamburg, Lynn, Ipswich, Bremen, Lubeck, Stralsund, London, Dortmund, Brunswick, Berlin, Bruges, Cologne

Chief Member Towns
Chief Agency Counters

Medieval commerce reached its apogee with such developments as the growth of the Hanseatic League *(top)*, a band of merchant-cities, which, as early as the 13th century, had virtually converted the whole of northern Europe into a single economic unit. At the height of its power in the 14th century, 160 towns belonged to the League, which had gained a near monopoly of the lucrative Baltic and Low Countries' trade, especially in fish, timber, furs, wax and amber. Its power was centred on the ports of northern Germany, but there were outlying agencies with special rights in such trading centres as Bergen, Novgorod, London and Bruges. Its aims were always commercial, but it pursued such an aggressive policy of embargo and blockade that it won exceptional trading privileges for its members. But, by the time that Holbein painted this Hansa trader *(above)*, the growth of nationalism had brought about the League's decline. Its unique trading privileges were gradually rescinded by one country after another, and finally, in the mid-16th century, the Dutch won control of the Baltic trade.

economy already had some division of labour and specialization based on skill. But that specialization was directed from above by the ruling authority and was not achieved through the market mechanism. It is the market, nevertheless, that has provided the big impetus to specialization.

The breakthrough in market development was reached when casual trading gave way to regular trading, which in turn led to the establishment of a specialist merchant class. Up to a point, the producer himself was able to carry out the merchant function. But with trade becoming increasingly distant and risky, the need grew for the specialist middleman. Even in the traditional and feudal economies specialist traders did exist. The feudal lord himself would employ a few to administer the manor's external trade. But the mercantile economy really began to flourish in places where there was considerable opportunity for external trade, such as the ports around the Mediterranean. Back in antiquity and during the Middle Ages, many of these developed into city-states whose rulers were themselves engaged in trade. They were small and independent as they had to be in order to adapt their institutions sufficiently to the special needs of foreign trade and to derive maximum advantage from it. But the medieval world also had many inland towns which were the centres of manufacture and trade. Many had been established by manorial lords who were keen to derive tax revenues from their expected prosperity. Independent craftsmen developed into regular traders selling manufactures to the manors and to distant parts for money. On the whole, nevertheless, the medieval economy remained mainly agrarian.

The nature of the traditional and, later, of the feudal society also dictated an ideology that was compatible with it. The ideology was a system of values and attitudes which rationalize and justify social institutions. As custom and/or command were the basis of these societies their ideology was naturally rather conservative, particularly in the Middle Ages when the Catholic Church was a dominant force. It was paternalistic in that it emphasized obedience to those who had been destined by birth for leadership and who in turn had paternalistic obliga-

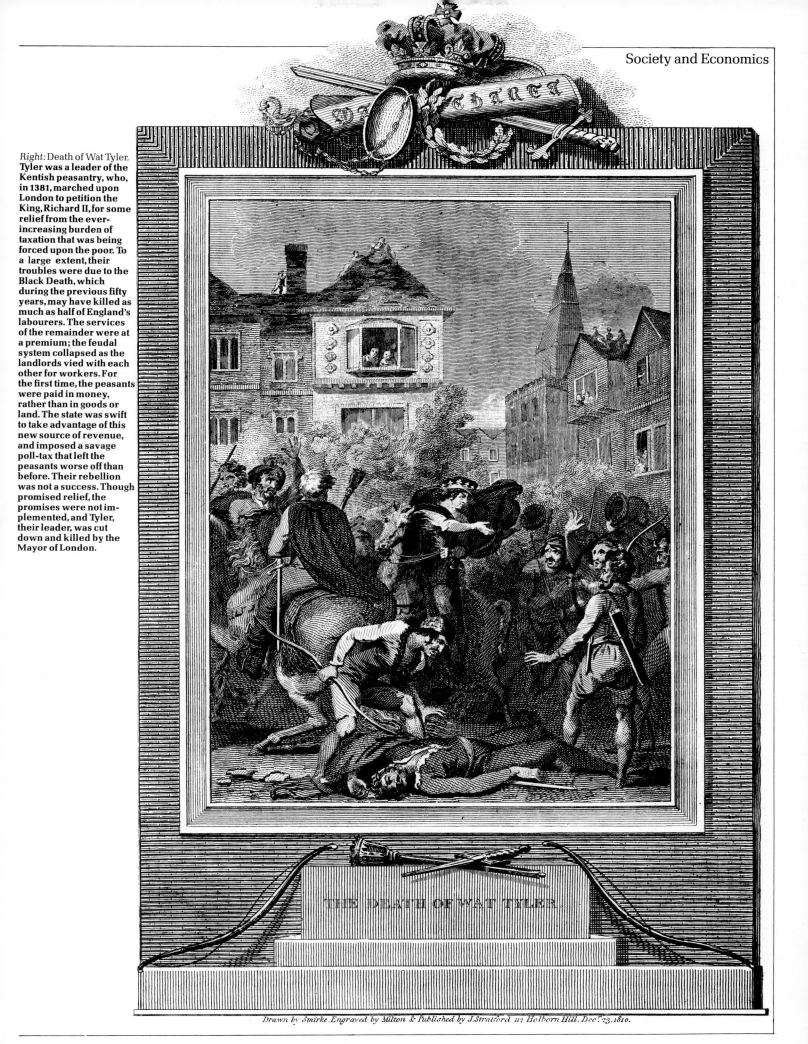

Right: Death of Wat Tyler. **Tyler was a leader of the Kentish peasantry, who, in 1381, marched upon London to petition the King, Richard II, for some relief from the ever-increasing burden of taxation that was being forced upon the poor. To a large extent, their troubles were due to the Black Death, which during the previous fifty years, may have killed as much as half of England's labourers. The services of the remainder were at a premium; the feudal system collapsed as the landlords vied with each other for workers. For the first time, the peasants were paid in money, rather than in goods or land. The state was swift to take advantage of this new source of revenue, and imposed a savage poll-tax that left the peasants worse off than before. Their rebellion was not a success. Though promised relief, the promises were not implemented, and Tyler, their leader, was cut down and killed by the Mayor of London.**

THE DEATH OF WAT TYLER.

Drawn by Smirke. Engraved by Milton & Published by J. Stratford, 112 Holborn Hill, Dec.r 23. 1810.

tions towards the poor and the needy. It condemned interest and profiteering and held in disdain the attitudes of acquisitiveness and greed which the growth of trade seemed to be inculcating. But it was those new attitudes that were eventually to prevail and to consolidate themselves in an ideology compatible with the new situation.

The changing role of money
The driving force behind these changes was, arguably, technical progress in the form of improved productivity in agriculture and transport which was added to a fortuitous improvement in climate. Greater surpluses of food were produced and manpower became available for manufacturing industry. Long-distance trade in both foodstuffs and manufactures became increasingly possible as a result. Changes in the institutions followed naturally. Cities grew as trade centres and gradually gained political independence from feudal authority. The use of minted, state-guaranteed money became universal and commercial contracts replaced feudal customs and traditions to form the basis of the new mercantile legal system. Both coinage and mercantile law were legacies of the ancient world, especially the Greek city-states and the Roman empire. But the use of both had diminished considerably following the Roman Empire's collapse and Europe's partial relapse into more of a customary and less global economy. But with the disintegration of the medieval society both became more important. Only Roman law became more specifically mercantile at this time and money was also changing in character. Its role was evolving and it was linking up with credit and finance. Credit dealings developed as the natural extension of trade dealings and modern instruments like the bill of exchange came into existence. Banks grew in importance and their functions became more and more extensive. Insurance businesses also emerged to form, with the banks, the nucleus of the complex modern financial system.

The new landowners
The market also penetrated agriculture. Landlords came to prefer receiving the peasants' dues in money but that could only be done if the peasants themselves could sell their produce. Marketization made it necessary also to define both the landlord's property and the peasants' rights in mercantile terms. Previously there was no land "ownership" as we understand it today and the peasant was tied to the land. In the new situation, he could be dispossessed for defaulting on his dues to the landlord. Tenant farming developed as a compromise to provide the peasant with some security. Free farming also started to appear as landlords who wished to sell their lands found in many peasants the most obvious buyers. In other cases a landlord would take direct control and operate the land with wage labour. Agriculture was becoming like a manufacturing industry. A return to the old ways was threatened around the fifteenth and sixteenth centuries when labour shortage following the ravages of the Black Death in Europe raised wages and reduced landlords' rents, prompting them to seek to tie the peasants to the land once again. Bitter conflict followed with different outcomes in Western and Eastern Europe. In the West it proved too late to turn the clock back. In fact population pressure in the countryside caused by agricultural revival eventually drove many peasants to the cities and the growing urban industries. In the East, the population remained stable, and landlords were generally successful in maintaining the basic system of lord and serf for considerably longer.

The birth of capitalism
The system that followed feudalism is the one that is loosely referred to as capitalism or a market economy. The fundamental principle of the system was free exchange. Market institutions were essentially non-hierarchial and the relation of buyer and seller, presumed on some basis of equality, replaced the earlier one of master and servant. Already in the previous regime the rule of the market was beginning to

Prosperity, purpose and God

Above: Port Sunlight, Merseyside, UK. **A village built by William Lever in 1888 for the workers of his soap factory.**
The Puritan philosophy produced, during the seventeenth century, an extraordinary race of men and women whom no disillusionment could sour, no worldly consideration shake, since God guided them in every single aspect of their lives.

It was this spirit that, during the next 200 years or so, was to produce the Quakers, the Frys and the Cadburys, who pioneered many of the ideas of decent working conditions, working-class education and prison reform that helped to establish the better aspects of the society in which we live.

Right: The stocking makers. **By the mid-19th century, the English Industrial Revolution was in full swing, most notably in the cloth and garment industries. New inventions encouraged the building of large factories, such as Owen and Ugton's stocking factory at Tewkesbury. Owen had invented a machine that reinforced stocking feet. By 1860, he was employing 600 workmen and 150 girls in his factory.**

extend to labour as well as goods. Now the use of wage labour became very widespread. The worker hired out his labour power to the capitalist or, more generally, to the entrepreneur for a specified wage to perform a specified job under the entrepreneur's direction and for a specified period of time. The contract was free and the worker was supposed to be highly mobile, both geographically and occupationally.

Capitalist industry came gradually to replace the earlier handicraft type industry in which the craftsman, who was often a farmer as well, owned the workshop, the tools and raw materials, sold the final product and generally functioned as an independent entrepreneur. At first, the capitalist furnished a craftsman with the raw material for processing into the finished product. This, the capitalist owned throughout the process and eventually sold on his own account. That was the putting-out system. But eventually the capitalist himself came to own the workshop and the tools and simply hired the craftsman's labour. It was now that he became the capitalist proper as the person who owned all the means of production, the capital stock. After a point, conditions became hard for the independent craftsman who often had to go out of business and become an industrial worker. Together with the peasants who had been driven out of the countryside, former craftsmen, equally propertyless, formed the new urban

proletariat, the labour force of capitalist industry.

Individualism and industry
The rise of modern capitalist industry, which is often referred to as the Industrial Revolution, started in England and the north of Europe. Its main distinguishing feature was a permanent increase in the range and variety of fixed capital goods used in production and the consequent dominance of capital. A key element in the process was also the constant accumulation of capital out of the reinvestment of profits.

Industrial development has itself helped to accelerate the pace of technical and scientific advance and important inventions found widespread commercial application. These gave further impetus to industrial development in a continuous feedback. Changes in ideology had to follow. The quest for profit became the accepted motive of economic activity. Self-interest was exalted and individualism was admitted as an ethical norm. Charging interest was no longer regarded as usury and the medieval concern with the just price receded. For the most part a new Protestant philosophy of work and thrift gained the ascendency over the old paternalism of the Catholic Church.

The State takes control
Most importantly, perhaps, there were

political developments. Big nation states emerged as monarchies, relying now on the new merchant/capitalist class defeating the feudal lords and unifying territories under a central power. A formidable administrative state apparatus gradually evolved. As it turned out, the marketization and monetization of the economy were conducive to the growth of the state's authority. It was now possible to assess much more accurately the subjects' tax-paying ability and to collect the revenue in the form of money. Financial developments also helped. Through the growing banking system the state could borrow from the population much more readily than before. Previously people were reluctant to lend to the state as they had little confidence in their ability to enforce their claims on it. Now they could lend to the banks instead and the state could borrow from the banking system on which it was relying more and more. The role of the state had already grown in the defining and guaranteeing of commercial rights. The point was finally reached where the central state apparatus was better able to offer protection at the local level, thus irrevocably replacing the feudal lords in that role.

Individual rights were increasingly consolidated with the growth of state power. Interestingly, the rise of capitalism coincided roughly with the abolition of slavery. There is, of course, an economic explanation for that.

Historical circumstances deprived, Western Europe at any rate, of its previous sources of slaves and the cost of slave labour gradually rose above the cost of free labour. The colonization of America produced a temporary revival in the demand for slaves and the opening up of Africa provided new supplies at a relatively late stage in the development of the market economy. But over the centuries people became increasingly hostile to the institution while the disintegration of the feudal economy had also brought to an end even the lord-and-peasant relationship. Slavery as an institution did not survive the combined effect of these developments. The free labour contract, certainly in the more advanced part of the world, became the norm.

The Marxist view

The Marxists, however, view both the employment of labour as well as the ascendancy of the state under capitalism in a somewhat different light. It is argued, quite rightly perhaps, that the "free" labour contract is hardly free exchange. The worker's bargaining position is often very weak, especially where the employer is the sole buyer of labour in an area and labour mobility is low, possibly due to geographical, educational, cultural and in some cases even legal barriers. The same is true under conditions of widespread unemployment, when the worker's alternatives are limited. Unionization over the last century or so has, of course, done a lot to improve the bargaining power of labour. But the Marxists would still maintain that the system of employment involves exploitation. It can hardly be denied that, in many instances at least, the worker in capitalist industry cannot easily be seen as as "equal" in a contractual relationship. The power of the state, in the Marxist view, is, in a sense, the power of the capitalist class, which since the Industrial Revolution has become the dominant one in the social fabric. According to this analysis there is a ruling class in every situation and class relations and antagonisms are

the key to the understanding of the nature of the state.

Contemporary industrial mixed economies and the planned economy

The economic system which evolved with the Industrial Revolution is known as capitalism or as the market system. The system is also known as the free enterprise system as, theoretically, it offers to all the possibility of setting up in business, which is a key aspect of individual economic freedom. But the system has undergone many changes since the Industrial Revolution. Early capitalist development was associated with the growth of state influence in the

Left: Worker ownership. **In 1848, a French states-man, Louis Blanc, suggested the creation of co-operatives in which the factory and plant would be the property of the workers. One such scheme – a tailors' shop – was housed in a disused prison.**

economy. That influence was to grow steadily and to alter fundamentally the character of most of the economies of the Western World. The term "mixed economy" has come to describe such as in the U.S., the U.K., or France. In Eastern Europe and China, following the Russian and Chinese Revolutions and the Second World War, the state has taken almost complete control of the economy. These countries are now loosely described as Socialist or Communist.

The distinguishing characteristics of these two groups is perhaps the structure of property rights. Capitalism can be defined as the system in which non-human means of production (including natural resources) are owned privately. Private ownership can be collective or co-operative as well as individual. It is only when ownership passes to society as a whole (in practice to the state) that we cross-divide into socialism. (Ownership, that is, of capital goods and natural resources. Consumer goods are still owned privately.) Capitalism and Socialism in their pure form, are the two opposites on the ownership spectrum. But they are impossible to exemplify in pure form. Most economies have sectors of public and private ownership and are there-fore mixed. The Western-type mixed economy has an extensive public sector but, on the whole, private ownership still predominates. To that extent, it is, on balance, capitalist. In contrast, state ownership predominates by far in the U.S.S.R. but there, too, there are pockets of private and fairly large areas of co-operative ownership of the means of production.

Profits or common wealth?

The ownership spectrum is not, how-ever, the only one. It is also important to see who controls or manages the means of production, and for whose benefit. In capitalism the driving force is, in theory, the pursuit of profit and the allocation of resources is by voluntary market exchange. Decision-making is decentralized and exercised by the owners of independent firms who generally respond to price signals. The price system is then the overall co-ordinating device. At the other extreme the economy can be planned, down to the minutest detail conceivable, by a central co-ordinating agency, a planning bureau. It would then be, in

effect, a command economy.

Resources are allocated by adminis-trative decision from above and decision-making is thus centralized. Production is for use and not for profit. Planning for the social good is the objec-tive of the state-owned firms and a mixture of rewards and penalties ensures some motivation. The role of markets, at the theoretical extreme, is limited or plays no part.

In reality, as with the ownership spectrum, it is impossible to find any actual examples of the extremes of the organizational alternatives.

The changing face of big business

In the Western economy the growth of the government sector has expanded the area where centralized adminis-trative decision rather than exchange is the norm and this has correspondingly reduced the importance of the market. Also in the private sector the system is not as competitive as it used to be. There has been a remarkable growth of big business and many industries are now very concentrated in that most of the output is produced by a few large firms. This is the oligopoly situation and it involves co-operation and collusion at least as often as it results in competition. The manufacturing and the financial sectors are examples. Big businesses are generally price-makers rather than price takers and they have, mainly through advertising, considerable control of the markets in which they operate. That enables them to reduce uncertainty and to ensure their long-term stability and growth. These are generally the objectives that matter to the managers of the big corporations. Profit is important to the owners of a business but not as important to its managers. In the modern joint-stock company the owners, who are the shareholders, are not in a position to exercise control and there has been a separation of ownership from control and an effective transfer of power to the managers. That transfer has led to a relative neglect of profit maximization, especially where competition is attenuated and maximum profits are not a condition for survival.

Management has the opportunity to pursue its own objectives. But when firms do not seek maximum profits the traditional rationale of the market economy as an efficient allocative device does not quite apply.

The power of the Multinats

The growth of big corporations is a striking phenomenon of recent times and perhaps comparable in significance to the growth of government itself. Government and big business have developed very close links in recognition of their obvious importance to one another. The government itself operates big quasi-commercial enterprises with monopoly power in the shape of the nationalized industries and works very closely with private industry on matters affecting investment and employment and on the design and production of goods for its own requirements (such as military equipment). The power of the biggest corporations, the multinationals, extends well beyond national boundaries and involves links with many governments. The increasing concentration of business has, however, largely been matched by the countervailing power of increasingly unionized

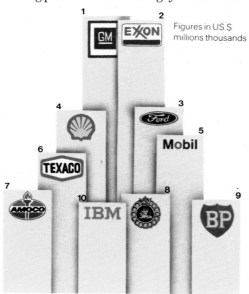

Figures in US $ millions thousands

1. General Motors (US) 54,961,300
2. Exxon (US) 54,126,219
3. Ford Motors (US) 37,841,500
4. Royal Dutch/Shell group (The Netherlands/UK) 36,087,130
5. Mobil (US) 32,125,828
6. Texaco (US) 27,920,499
7. Standard Oil of California (US) 20,917,331
8. National Iranian Oil (Iran) 19,671,064
9. British Petroleum (UK) 19,103,330
10. International Business Machines (US) 18,133,184

Above: The sales of the world's 10 leading multinational companies during 1977. **Such companies, largely a phenomenon of the post-war era, operate mainly through subsidiary companies outside the country of origin. Decisions are therefore made in a global context.**

Right: Areas of influence. **Though a multinational subsidiary may be the richest company in a country, it may not always be working in that country's best interest, since the company's first allegiances are to its head office and ultimately to its shareholders.**

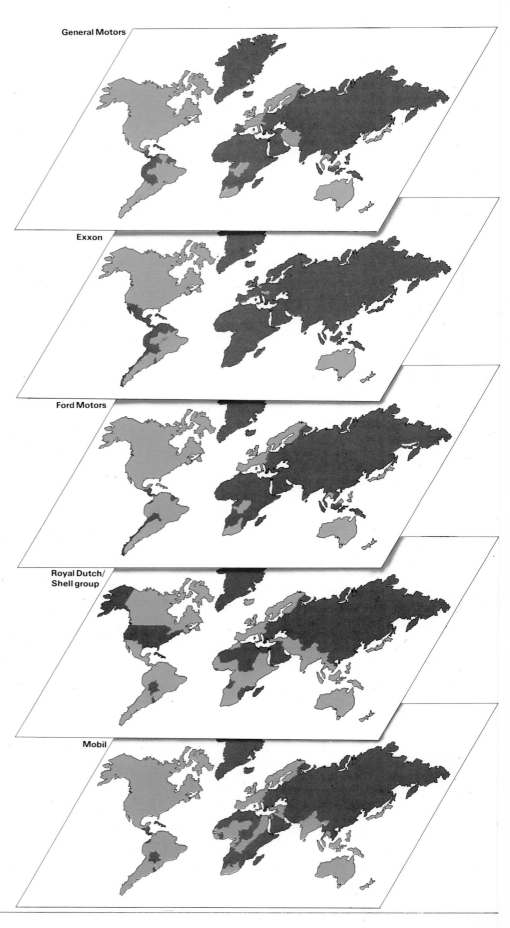

General Motors

Exxon

Ford Motors

Royal Dutch/Shell group

Mobil

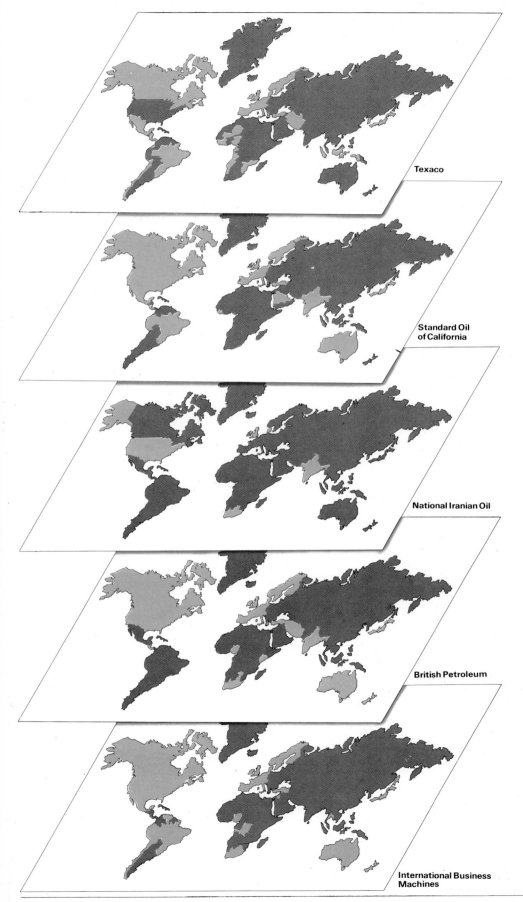

Texaco

Standard Oil
of California

National Iranian Oil

British Petroleum

International Business
Machines

labour. This development has been of obvious importance for the security and the standard of living of the working class but has further reduced the role of the market in the system. It has created, in many cases, what the economists refer to as bilateral monopoly and a group-competitive situation, based on collective bargaining, rather than competition among individuals in the market place.

Also inside companies, even small ones, market allocation is in any case superseded by command. Overall the area of market allocation in the mixed economy is not as large as might be expected and is also probably shrinking. The complex reality of the new industrial state does not fit any simple model of the market. The operation of big business has a certain planning aspect in that it seeks to suppress competition and uncertainty. The importance of capital and the capitalist entrepreneur has somewhat diminished in the process. The managerial and technical specialists of the big corporations and the big organizations in general have come to be the key factor of production. That picture, however, which emerges, particularly in the works of J. K. Galbraith, is not one that everyone finds convincing. Some regard the changes that have been taking place as relatively superficial and deny they have fundamentally changed the character of the capitalist market economy. According to the Marxist view the system continues to be, basically, one of class antagonism and exploitation. The new industrial state has at its side a large competitive sector as well, with many small and medium-sized businesses. Not all industry is dominated by the giants and their elites. The mixed economy is thus truly mixed.

Western economy and the State
The best way to understand the Western mixed economy is to survey quickly the role of the government, which has grown enormously. From simply providing a monetary and legal framework, individual protection and national defence, the state has now come to intervene in practically every aspect of economic life. Three main objectives can be discerned in the maze of government activities:

1. Correction of resource allocation when the market fails. Some goods are difficult to provide privately because

their technical characteristics make it hard to concentrate the benefit on those prepared to pay. Examples are national defence and street lighting. In other cases, such as health and education, the total benefit to society exceeds the benefit to the immediate recipient, which is all that he is prepared to pay for. The government then tends to provide these goods free or to subsidize them. The reverse holds with harmful activities like pollution which the government can discourage through taxes or fines.

2. Maintenance of full employment, stability and growth. Fluctuations are an unfortunate feature of the free enterprise economy which tends to alternate between boom and inflation and stagnation and unemployment. But since the big recession of the 1930's governments have learned to cope with these problems much more successfully than before. This has largely been due to the works of J. M. Keynes. By controlling its taxation and spending (fiscal policy) and the money supply (monetary policy) the government can generally help the economy to pull out of a recession or it can slow down a boom that threatens stability. Although the simultaneous stagnation and inflation of recent years has cast doubts on the efficacy of these policies The addition of prices and incomes policies to the governments' armoury may prove decisive in the control of the economy.

3. Correction of income distribution. Inequality is another result of the free working of the market system which many find very objectionable. The government seeks to reduce it to an acceptable level through payments or welfare services to the poor or subsidies for certain necessities which are of special importance to the lower income groups. The tax burden is also organized to redistribute income on the criterion of 'ability to pay', and income and wealth taxes are typically progressive. Concern with poverty and inequality is now prominent in our consciousness and the term 'welfare state' is becoming a fashionable synonym for the mixed economy.

The development of tax revenue has parallelled the growth of government expenditure. It is also now collected from a far greater variety of sources than before (such as on property, income and expenditure) and on corporations as well as individuals. The increased ability of the state to tax is perhaps the best single indicator of the growth of its influence.

Private monopoly or nationalization?
The government also engages, however, in regulatory and commercial activities. Anti-trust legislation has been passed in most countries to preserve competition and many industries with monopoly power or with monopoly potential have either been nationalized

or have come under regulation. The assumption is that a public monopoly is more benevolent than a private one. Public utilities come in this category as, for technological reasons, they tend to grow more efficient as they grow larger until one firm comes to dominate and there is no room for competition. In the UK and France nationalization of such industries as electricity, gas and the railways has been the preferred policy and the nationalized sector is now so large that it can be used, like the budget, as an instrument of general economic policy. In the US regulation has been found sufficient so far, except for the postal service which is nationalized. In other cases governments intervene to encourage a merger which may be judged desirable for efficiency.

Governments also have the responsibility for maintaining the external stability of the economy. If a country buys more from abroad than it sells that creates problems with inter-

Right: Labour heroine. **In the USSR, medals and press acclaim are the rewards of high productivity. Olga Diptan, team-leader at the Ilyich Collective Farm, Kiev, proudly wears her two decorations as Hero of Socialist Labour.**

Below left: A pennant for Socialist Emulation. **Presented to the winning Assembly team at Gorky Autogaz for exceeding their productivity target.**

national payments. External disequilibrium can have a serious inhibiting effect on the domestic economy, as has been amply shown by the sterling and lira crises of the last decade or so in the UK and Italy and the restrictive policies that these have dictated. At one time during the early period of capitalist development government policy assigned top priority to the achievement of a surplus in international trade with a view to accumulating as much gold as possible for the state coffers (mercantilism). Nowadays the emphasis is on equilibrium rather than on surplus and that, too, is a constraint on policy rather than an objective. But keeping within the external constraint is not easy.

Controversy is always present in economics and governments in a mixed economy have to accept that some policies are doomed to remain ineffective, so long as the basic capitalist structure of the system remains unchanged. The Marxist view urges attention to the disease itself rather than the symptoms.

Central planning and individual choice

The economies of the Soviet Union and of the other Eastern European countries in general do not conform to the standard model of the planned economy any more than Western ones

do to the simple model of the market. They comprise a large number of market institutions which exist side by side with the main planning apparatus, especially markets for consumer goods. But the main allocative decisions are made by the planning authorities and targets are handed down to the state-owned firms to fulfil, on the basis of these allocations. Following the reforms in recent years targets are increasingly specified in terms of sales rather than in strict quantities for each type of goods but the plan is still strict as regards the main priorities. For a long time the main priority was the building up of heavy industry at the expense of consumer goods but this is now changing. Prices and wages are also generally fixed centrally but consumers are free not to buy the goods and workers not to take the jobs offered. Yet the reactions of the market do not lead as readily to changes in prices or in the quantities produced as they would in the West. The process of plan revision is a slow one. The plan largely covers agriculture as well as industry but ownership of the farms is essentially co-operative, for the most part, and a considerable amount of cultivation for sale or for private use is permitted. With the exception of the Soviet Union, many private farms still exist. The profit motive is hardly absent. In the state sector, however, as quantities and prices of inputs and outputs

Left: Soviet shopping. **In Russia and other Eastern bloc countries, collective farms are permitted to sell a large amount of their produce in nearby markets. Prices are fixed by the government, but shoppers are free to refuse the goods offered, as workers are free to refuse jobs.**

Below: The percentages of the Gross National Product that is deducted as tax in various countries to provide government revenue. **In general, the developed countries pay a far higher percentage than developed ones.**

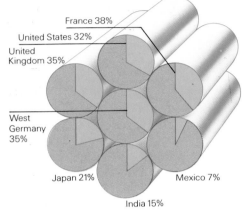

France 38%
United States 32%
United Kingdom 35%
West Germany 35%
Japan 21%
Mexico 7%
India 15%

instrument of planning. Companies can draw funds from the bank generally only in conformity with plan allocations, such as for an authorized purchase of capital equipment. The firms' accounts are under close supervision by the bank and their money profits revert automatically to the state budget. So, although the economy shows all the outward signs of a fully monetized one, the significance of money is somewhat smaller than in the West. Money is passive in the Soviet-type economy.

State capitalism
The influence of the state in the economy is rather more pervasive in the East. In practice, although perhaps not by necessity, that is accompanies by a rather more authoritarian political system. But there is exchange as well. The state sector of industry can be thought of as trading, in a broad sense, with the private or co-operative sector in agriculture, with the relative prices of the two categories of goods being a matter for political bargaining as well as of supply and demand. Also, when it comes to foreign trade the state agencies are having to operate increasingly like their Western trading partners. Recent reforms have been pushing the economy, slowly, in the direction of greater commercialization. As a result, perhaps, the term state capitalism is increasingly applied in

are generally planned, so are profits, by necessity. But with the reforms, companies are acquiring increasing discretion in the use of the profits which they generate.

One of the main objectives of socialism and one of the potential areas of superiority of the planned economy is that it can produce more easily than capitalism a desired state of distribution, and presumably a more egalitarian one. As private ownership of the means of production is largely excluded, the accumulation of large fortunes and of large incomes is generally difficult whereas the planning mechanism can fix wage rates such as to restrict inequality in earned incomes as well.

But experience has shown some inequality to be essential as an incentive. Consequently earned incomes are unequal.

Money in the Eastern bloc
As in the West, the role of money in the Soviet-type economy is the medium for all transactions and also the universal unit of account. There are notes and bank deposits, as in the West. But whereas households can spend their money and draw on their deposits freely, enterprises can do so to a much lesser extent. This is because the government uses money and the credit system, over which it has complete control through the state bank, as an

some quarters to describe the system. But the term is also applied, sometimes, to the nationalized sectors of the Western economies.

Planning as such is not wholly unknown in the West either. But it is indicative and not directive as in the East. As practiced in France and also in the U.K. during the 1960s, Western-type planning is a process whereby the government collects together the growth forecasts and investment plans of the various sectors of industry, checks them for mutual consistency, suggests revisions and, after a series of successive approximations, produces a set of feasible targets for each sector and for the economy as a whole. Private industry is not obliged to carry out its target investment but has every incentive to do so as the planning process reduces uncertainty and ensures the overall expansion on which the profitability of investment depends. Indicative planning is not yet highly developed in the West but it does suggest that there is more similarity between economic systems than is immediately apparent.

Markets in the socialist system

To complicate the picture even more, the Soviet-type economy does not apply very closely to two important countries in the socialist camp: Communist China and Yugoslavia. China is the more important quantitatively in view of its vast population, but its institutions are not stable enough or well enough understood to allow a simple example. Yugoslavia, however, is of more interest than its size would

suggest as it is the only actual approximation of a rather distinctive version of socialism.

The basic disadvantage of the so-socialist economy is supposed to be that, unlike the competitive market economy, it cannot easily produce an efficient allocation of resources. The task is too vast to be performed centrally in the absence of markets. The most that can be hoped for is a coherent plan which would not, however, necessarily best satisfy consumer preferences. The early experience of the Soviet economy gave some substance to these criticisms and some socialist writers started to think in terms of using the market not in a supplementary role but as a basic organizational device of the socialist economy. State-owned firms surely could be instructed to behave like capitalist ones in perfect competition and then the same allocative efficiency would be achieved.

From another angle, objections to the planning process were raised on grounds of alienation. Planning involved centralization and the vast majority of people did not participate in the decisions which affected them. Under capitalism many people, basically the working class, were also alienated in that sense. But that was one of the wrongs that socialism could be expected to put right. It was even suggested, and still is, that social control of the means of production by the producers themselves rather than state ownership, is the true distinguishing characteristic of socialism.

The participative ideal is historically associated with the co-operative

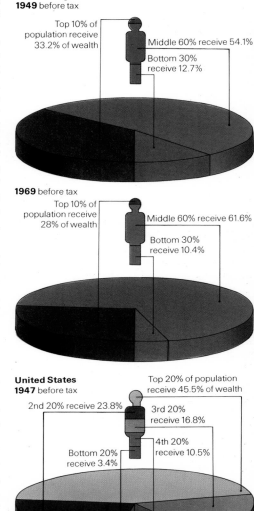

United Kingdom
1949 before tax

Top 10% of population receive 33.2% of wealth

Middle 60% receive 54.1%

Bottom 30% receive 12.7%

1969 before tax

Top 10% of population receive 28% of wealth

Middle 60% receive 61.6%

Bottom 30% receive 10.4%

United States
1947 before tax

Top 20% of population receive 45.5% of wealth

2nd 20% receive 23.8%

3rd 20% receive 16.8%

4th 20% receive 10.5%

Bottom 20% receive 3.4%

1972 before tax

Top 20% of population receive 43.9% of wealth

2nd 20% receive 24.6%

3rd 20% receive 16.8%

4th 20% receive 10.5%

Bottom 20% receive 4.2%

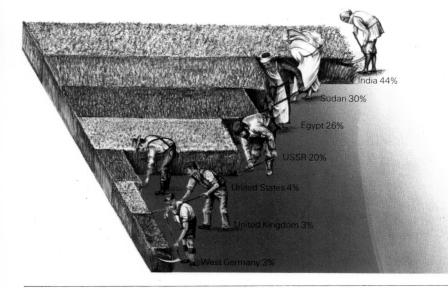

India 44%

Sudan 30%

Egypt 26%

USSR 20%

United States 4%

United Kingdom 3%

West Germany 3%

Left: A comparison of the percentage of Gross National Product (GNP) that is derived from agriculture in different parts of the world. **In the under developed countries, most of the land is in the hands of peasant subsistence farmers.**

Above: A comparison of the share of total national income received, before tax, by different income groups in the UK and the US. **Since the upper income groups are taxed most heavily in both countries, the contrasts become less marked once tax is deducted.**

movement. That in turn has been market-oriented and, on the whole, not particularly socialist. But awareness of the possibility grew that there could be participative decision-making in state-owned firms operating in a competitive market. The mixture would result in a socialist economy free of allocative inefficiency and alienation. That is what the Yugoslavs have tried to do.

The Yugoslav experiment

Since the 1950's, Yugoslavia has operated a system of participative socialism. The means of production are ultimately owned by the state, but workers' collectives make the decisions regarding their use and share the profits or losses. The workers are in a sense the collective entrepreneurs. In reality, worker-managed firms are not all that independent of government direction and the details of the system are nowhere near stable. But the Yugoslav experiment is a genuine attempt to deal in an original way with some of the most vexing problems of socialism and has attracted much interest.

Common ground for East and West

There are, therefore, the changing capitalist market economies, the planned socialist economy under reform and the participatory market socialist experiment somewhere in the middle. The transition from capitalism to socialism has so far happened only in what has been an essentially violent way, following a revolution or, in the case of Eastern Europe, Soviet victory in the Second World War. But for a long time people have been wondering whether such a transition is inevitable. Also if it can be non-violent, then the reverse change might be possible. The questions are fundamental but there is not enough evidence at present for definite answers. Certainly, the mixed economy looks at times distinctly unhealthy. But the economies of the East also face difficulties from time to time. Some of the problems (inflation and pollution) crop up in both systems. Interestingly, while the debate on the two systems is still raging, we are witnessing increasing political and economic links between East and West. Plan and market have come to co-exist in both camps while still competing as alternatives. Some people are suggesting that a convergence of systems may be taking place.

The various economies of the developing world

There is another striking division, between developed and less developed countries. Living standards are clearly rather different between London, New York or Sydney on the one hand, and Cairo or Calcutta on the other and the difference between the respective countries is even more pronounced. Economists usually measure living standards by Gross National Product per capita. GNP is the sum of the market values of all consumer goods and services produced in a year plus the value of investment minus depreciation. The figures need to be adjusted considerably and interpreted with care before they make sense for comparisons, and obviously, different societies have not exactly the same needs or tastes. Warm clothes are necessary in Finland but not in the tropics and the British, in contrast to the Germans perhaps, may require more leisure and fewer material goods. Things are also complicated by the fact that much of the

Left: Gross investment. **A summary of the percentage of Gross National Product that different countries invested in 1977 in improving production. The amounts include expenditure on new machinery and on replacing obsolescent or worn out equipment.**

Egypt 11%
India 15%
UK 18%
USA 18%
W Germany 25%
France 26%
Italy 27%
Japan 37%

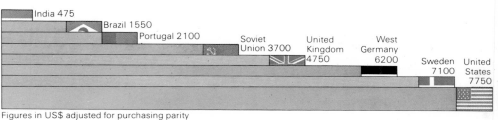

India 475
Brazil 1550
Portugal 2100
Soviet Union 3700
United Kingdom 4750
West Germany 6200
Sweden 7100
United States 7750

Figures in US$ adjusted for purchasing parity

Above: Gross National Product is divided here on a per capita basis to show the purchasing power of individuals in different parts of the world in 1976. **This helps to highlight the staggering contrast between developed and emerging nations.**

economy of many poor countries is still rather primitive, with few money transactions to serve as a basis for income measurement and, further, by the need to translate data expressed in one currency into another with very different purchasing power. Finally, a high GNP per capita may conceal colossal inequality and a low standard of life for the majority. But even with these reservations and following some adjustments it is clear that standards of living differ enormously between different countries.

The vicious cycle of poverty

Apart from low GNP per capita, the main characteristics of underdevelopment are that, like the pre-capitalist economies of the now advanced countries, poor countries are mainly agricultural or, in any case, primary producers. In some cases there is heavy dependence on one ot two products whereas there is often a marked contrast

Above right: Kashmiri farmer. **A low Gross National Product and a poor rate of investment ensures that growth is slow or non-existent. The subsistence farmer has no money for machinery or fertilisers; therefore, his farm can never increase in size or be made more productive.**

between a large traditional sector and a smaller modern industrial one, creating what has become known as a dual economy. The predominance of agriculture or mining is not in itself bad, of course. But low productivity in primary production does not leave enough surpluses of food and manpower for industrialization.

Secondly, there is usually faster population growth than in advanced countries. Cultural attitudes as well as the need to produce children as security for old age have kept the birth rate high whereas recent medical advances have been reducing the death rate and increasing life expectancy. As a result, the typical poor country suffers from population pressure.

Thirdly, poor countries suffer from a severe lack of perhaps the most important prerequisite for development: capital. They are typically caught up in a vicious cycle of low incomes, from which only little savings can be generated, leading in turn to a low rate of investment and capital accumulation. Whereas in rich countries 20 per cent of GNP may go into capital formation, in poor countries the rate can be as low as 5 per cent. Low investment also entails a slow introduction of new technology and skills and investment is not always channelled to the most useful projects, due to lack of entrepreneurial and administrative ability.

It is hard to be confident about the causes of underdevelopment. Unfavourable geography and climate is a fairly common but superficial explanation. Inadequate natural resources may be a serious inhibiting factor although availability of natural resources does not guarantee development, as is shown by the experience of certain oil-producing countries. Race and associated cultural factors provide another explanation that is favoured by some but is hardly a convincing one. At the other extreme, colonialism has been seen as a serious obstacle to development, an explanation which seems to be supported by the observation that most poor countries were colonies of the advanced ones in the not too distant past. But again, there are others who think that colonial institutions may have actually promoted development.

Many developing countries acquired their independence only recently and their leaders have been faced with the dilemma of choosing between the capitalist or the socialist road to development. The ideological battle is often fierce but the majority seem to be choosing a mixed path, albeit with a definite bias towards planning and state direction of the economy. That seems appropriate under modern conditions. Nowadays it does not seem very promising to sit back and rely on the spontaneous forces of private initiative to work out an industrial revolution in the typical underdeveloped country. At best, it would be a slow process and would not satisfy present aspirations to accelerate development as a matter of urgency. Even with planning there is the problem of penetrating world markets already dominated by producers from the advanced world and, in many cases, there is also the problem of shaking off what some would regard as neo-colonial dependence on the multinationals. It is not appropriate to simply copy the technology of the advanced countries. Intermediate, labour-intensive techniques of production are required and these have to be developed to fit the particular conditions. It is, however, a fair generalization, that developing countries are adopting flexible strategies in their choice of technology and of economic systems in general. Even those which show a strong inclination towards the socialist road are visibly reluctant to align themselves politically in any permanent way with the Eastern bloc.

International comparisons of achievements

It is hard to generalize on how economic performance under socialism compares with Western performance or the success of developing countries.

The growth in some Western countries (such as Italy, France and West Germany) since the Second World War has undoubtedly been impressive. In addition, Japan's growth performance has been spectacular. At the same time, the growth rate of the US has been moderate and that of the UK positively low. On the other side, there is little doubt that the growth record of the USSR since 1917 has been very good. But it has also been distinctly uneven, with massive progress in the industrial/military field and relative stagnation in agriculture. In any case the USSR is certainly closing the gap in living standards vis à vis the US, although Soviet and Western experts tend to disagree as to the speed at which this is happening. One complication is that the Soviet Union is devoting a greater proportion of its GNP than the U.S. to investment and to military spending. The same picture of industrial growth and agricultural stagnation generally applies to the other countries of Eastern Europe as well and has led many to doubt the suitability of socialist/collectivist organization for agriculture has been uneven, following Communist China. China's overall growth rate is, as far as can be established, high but experience with its agriculture has been uneven, following considerable institutional instability.

On the whole socialist countries are probably reducing the gap between themselves and the advanced countries of the West.

Planning for tomorrow

In the USSR successive five-year plans have been in operation since 1928, setting out in broad outline the allocative decisions for the period and incorporating growth targets. Comparison of the actual growth rates with the targets shows some overfulfilment in the early part of the period at least. But over- or under-fulfilment may also have something to do with the realism of the targets themselves and cannot, without qualification, be regarded as a measure of success. Also, plan targets have tended to be revised during the corresponding periods so that it is generally hard to identify one operative target in each case. The Chinese experience presents much the same picture, with the first five-year plan apparently the most successful in terms of growth. In the West, where indicative planning is practiced, the plan can be seen primarily as a forecasting document and again can be compared with actual performance. In France growth rates and targets have been reasonably close although not on a sector-by-sector basis. In the UK on the other hand, growth

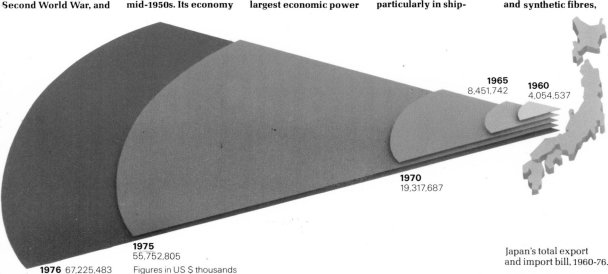

The Japanese miracle

The best sustained growth performance in history has taken place in Japan during the last three decades. Devastated in the Second World War, and only saved from mass starvation by US aid, Japan had regained its high pre-war per capita levels of output and living standards by the mid-1950s. Its economy maintained an average annual growth rate of nearly 12 per cent throughout the 1960s, and, by the 1970s, Japan ranked as the third largest economic power after the United States and the Soviet Union. It achieved this phenomenal progress by rapid expansion of industrial production, particularly in shipbuilding and manufacturing. By the end of the 1960s, it led the world in the production of ships, motorcycles, cameras and synthetic fibres, and was second in world automobile production. Its success, which is due above all to competitive adaptation of Western technological innovations, is shown by its exports, which increased fourfold during the 1960s to take seven per cent of the total world market. After 1973, the picture changed somewhat following the unprecedented rise in oil prices. For the first time since the war Japan, which imports 99 per cent of its oil, saw a fall in 1974 in its Gross National Product, and in a 1975 White Paper, the government advocated the virtues of frugality, and of a smooth change from a high rate of growth to a low, but stable, growth pattern. Nevertheless, Japan remains the world's third major economic power.

1965 8,451,742

1960 4,054,537

1970 19,317,687

1975 55,752,805

1976 67,225,483

Figures in US $ thousands

Japan's total export and import bill, 1960-76.

Right: Workers committee, Chinese dying and printing mill. **Although in China all means of production are ultimately owned by the state, the day to day running of the factories, the setting of short-term targets and disciplinary matters are in the hands of a workers-committee.**

during the period of the National Plan in the 1960's fell well short of the target of 4 per cent.

Aid from overseas

The second comparison, between the developed and the developing groups of nations is crucially affected by the presence of Communist China. China's growth rate since 1949 has been relatively high but it is difficult to quantify

that for a reliable comparison with the West, especially as its birth rate is among the highest. In other developing countries, such as India or Pakistan, moderate growth rates combined with fairly high birth rates make for rather modest growth in per capita terms. On the whole, it is quite possible that the gap in living standards between rich and poor nations may be widening rather than narrowing although inequality of

incomes within the advanced countries seems to be diminishing. Governments of the advanced countries may therefore wish to devote more of their tax revenues to international aid programmes than to relief for their own poor. It is probable that foreign aid will need to be increased massively before it makes any impression on the present picture of international inequality.

Right: Since 1935, the importance of gold to the Australian economy has changed dramatically. **In 1935 gold ranked second only to wool in economic importance, but by 1969 it was contributing a mere 0.6% of the economy. In contrast, the production of other minerals rose sharply through the same period, starting at a lower figure than gold and speedily overtaking it. Iron ore was a major contributor to this change in emphasis, as new deposits were exploited. In 1975-76 over 62 million tonnes were exported to Japan alone.**

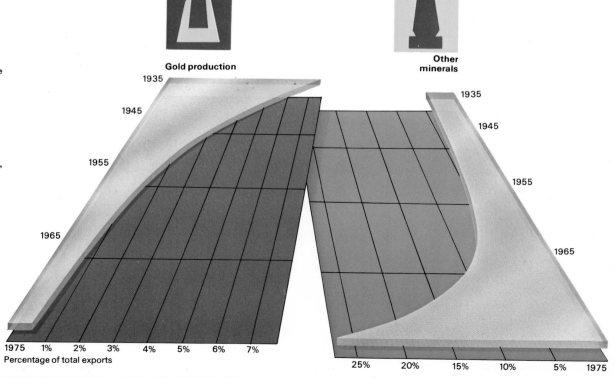

Gold production

Other minerals

Percentage of total exports

Ships and railway
wagons at the dockside
in Dar-es-Salaam,
Tanzania.

4.

FINANCING ECONOMIC ACTIVITY

The basic facts of economic life mean that no economy can survive without some form of monetary control. This applies even more to nations than to individuals; monetary policies govern how much is spent, how much earned, how much invested, how much is raised in taxation, and so on. Largely, such controls are today the province of the state, which, usually through an annual budget, controls taxation, and tries to deal with such problems as inflation and unemployment. Yet, the world economy is now so complex that no country can deal with such economic issues in isolation, a fact summed up by the balance of payments, the ultimate barometer of economic well-being.

FINANCE AND THE HOUSEHOLD

Below: Theory. The simplest way of measuring the national income of the economy. Here, the expenditure of households–the Gross National Expenditure (GNE)–and their total income from industry–the Gross National Income (GNI)–exactly balances, as it would do in an ideal economic situation. If this was so, the two flows could continue indefinitely. Economists refer to this as the circular flow of income.

How the system works

A typical breakdown of a national economic system would include the household sector, the industrial sector, the public sector, the overseas sector and the financial sector. An analysis of the economic system can then proceed either by analysing the income and expenditure pattern of each sector, or at the national level by a process of aggregation over all sectors. It is then possible to highlight the various relationships that exist between the different sectors, of which perhaps the best known example is the relationship between national income and total expenditure.

National economy can be measured either in terms of the total value of goods and services supplied by firms (Gross National Product, GNP); in terms of the total expenditure outlayed by households (Gross National Expenditure, GNE); or in terms of total incomes received by households (Gross National Income, GNI).

Below: Reality. In actual economic terms, the measurement of the national income is complicated by various factors. These include elements such as savings, investment at home and overseas, government taxation and expenditure, and imports, all of which serve to complicate the simple economic model.

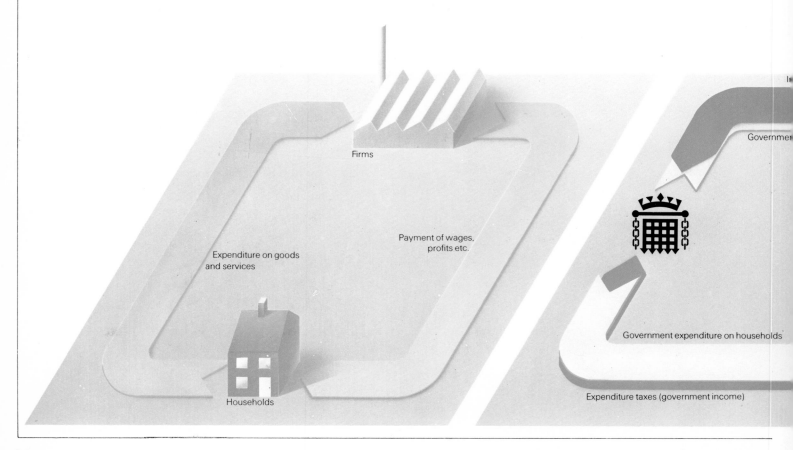

Firms

Payment of wages, profits etc.

Expenditure on goods and services

Government

Government expenditure on households

Households

Expenditure taxes (government income)

If households spent their entire incomes on purchasing goods and services from firms, and if firms spent all their receipts on paying salaries, then income, output and expenditure would balance each other and the situation could continue indefinitely.

However, in the real world the situation is complicated by a number of factors: (a) households save part of their income, (b) firms also save part of their receipts and spend a proportion on capital assets, (c) a government sector exists which taxes both households and firms and also undertakes expenditure on current goods and services, and (d), an overseas sector exists within which account has to be taken of domestic expenditure on foreign goods and foreign expenditure on domestic goods.

In the complex interrelationships of modern economic systems, the financial sector plays an indispensable role in co-ordinating the income and expenditure patterns of the other sectors. For example, if the total capital investment plans of firms were to exceed current business saving then the excess will need to be financed; this will normally require the issuing of a new debt by the industrial sector. Financial institutions will then have to find holders for this debt. Frequently, they will turn to the household sector because this, as a rule, is in financial surplus – that is, its current income exceeds its current expenditure. In this way, the financial sector attempts to reconcile the asset requirements of the household sector with the borrowing requirements of the industrial sector, or, indeed, of any other. Furthermore, financial institutions also attempt a reconciliation between different units within each sector. For example, some households will be net lenders and others net borrowers, and to bring the two together, some form of financial intermediation is required. The financial sector provides this intermediation at minimal cost, so providing an invaluable service.

In the process of financial intermediation, the financial sector enables some sectors to spend in excess of their current income and therefore has an important effect on current expenditure levels. Output, income and expenditure are all closely interrelated. In fact, the level of national income (GNP) is largely determined, in the short run, by the level of total expenditure on goods and services. Therefore, since expenditure is a major determinant of the size of national income, it is important to be able to explain and predict the expenditure level in each sector.

The next four chapters investigate the expenditure pattern of each sector and attempts to highlight the important role played by financial institutions in this area. For example, it may be possible to throw some light on expenditure plans by analysing the relationship between household expenditure and the availability of credit and show to what extent the former is influenced by the latter. Similarly, the relationship between saving and investment, taxes and government expenditure, exports and imports, are examined to discover the degree to which each finances the other. If investment exceeds savings or government expenditure exceeds tax revenue, then the financing of the excess may be a crucial link in the chain. In order to highlight the important processes involved, it will be necessary to investigate the flow of funds both within and between each of the various sectors.

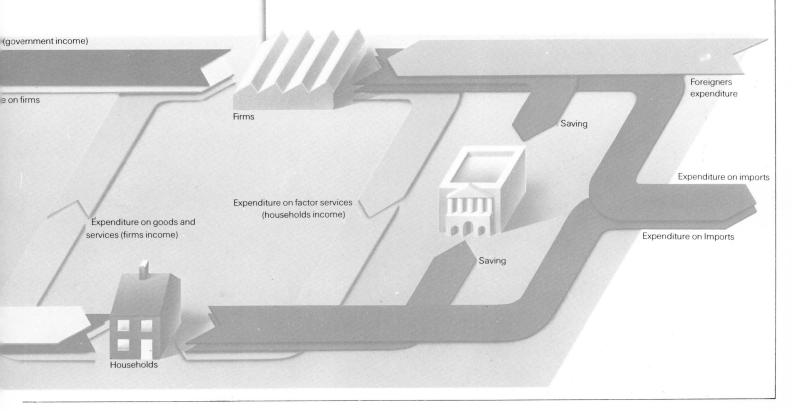

In most countries expenditure by the household sector is the largest component of total demand and accounts for about 60 per cent of the Gross National Product (GNP). Household expenditure – often referred to as consumers' expenditure or simply consumption – has remained fairly stable as a percentage of GNP over long periods and in many different countries. However, since it accounts for such a large percentage of the total, even relatively small changes can have far-reaching effects on the expenditure plans of the other sectors and on the level of GNP itself. The ability to explain and to some extent predict household expenditure is an important objective of economic and financial policy.

The original stimulus to research in this area came from Keynes who said "that men are disposed, as a rule and on the average, to increase their consumption as their income increases, but not by as much as the increase in their income". *(The General Theory of Employment Interest and Money, p. 96)* This suggests that the main determinant of consumer expenditure is household income, and the statistics to some extent support this view. For example, an estimate of household income is provided by government statistics on personal disposable income (PDI). This is the sum of all incomes received by households from employment, self employment and dividends, and less income taxes and social security contributions. In most countries these deductions from personal income amount to 20 per cent and consumers' expenditure then comprises between 80 per cent and 90 per cent of PDI.

Patterns of saving

The measurement of consumption as a percentage of PDI is known as the average propensity to consume. A corresponding measure of this trend in consumption can be obtained by looking at the pattern of savings. An average propensity to consume of 90 per cent implies a savings level of 10 per cent and this is referred to as the savings ratio.

Many countries have experienced an increase in their savings ratios during the 1970s but the UK and Japan have experienced a dramatic increase of about 50 per cent. However, there are also great disparities that exist between the savings ratios of different countries, ranging from 28 per cent in

Japan to 8 per cent in the US.

But too much significance should not be attached to the absolute level of these ratios because the categories of savings differ considerably between countries. For example, while by definition savings equal PDI minus consumers' expenditure, much depends on how expenditure is defined.

Saving by mortgage

It can be said that consumers are really saving when they pay off a debt because they build up equity in, say, a house, when they make a mortgage payment. Part of this payment is for interest on the loan and part goes towards paying off the principal. In this way, instead of saving to buy a house, a debtor first purchases the property and then saves to pay for it (the interest payment

Left: Workers in Lombard Street, close to the heart of the city of London. **In any technologically-advanced, money orientated society, the weekly wage is an essential for survival. Recognizing this, many governments have tried to control the amount that can be earned, but many workers resist this, preferring instead the process of "free, collective bargaining."**

Above: Shoppers in the market place. **Consumer spending is an essential element in the operation of any economic policy. Keynes argued, for instance, that it was a "fundamental psychological law" that consumption would rise as incomes rose. But he also believed that a proportion of the income would be saved.**

being a penalty for preferring current to future consumption). This applies to any durable goods bought on credit, and the servicing of such a debt should be counted as saving. In the national income statistics, however, consumers' spending that is financed by borrowing from banks and hire purchase companies appear as consumption and to the extent that consumers in, say, the US make greater use of credit, the savings ratio in the US will appear lower than elsewhere. Consumer credit (excluding mortgages) in the US in 1975 was nearly 20 per cent of PDI – much higher than in other countries, and this to some extent explains the low savings ratio.

The changes that have occurred in

the savings ratios in various countries cannot be entirely accounted for by Keynes's proposition that expenditure is influenced mainly by current income. Milton Friedman's 'permanent income hypothesis' suggests that households are influenced more by expected future income based on some kind of average or normal income level than by current receipts.

Inflation and the householder

A complicating factor in explaining consumers' expenditure during the current decade has been the presence of accelerating inflation. It is often argued that inflation undermines the

There are a number of channels through which financial markets can influence consumers' expenditure.

If the household sector alters its consumption pattern independently of changes in PDI, the financial markets will be affected. Specifically if consumers' expenditure is increased without any change in PDI, the increase will have to be financed from somewhere, and there are basically three main sources of finance for the household sectors – households' financial surplus, borrowing and the sale of financial assets. Households' savings less capital expenditure on housing equals the financial surplus of the

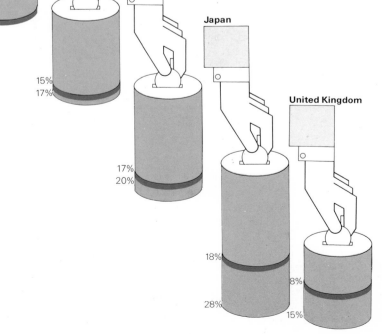

United States

1960's   6%
1975   8%

West Germany

15%

France

15%
17%

The Netherlands

17%
20%

Japan

18%
28%

United Kingdom

8%
15%

incentive to save but in many countries from 1971-77 there was a sharp rise in the savings ratio at a time when inflation was accelerating. Inflation reduces the real value of a household's liquid financial assets, such as deposits with banks, savings banks and building societies, and if households desire to maintain a specific ratio of these assets to money income they will be forced to increase their saving in order to build up their financial assets in line with the growth of their money income and the fall in the real value of money. It is likely that savers have been trying to compensate for inflation by restoring the real value of their stocks of financial assets.

Left: An international comparison of savings ratios – the ratio of the amount saved to the amount consumed – in six major industrial countries. **It is based on actual figures for 1975 and an average over the 1960s. During this period, savings levels in all the countries have increased, with a dramatic jump in the UK and Japan.**

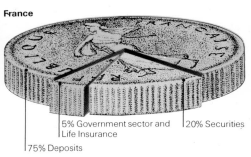

United Kingdom

60% Deposits

40% Government sector and Life Insurance

France

5% Government sector and Life Insurance

20% Securities

75% Deposits

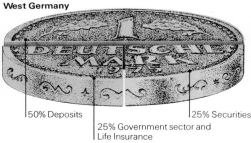

West Germany

50% Deposits

25% Securities

25% Government sector and Life Insurance

household sector. Borrowing can be made either long-term from savings banks and building societies, or short-term from commercial banks and hire purchase companies.

Savers in all countries demonstrate a strong preference for liquidity and this is reflected in the large demand for liquid deposits, even in inflationary times when these assets provide little hedge against inflation. The financial markets must reconcile the desire for liquidity with the needs of borrowers for long-term finance; this is often spoken of as the transformation problem.

New housing and finance
New housing in most countries is financed on borrowed money which is particularly responsive to changes in the availability and cost of credit. Changes in financial conditions largely explain the very uneven trend of new

house-building. The finance for the construction of houses for owner occupation – the largest sector of the housing market – is raised by private companies through retained profits and bank loans. However, this is only the short-term finance needed during construction. The financing of the acquisition of the completed property is by far the most important element and this is provided by long-term loans mortgaged on the property. In this way the funds for construction are effectively provided by the long-term savings of the potential purchaser, with the availability of mortgage finance significantly affecting the construction of new houses.

There are two main types of mortgage finance – those backed up by short-term deposits which are customary in the UK and France, and those backed up by longer term deposits and bond issues which are generally

Above left: The German Savings Bank. **This type of bank originated in Scotland in 1810; one of its main functions is to attract small savers with the offer of interest on all deposits. In Britain, the best-known savings bank is run by the Post Office, which has now developed its banking services to compete with those offered by commercial banks.**

Above: The areas which attract savers in the UK, France and West Germany. **Savers in all countries show a strong preference for liquidity, a fact reflected in the high percentage of money that remains on deposit. Such funds are often more readily available, if the need arises, than funds invested in the other sectors.**

favoured in Germany and the US. With short-term deposits the transformation problem is highly acute, and to maintain the supply of short-term deposits the institutions have to be prepared to vary interest rates offered to depositors and alter the rates charged to borrowers. Countries like the UK and France, which finance house purchase by short-term deposits and variable rate mortgages, will often be faced with the problem that the construction industry will suffer disproportionate swings in the level of its activity whenever savings banks have difficulty attracting short-term funds. Where long-term lending is matched to a greater extent by long-term deposits and bond issues, as in Germany and the US, fixed rate mortgages will usually operate, and consequently a more stable level of activity in the construction industries will prevail.

The role of government
Because of the transformation problem and its implications for the construction industry, a common feature of all countries is government intervention to keep mortgage interest rates low to assure an adequate supply of funds. Savings for home ownership are encouraged in most countries by the operation of national savings banks, provision of tax concessions and subsidies to interest rates. These concessions usually result in privileged sources of funds developing within the financial system which are exempt from the usual credit market restrictions. Such concessions also apply in the UK to life assurance contributions. The UK is unique in being the only country where the household sector is consistently a large net seller of securities; long-term household asets are channelled increasingly into insurance and pension funds, which provide the main source of long-term external finance for industry and the public sector.

In general, governments encourage certain forms of saving and encourage house purchase, but this is not extended to other forms of saving, nor to the purchase of other consumer durables. Government action in the housing market is usually in sharp contrast to its actions in other markets. While house ownership is encouraged, there are often credit restrictions and hire purchase controls on the purchase of other durable goods. It could be said

Top left: A bricklayer at work, *below:* Chinese housing under construction, *top right:* New housing in Telford, one of Britain's "new towns." *below:* Low cost housing in Nigeria, *above:* Building in Geneva. **In most countries, new housing is usually financed on borrowed money and** thus the building industry is usually one of the first to be affected by any downturn in the economy. In Britain, for instance, the number of "starts" on housing in both the public and private sectors has declined dramatically over the last few years. As far as private housing is concerned, one of the chief reasons for this has been the difficulty in obtaining mortgages for "first time" buyers; in the public sector, the major problem has been the difficulty of raising adequate finance, either from government funds or on the loan market.

that public policies seem to be in favour of house purchase, but against allowing the houses to be stocked with expensive goods bought on credit. Restrictions on consumer credit have been imposed extensively, but these regulations have caused only temporary fluctuations in the demand for durable goods. Usually they lead to a postponement of purchases rather than a net decline in demand and they appear to have been necessary because the demand for short-term loans does not appear very sensitive to changes in their cost. Credit restrictions have not had as disastrous effects on the durable goods industry as similar restrictions would have had on the housing market.

From the point of view of the household, usually the greatest form of expenditure undertaken on credit is the purchase of a house. But as this form of expenditure is regarded as a form of saving – because the householder is gradually building up equity in the house – this type of expenditure is not included in government statistics on current household expenditure. Instead, it is included as part of investment or capital expenditure. A house purchase is regarded as consumption taking place over time and the price needs to be considered in terms of the outlay over a long period.

How mortgages work

Normally a house is purchased on a mortgage which is a loan secured by the property. In most countries there are specialist financial institutions engaged in the provision of housing finance – the building societies in the UK, the building and loan associations in Germany and the saving and loan companies in the US. There are two main methods of raising a mortgage and paying it off – a repayment mortgage or an endowment mortgage.

A repayment mortgage is most common and is obtained from a building society, or in some countries from local public authorities, such as in the US through the Federal Home Loan Banks, or in Germany from the public mortgage banks. A repayment mortgage involves the purchaser making a regular monthly payment to the lender, part of which is interest and the other part repayment of the principal. In the early years, a high proportion of each payment is interest and, as the amount outstanding gradually declines, the proportion of each payment needed to pay the interest goes down while the proportion going towards paying off the principal increases.

A typical mortgage is spread over 25 years and the monthly cost of each £1000 of mortgage is calculated at different interest rates. However, taxpayers in virtually all countries obtain tax relief on the interest they pay on mortgage loans. In fact, the tax status of home ownership is quite lucrative and the tax deductions offer a tax benefit to owner-occupiers for which households living in rented accommodation are not eligible. The after-tax cost of a mortgage is usually far less than the calculated interest charge, but since it is only possible to get tax

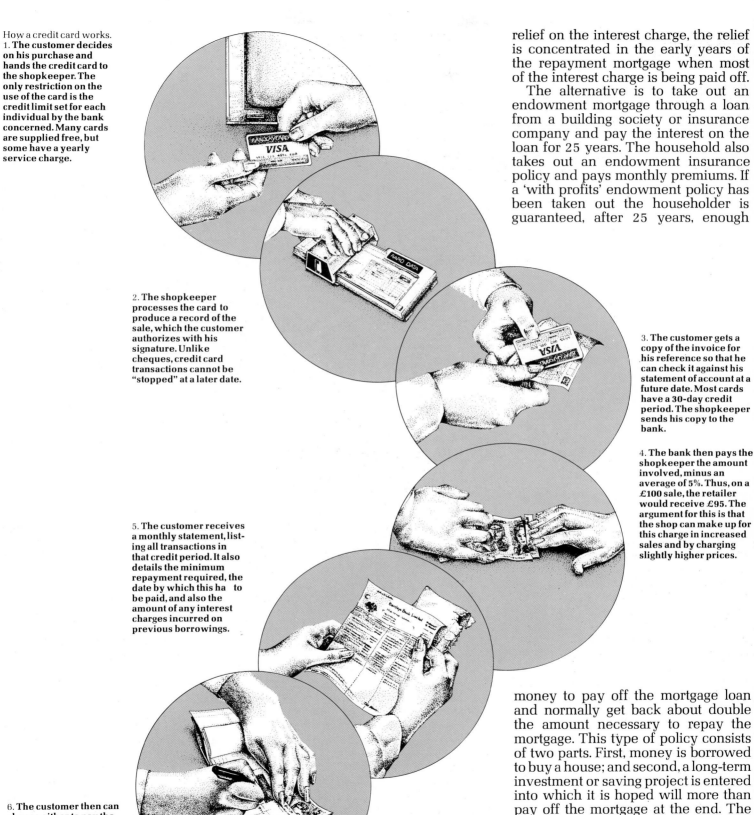

How a credit card works.
1. **The customer decides on his purchase and hands the credit card to the shopkeeper. The only restriction on the use of the card is the credit limit set for each individual by the bank concerned. Many cards are supplied free, but some have a yearly service charge.**

2. **The shopkeeper processes the card to produce a record of the sale, which the customer authorizes with his signature. Unlike cheques, credit card transactions cannot be "stopped" at a later date.**

3. **The customer gets a copy of the invoice for his reference so that he can check it against his statement of account at a future date. Most cards have a 30-day credit period. The shopkeeper sends his copy to the bank.**

4. **The bank then pays the shopkeeper the amount involved, minus an average of 5%. Thus, on a £100 sale, the retailer would receive £95. The argument for this is that the shop can make up for this charge in increased sales and by charging slightly higher prices.**

5. **The customer receives a monthly statement, listing all transactions in that credit period. It also details the minimum repayment required, the date by which this ha   to be paid, and also the amount of any interest charges incurred on previous borrowings.**

6. **The customer then can choose either to pay the full amount on the statement, in which case no interest is charged, or to pay an installment. In the second case, his next statement will have interest charged on the outstanding balance.**

relief on the interest charge, the relief is concentrated in the early years of the repayment mortgage when most of the interest charge is being paid off.

The alternative is to take out an endowment mortgage through a loan from a building society or insurance company and pay the interest on the loan for 25 years. The household also takes out an endowment insurance policy and pays monthly premiums. If a 'with profits' endowment policy has been taken out the householder is guaranteed, after 25 years, enough money to pay off the mortgage loan and normally get back about double the amount necessary to repay the mortgage. This type of policy consists of two parts. First, money is borrowed to buy a house; and second, a long-term investment or saving project is entered into which it is hoped will more than pay off the mortgage at the end. The advantage is that normally both the interest on the mortgage is tax deductible and the premiums on the insurance element qualifies for tax relief. A lump sum is thereby saved over 25 years at low real cost to taxpayers, particularly the higher rate taxpayers.

As higher rate taxpayers benefit most from these schemes, many governments have instigated various other schemes aimed at those households who pay income tax at less than the standard rate, because they are being discriminated against and forced to pay a higher real cost of mortgage finance than households in high tax brackets. One system is an option mortgage which is similar to a repayment mortgage but tax relief is not given on interest payments. Instead, the householder pays a lower rate of interest and the government pays a subsidy to the lender.

The interest paid on mortgages is not normally at the true rate of interest. The interest charge for one year is based on the amount outstanding at the beginning of the year and takes no account of the reducing balance over the year. This has the effect of increasing the interest rate from, say, 10 per cent to a true rate of about 10.2 per cent.

Paying later
Although the household sector in general is in surplus, individual households at one time or another will be in deficit as net borrowers of funds. There are numerous financial alternatives available to deficit households to enable them to undertake expenditure. In modern economic systems the exchange of goods and services is facilitated by money which is usually defined as cash and bank deposits. When households use their current income or previously accumulated savings to purchase goods, they use money; this simplifies the process of exchange. There is only one stage involved in the transaction when money is exchanged for a particular item. However, if the household intends spending in excess of current income and savings, it requires some kind of credit instrument to finance its resulting deficit. Where goods are purchased on credit there are two stages involved in each transaction – the first between buyer, creditor and supplier to finance the purchase and a second between buyer and creditor to pay off the debt.

There are many different sources of consumer credit – trade credit, credit cards and hire purchase, or instalment credit.

The most common is trade credit, where a retailer allows a customer to build up a deficit over a period of a month and usually charges no interest if the account is settled within a certain time. In this case, the seller is also the creditor and this form of credit is common in both the household sector and the industrial sector for wholesalers and component suppliers extend the same form of credit to industry.

Credit card or HP?
Another form of credit is provided by credit cards, in which the creditor is usually a commercial bank. *Visa card* is run by the Bank of America and *Barclaycard* is organized by Barclays Bank. Credit cards are financed by charging both the purchaser and the supplier. At the initial stage of the transaction, the supplier may receive from the Bank of America only 95 per cent of the purchase price with a 5 per cent discount being accepted by the supplier in the belief that credit cards boost sales. The added cost is passed on to all customers in the form of higher prices. At the second stage, the purchaser is charged interest on the loan at about 20 per cent a year unless it is paid off within, say, a 30 day period. A credit card holder is allowed to extend credit up to a certain limit without entering into fresh negotiations for

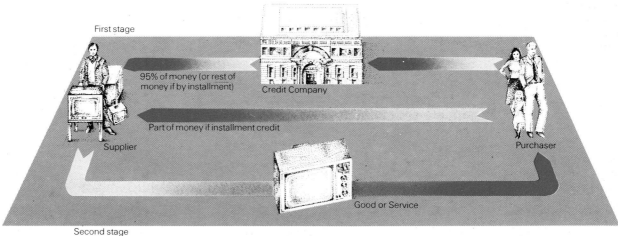

First stage

95% of money (or rest of money if by installment)

Credit Company

Part of money if installment credit

Supplier

Good or Service

Purchaser

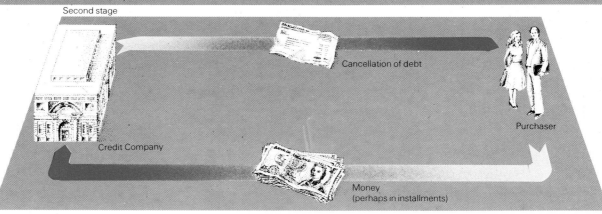

Second stage

Cancellation of debt

Credit Company

Purchaser

Money
(perhaps in installments)

Below: The purchase of a car is often a major drain on the average family budget and so it is often a hire purchase transaction. **The government regulates the amount of money that has to be deposited as a down-payment; interest on the outstanding balance varies according to the time taken for complete payment of the purchase price. As part of increased consumer protection, the full purchase price must always be shown on any advertising.**

each separate purchase. This greatly simplifies the process of borrowing and is an example of revolving credit which encourages the use of credit and leads to quite significant increases in consumers' expenditure. Governments have tended to put some restrictions on the growth of this sector by stipulating the amount of credit that can be generated at one time and by setting minimum pay-back periods.

Another common form of credit is provided by hire purchase companies that provide instalment credit. At the first stage of a transaction, the consumer makes only a 'down payment' of, say, one-fifth of the purchase price and obtains the goods on condition that a loan is taken out with a finance company. The finance company technically owns the product until the loan is paid off, and the goods will be re-possessed if the purchaser fails to repay the debt. The term 'hire purchase' means that goods bought in this way are regarded as on hire until the debt is finally paid. Hire purchase controls are commonly introduced when governments are attempting to restrict credit.

Above: The two stages of a hire purchase transaction. **In the first stage, the purchaser negotiates a loan with a credit company, which then pays the retailer. The goods are then supplied to the purchaser. In the second stage, the purchaser pays off the loan – usually in instalments – until the debt is paid. The chief penalty is the interest charge on the amount borrowed; this can be as high as 40% a year.**

INDUSTRY AND THE STOCK EXCHANGE

In most countries, expenditure undertaken by the industrial sector is the most volatile element of total demand. In general, there are two reasons why companies need to raise finance during their trading cycle – to finance working capital and to purchase long-term capital assets.

The requirement to raise working capital arises because companies incur costs during the production and distribution of their products, and these operating expenses have to be covered before any revenue is received from sales. The financing of this 'work in progress' is an essential element of business activity and the most common method of solving this problem was, in the past, to issue a bill of exchange. This is a financial instrument which allows the purchaser of, say, raw materials to defer payment for three months until processing and re-sale are complete. These bills of exchange provided an important impetus to the growth of financial institutions during the nineteenth century, but now most of the finance for this type of working capital is provided by commercial banks and trade credit. However, bills of exchange are still important in financing international trade.

In an established company, the cash receipts from earlier transactions are normally sufficient to finance current operating expenses. Work in progress is usually financed internally, but some form of external finance may still be required if the firm plans to expand output. Another important form of working capital requiring finance is unsold stocks of goods, and this has been a particularly common problem recently because of high inflation. The problem

arises when the value of these stocks appreciates during inflationary times and provide purely paper profits which are liable to tax. Consequently, serious problems involving inflation accounting have to be surmounted if a firm's cash flow and profits figures are not to be seriously distorted. Again, most of the finance is provided by banks.

Financing capital assets

The most important reason for raising finance is to purchase long term capital assets such as machines and buildings. Although these assets enable the final product to be efficiently and cheaply produced, the value of their contribution to production in any one year is almost always less than their purchase price. Therefore, the company has to obtain finance for their initial purchase and hopes that their contribution will eventually make their purchase profitable. New capital assets are required for the replacement of worn out assets in old production processes and for setting up new processes of production. Capital assets are referred to as replacement investment as in the case of new processes as net investment.

Left and *above left:* Petrochemical plants under construction in Brazil, *top right* the skeleton of a new British factory – the Courage brewery at Reading – and *bottom right* part of a new civic centre at Port Harcourt, Nigeria. **Modern industry frequently cannot finance such expansion – particularly in the so-called third world – without large-scale loans. These are raised either for financing work in progress, though this is done internally whenever possible, or for major development programmes which cannot be financed out of current revenue. In the latter case, the investment required is known as replacement investment, when the loan is needed to replace worn-out machinery, for instance, and as net investment, when a totally new expansion programme is being planned.**

The two forms of capital investment are together referred to as gross investment.

In general, companies require finance for working capital and for gross investment. The main sources of finance available to firms to meet these requirements are either internally generated funds or external funds.

Profits and depreciation

Internal funds are generated from retained profits (after payment of interest, tax and dividends) and depreciation allowances. The importance of these two items differs greatly from country to country because of tax considerations, especially those applying to depreciation, which is an allowance made to cover worn out assets and should therefore provide finance for replacement investment.

However, in some countries the total depreciation charges cover only the 'historic' cost of the machine and this may bear little relation to the current replacement cost. Also, in some countries, the depreciation allowance provided by the tax authorities may bear no relation to either historic or

replacement cost, but may instead be over-generous and act as an investment incentive by encouraging companies to retain a greater percentage of gross profits. The tax structure can also encourage retention if dividends are further taxed. The sum total of retained profits and depreciation provides the company's cash flow or undistributed income, which may not cover its planned expenditure on working capital and capital goods, so that some form of external financing will still be required. However, even if the cash flow exceeds planned expenditure, the company can still resort to external financing and keep part of its cash flow as a liquid cash reserve.

Borrowing for expansion

External funds can be viewed as falling into two main groups – short and long term borrowings, and equities.

Borrowings are a debt for which interest payments have to be made and these payments have the prior claim on the company's profits. Equities are financial instruments which confer ownership of the company and usually carry voting rights and a residual claim on profits in the form of dividends. But, unlike interest payments which have to be paid, there is no obligation to pay dividends.

Short-term borrowings are usually obtained from commercial banks and have increased in significance during the last decade. This is partly because short-term borrowings tend to increase during inflationary periods to finance the rapid rise in the value of working capital, particularly stock appreciation. It is also due to high long-term interest rates and depressed stock markets. This has forced companies to rely on short-term financing. In 1973, both these factors occurred simultaneously in most countries and the proportion of short-term debt increased enormously. It was most commonly supplied by the commercial banks in the form of overdraft facilities and the rate applying to these types of loans are variable at the discretion of the banks.

To avoid the uncertainties inherent in short-term finance at variable interest rates, many companies prefer to borrow long-term by issuing debentures and preference bonds at fixed percentage interest rates or by negotiating long-term loans with banks and other financial institutions. In some countries,

notably Germany, the commercial banks are more involved in the provision of long-term finance than in other countries.

The issue of equities or ordinary shares is often referred to as risk capital. Equities are not classed as a debt because ordinary shareholders are co-owners of the company and are eligible to receive an annual dividend. However, shareholders receive dividends from net profits, and these may be zero or negative making the return to the equity holder uncertain, and paid at the discretion of the company. This is in contrast to bond holders and other creditors whose return is fixed and certain.

The total finance generated through both internal and external sources can

Third world investment is seen *right* in tractors ready for delivery to farms in Angola, and *below* in stacks of groundnuts in Nigeria awaiting shipment to a factory for extraction of their oil. **Both developing countries and companies investing in them have sometimes their own special problems to face. Many newly-emergent nations do not have the domestic financial resources to fund investment for growth and they can also find it difficult to attract international financial support for expansion on ordinary commercial terms. In addition, their agriculturally-based economies are often dramatically affected by fluctuations in the world commodity market, which, in the past, have sometimes even forced countries to default on repayment of international loans. World shortages, as in the case of coffee, for instance, can lead to fantastic short-term gains, but a world glut can lead to an equally dramatic fall.**

How company finance works **After money has been set aside for depreciation in the value of physical assets, and tax, interest on loans and dividends to shareholders have been paid, the undistributed income is left as working** capital. **Funds for development can be provided by bank borrowing – in the form of short or long-term loans – and by the issue of two types of share, debenture, or pre-ference, and equity, or ordinary.**

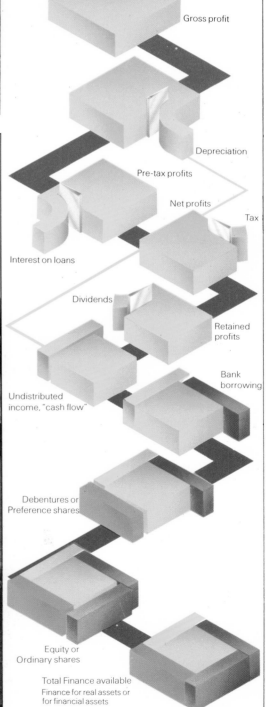

Gross profit

Depreciation

Pre-tax profits

Net profits

Tax

Interest on loans

Dividends

Retained profits

Bank borrowing

Undistributed income, "cash flow"

Debentures or Preference shares

Equity or Ordinary shares

Total Finance available
Finance for real assets or for financial assets

be used to finance an increase in working capital, to purchase long-term capital assets, to pay off current liabilities or to build up financial assets. Funds which are not used to finance long-term investment projects or to build up stocks of finished goods are usually held in liquid form as bank deposits or in short-term assets.

Self-financing is vital to companies and accounts for about 50 per cent of total funds. In relation to non-financial assets, the self-financing ratio is even more significant.

Retained earnings are a very important source of investment finance ranging from 93 per cent in the UK to 55 per cent in Japan. But there are major differences between countries in the methods of raising debt finance.

Industry and interest rates

A low self-financing ratio means that the industrial sector has to raise larger amounts of funds in the form of debt or equity, and this in turn has implications for the cost of funds to the company.

Interest payments on loans can be offset against tax, making the effective cost of borrowing often relatively low compared to other forms of finance. It is normally assumed that the average cost of capital will be lower, if the proportion of debt finance in the total is higher. The percentage of debt finance in the total is known as the gearing ratio. The higher this ratio becomes, the lower is the average cost of capital. However, the higher gearing implies a greater risk for ordinary shareholders, because interest payments will be high relative to dividends. Any fall in profits will increase the probability of dividends being cancelled, because they are paid at the company's discretion. The company is also placed at considerable risk because, since interest payments are a legal obligation, any default will lead to bankruptcy. This risk will be reflected in a higher cost of equity capital and there should be some optimal gearing ratio which both reduces the risk of bankruptcy and mimimizes the over-all cost of capital.

The industrial sector in the UK relies far more on short-term debt than either Germany or the US, and this has important repercussions on the type of investment undertaken. For example, because German and US banks are more prepared to lend long-term, they provide a more permanent source of finance for industrial companies – that is, more in line with the long planning periods of capital investment projects. Because of the absence of this type of finance, UK investment has been more short-term in nature. The high dependence on short-term finance (usually automatic overdraft facilities), coupled with a high self-financing ratio, has effectively immunised the UK industrial sector from the discipline of the capital market. This has led to an inefficient use of capital resources.

The role of the stock markets

The stock market plays a relatively minor role in financing the investment requirements of industrial companies, although long-term borrowings are included in the issues of debenture and preference shares, and other private bond issues which do not offer equity holdings.

Despite the minor role played by stock markets in financing the investment of the industrial sector, most countries attach immense importance to them. There are two separate parts of the stock market – the secondary market and the market for new issues.

The secondary market trades in existing stocks and is usually the most active. It provides an organized market on which shareholders can quickly divest themselves of any stocks they wish to sell. So long as it does this efficiently, the secondary market provides a useful function.

The new issues market is relevant for companies planning to raise finance to undertake capital investment. New issues are marketed through investment bankers and underwriters, or through merchant banks. These are specialist organizations which accumulate expertise on potential buyers and market characteristics, and advise on the timing and pricing of new issues. For these services they receive a fee. The cost of new issues, especially when the secondary market is depressed, can be quite high, and in order to avoid these costs and also to avoid brokerage fees, it is usual for existing firms to by-pass the new issues market by making a rights issue, and placing new issues directly with stockholders. This is done by offering existing stockholders the right to buy a proportion of the new issues at a preferential price.

Both the new issues and secondary markets deal in equities, which have a

Economic contrasts *right* a dumper truck in Zambia and trucks in the United Arab Emirates **Zambia is one country whose economy – based chiefly on copper – has suffered because of a reduced world demand for the metal.**

In the United Arab Emirates, however, oil revenues are transforming what was once one of the poorest areas in the world into one of the richest, as full-scale industrial development gets under way.

claim on the profits of a company and on bonds, which are debt instruments with a fixed interest rate. The price of equities fluctuates more extensively than bonds, making the holding of equities more of a gamble. The price of equities fluctuates in relation to profit expectations which can change markedly, while the price of a bond fluctuates mainly in relation to other market interest rates. The relationship between the new issue market and the secondary market is very important (for both bonds and equities), because the prices that are set in the secondary market determine to a large extent the cost of raising funds in the new issues market.

Stocks and flows

The interaction between these two markets is at the very heart of economic analysis in that it illustrates a relationship between two vital concepts – stocks and flows. The volume of existing securities at any time is a stock, which is measured at a particular time, while the volume of new issues is a flow that is measured over a longer period – say one year. In all countries, the value of the annual flow of new issues is small in relation to the total value of the stock of existing securities. This is the reason why the secondary market tends to dominate the price of stocks and bonds and, through these, rates of interest. But the flow of new issues can at times be quite large relative to the existing stock, and exert a separate influence on the price. This happens especially when there are large issues of government debt.

In the secondary market, prices are strongly affected by the pattern of ownership security, in which it is usually possible to identify two extremes. A market is said to be 'broad' when

Finding the money **How five of the world's leading industrial nations – the USA, the UK, West Germany, France and Japan – tap sources of funds to finance their investment programmes. West Germany manages to raise the highest proportion of funds internally, while Japan gets 75% of its funds from external sources, chiefly in the form of short-term loans. These loans fuelled the dramatic Japanese industrial expansion of the 1950s, 1960s and 1970s.**

Below the London base of the Chinese-financed Overseas Trust Bank **The international banking community is playing an increasingly important part in the funding of international loans, both short and long term. Their help frequently takes the form of overdraft facilities. Short-term loans have greatly increased in number over the last decade, as inflation has forced an increase in long-term interest rates and also led to stock market depression.**

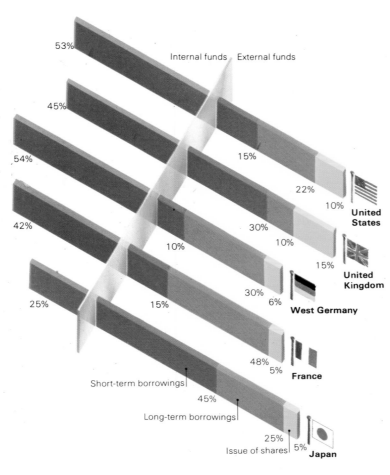

Internal funds   External funds

53%

45%   15%
                  22%
                    10%
                  United States

54%   30%
                    10%
                  15%
                  United Kingdom

42%   10%

25%   15%   30%   6%
                  West Germany

              48%
                    5%
                  France

Short-term borrowings

Long-term borrowings   45%

                  25%   5%
Issue of shares   **Japan**

securities are scattered among a large number of relatively small holders, and 'thin' where ownership is concentrated in a small number of financial institutions. In a broad market, securities prices are more stable because it enables large transactions to be spread over a great number of holders without much disturbance to prices.

The new stockholders

The US and UK stock markets are regarded as much broader than their European counterparts. But in all countries the pattern of ownership has been gradually changing since 1950 in such a way as to make stock markets rather 'thinner'. For example, until 1950 the direct ownership of shares and bonds was heavily concentrated in the hands of individuals; but the rise of unit and investment trusts, and life assurance and pension funds has caused a large diversion to financial institutions. Unit and investment trusts allow individual holders to acquire a reasonable spread of securities without incurring high brokerage fees. The purchase of a single unit offers the investor a share of a large number of companies through a wide portfolio which safeguards the investor from possible large capital losses. This reduces the risks to indivi-

OVERSEAS TRUST BANK LTD.

行 銀 記 信 外 海

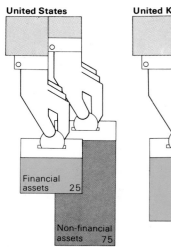

United States

Financial assets 25

Non-financial assets 75

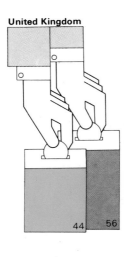

United Kingdom

44 56

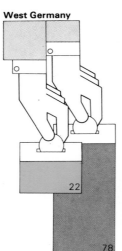

West Germany

22

78

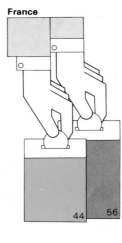

France

44 56

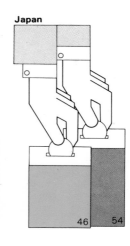

Japan

46 54

How the USA, the UK, West Germany, France and Japan use the funds they raise for investment **West Germany and the USA lead in the amount of money they invest in non-financial assets; in the other countries, the two forms of investment are much more closely balanced. Quite frequently, capital surplus to immediate requirements will be invested in the financial field to produce a short-term yield.**

dual share-holders and, because of this, a greater proportion of households invest in shares through unit and investment trusts. Life insurance and pension funds have consistently been increasing their share of securities, and in some countries, where households have been net sellers of securities for many years, these institutions have built up their proportionate share to over 50 per cent. In the US, life insurance and pension funds hold around 30 per cent of stocks and 60 per cent of corporate bonds. In France and Germany the pattern is similar and, although the relative importance of life insurance and pension funds is less than in other countries, their role is steadily increasing.

The trend is for a greater proportion of households' saving to be channelled indirectly into industrial investment through pension funds and insurance companies, rather than directly through individual holdings.

Although stock markets in general provide the same function – an organized market for the purchase and sale of existing securities and as pace-setters for the issue of new securities – their organization differs considerably from country to country. The world's oldest stock market is the London Stock Exchange, which can be traced back to the London coffee houses of the seventeenth century. The Exchange established its first permanent home in Threadneedle Street in the City of London in 1773, just before the US War of Independence, and its constitution has not changed very much over the centuries. Membership is still confined to two distinct types – 'job-

bers' and 'brokers'. Brokers deal on behalf of the public and buy or sell shares on the best terms available. Jobbers deal as principals trading on their own account with brokers, but do not deal directly with the public. The object of this system is to ensure that prices remain competitive and that short-period fluctuations in price are minimized.

The main differences between the major stock exchanges are that in the US, there are no jobbers but, like the UK, there are a very large number of independent brokers. In Germany and

France there are no jobbers either, but the number of brokers is smaller, which contributes to the thinness of the stock markets in these countries. In Germany, the banks are the only members of the stock exchange who are allowed to deal on behalf of the public.

In all countries, in addition to the normal supply of funds generated and distributed through private financial markets, there are additional funds provided by publicly owned or organized credit institutes.

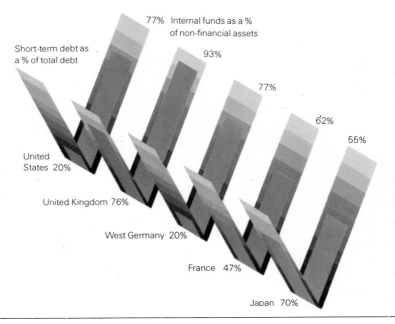

77% Internal funds as a % of non-financial assets

Short-term debt as a % of total debt

93%

77%

62%

55%

United States 20%

United Kingdom 76%

West Germany 20%

France 47%

Japan 70%

How the USA, UK, West Germany, France and Japan balance short-term borrowings and self-financing from internal funds **The relationship between the two is known as secondary gearing. When self-financing ability is inadequate, the need to borrow is proportionately increased, and this can have major consequences on industrial finance. Borrowing is often attractive because the debts concerned can be offset against tax. However, this means that shareholders take a higher risk, as such debts have a legal obligation over dividends.**

No small company, however vigorous, can progress very far unless capital is available to provide the machinery, transport and labour it requires for expansion. Banks will gladly supply finance up to a point, but if large sums are required – say, to build a factory – then the business must be converted into a public company. shares are offered to investors via a merchant bank or the Stock Exchange; the company's founder gets the money he needs, but relinquishes ownership to the shareholders who are free to sell or re-purchase their shares according to the rise and fall of the market.

The notion of a number of merchants pooling their resources to finance some venture beyond the reach of any single one of them, is a fairly ancient one. Each would invest in the venture – say, a trading voyage – according to his means, and if the voyage was a success, would gain a profit proportionate to his share of the investment.

Sometimes, if the ship was overdue, or the investor wanted his money back, he would sell his shares to someone else who was prepared to take the risk. In seventeenth century London, one or two City coffee houses became well known as centres for such transactions; and so the Stock Exchange was born.

Today, every major industrial nation possesses a market in which stocks, shares and other securities are bought and sold, ensuring that the life-blood of finance continues to flow through the veins of commerce. Paris has its Bourse, for instance, and London and New York their Stock Exchanges. Many evolved from informal beginnings – the New York Exchange began in the 1790s with a gathering of businessmen under a tree in Wall Street – and in consequence, the weight of tradition, rather than law, lies heavily upon those that have dealings in them. This is no bad thing; due to its complexities, much of the world's financial dealings must be conducted in a spirit of trust between seller and buyer, broker and dealer, that is summed up in the motto of the London Stock Exchange – 'My word is my Bond.' All transactions, even those involving millions of dollars or pounds, are settled, at least initially, by a verbal agreement on the crowded Floor of the Stock Exchange.

People on 'Change

Customs, methods and degrees of governmental supervision differ considerably between the exchanges of one country and another. The Milan exchange, and part of the Paris Bourse are supervised by government officials, while the exchanges of London and New York are largely self-governing.

Membership of stock exchanges is generally gained by election; the qualifications required are a reputation for honesty in business affairs, a knowledge of the functions of the exchange, financial stability, and a purpose for becoming a member other

The world's main stock exchanges. **From left to right, Copenhagen, Amsterdam, Frankfurt, London, Zurich and New York.** *Below,* **the Paris bourse.**

than sheer speculation. In London, prospective members also have to pass a stiff written examination.

Only members may deal on the exchange, though their functions differ somewhat from one country to another. In London, for example, there are two distinct classes of member, brokers and jobbers, neither of which would dream of usurping the other's function. Brokers deal directly with the public, buying and selling shares for their customers at the best terms available, and offering them the benefit of their expertise on a commission basis. Jobbers, on the other hand, have no contact with the public, but buy and sell to the brokers on the floor of the exchange. It is a rule in dealing that the jobber does not know whether the broker is buying or selling until the transaction is completed, and therefore quotes both a buying and a selling price; this ensures he does not under or overstate one or the other. Jobbers tend to specialise in particular kinds of shares – say, aircraft or oil – and

make their profits, like any other dealer, from the difference between their buying and selling prices.

In most other exchanges, including that in New York, jobbers do not exist. Instead, the broker both deals with the public and buys and sells shares directly in the exchange. West Germany is an exception in that only the banks are allowed to deal on behalf of the public.

Investing through the exchange

Stock exchanges deal in two kinds of business, the buying and selling of shares in existing companies, and new issues – selling shares in new companies that wish to raise capital for expansion.

In the latter case, the owner of the company must first go to an investment banker or merchant bank who, in the light of their specialised knowledge. will advise him about potential buyers, the price he should charge for his shares, and the time he should put them

on the market. For this, the banker charges a fee, which includes all the paperwork – advertising in the press, issuing share certificates, informing brokers – involved in the launching of a new company.

Ordinary, or equity, shares are sold to buyers, which in effect, makes them part-owners, sharing in the ups and downs of the company's fortunes. The company cannot be sold without their consent; new shares cannot be issued without their approval; and they can, if they wish, dismiss the company's directors On the other hand, they are taking a gamble; if the company makes no money, or the profit it does make is required for investment in new machinery, then the shareholders may see no return on their money for years.

The other role of the stock exchange – that of dealing in the shares of established companies – is, in some ways, the more important, for this is the business that keeps the exchange active. It provides the market

The world's major stock exchanges, with their opening dates. **London's stock exchange is the oldest, being officially established in 1773,** though its origins go back for at least a century before that. New York's stock market is located in Wall Street.

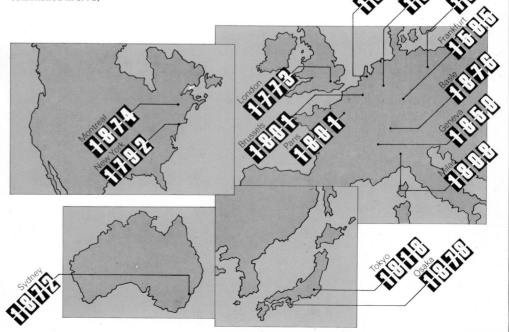

where investors can buy and sell quickly, advancing or denying money to particular industries depending on a delicate balance of prices, profits, world needs, world events and even the weather.

The customers

Until a few years ago, the stock exchange and all its works and dealings was regarded, probably correctly, as the rock on which the upper middle classes stood, and from which upper middle class blessings flowed.

Nowadays, very few of us are not investors in the stock exchange. Trade unions, building societies, insurance companies, pension funds and friendly societies all invest the funds they collect from members and between them, control an enormous share of the market.

The stock exchange, as always, bent with the wind, and wooed the newcomers just as assiduously as it wooed the Forsythes 70 years ago. It changes, but remains the same. Less formal, perhaps, but its motto stands: 'My word is my bond.'

Below: **The small producer, a baker, makes a living by selling his product – bread – direct to the consumer. Both the bakery and the baker are financed from the profits gained from sales.**

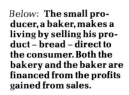

Right: **Customers multiply as the baker's fame spreads. He employs more labour and buys better transport and equipment; but still he cannot expand beyond the limit dictated by the profit he makes from over-the-counter sales.**

Above: **Better business encourages the baker to seek outside capital that will enable him to build a much bigger bakery and reach a greater number of customers. His local bank and a finance house both see him as a good investment, but their loans are short-term, and his plans are still limited.**

Right: **To obtain more capital, the baker decides to turn himself into a public company. A merchant bank 'floats' the company – that is, it offers equity or ordinary shares to the public through advertisements in the press or through the stock exchange. The baker gets the capital he requires, but now shares ownership of the company with the shareholders, each of whom expects a dividend on the bakery's profits. The shareholders may be private investors, unit trust managers, pension funds, insurance companies or representatives of other interests.**

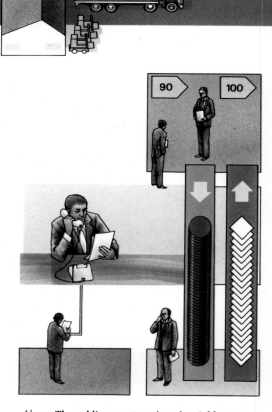

Above: **The public cannot deal directly in shares, which must be bought or sold through a broker. A shareholder wishing to sell contacts his broker** who asks a jobber – a stock exchange dealer – for his prices on the shares. If the buying price is satisfactory, the broker sells to the jobber.

*Left:*Dealing in progress on the floors of stock exchanges in, left to right, Paris, Zurich and Sydney. **At Zurich, bidding is in progress, while in Sydney dealers are watching share prices as news of a new mineral strike is announced. Since 1950, the pattern of who actually owns stocks and shares has been changing. Before that date, the ownership of stocks and bonds was chiefly the preserve of individuals, but now a larger and larger proportion is held by institutions – in particular unit and investment trusts and life insurance and pension schemes.**

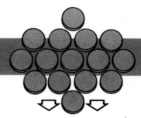

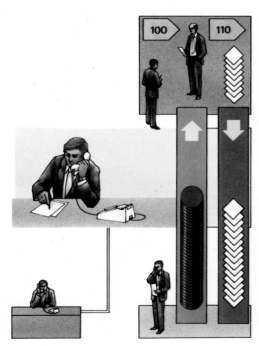

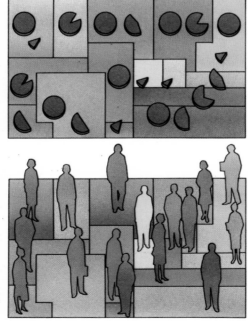

Above: **Buying shares follows the same procedure through broker and jobber. When a bargain is struck, the shares pass to the purchaser and the** proceeds to the jobber, whose profit is derived from the difference between his buying and selling prices. These may fluctuate daily.

Above: **Each year the company declares a dividend which is divided among the shareholders in proportion to their investments. The shares** may have changed hands. so the original shareholders will not receive a dividend. Their profits will have come from selling their shares.

Above: **A sharp drop in the value of shares – brought about, perhaps, by the company founder's death – brings in the 'bulls' and the 'bears'.** The former buy at the lowest ebb, hoping for a profit as prices rise, while the latter sell, hoping to repurchase as prices drop lower still.

THE FINANCE OF GOVERNMENT

Public sector expenditure is financed mainly in two ways, either internally through the income that the government receives from tax revenues, or externally by borrowing. Each financial year, governments publish their expenditure and taxation proposals in the form of an annual budget. This normally reviews the government's income and expenditure for the previous year and makes forecasts for the year ahead. If any changes in taxation are proposed to achieve new expenditure plans, they are introduced in the budget.

The budget statement provides more than just a formal statement of income and expenditure plans for the coming year. Nowadays, it often includes an indication of the policies that the government intends to pursue in order to achieve the stated objectives of its economic policy, such as a reduction in the level of unemployment. The budget also provides a summary of fiscal policy, one of the major economic weapons available to modern governments. By means of fiscal policies, governments can attempt to influence the level or distribution of the Gross National Product (GNP). They do this through changes in expenditure or tax revenue.

Government in debt

If a government's planned expenditure exceeds its estimated tax revenue, then the budget will be in deficit and the government will have to resort to borrowing to cover the excess expenditure. Such expenditure is said to be deficit-financed; this is likely to occur in times of depression or stagnation when the government is attempt-

*Left:*Spending on schools In all developed nations, education is one of the highest national priorities and it also takes its share of state spending. An increase in the birth rate means an eventual increase in the number of school places required – and the majority of these have to be provided by the state. In Britain, education is financed and controlled both at a national level and by local authorities. Cuts in this field, together with attempts to recover some revenue by charging for school meals, for instance, have proved an emotive political issue over the last decade.

*Right:*A motorway under construction in Cambridgeshire In Britain, the road programme has been a major consumer of government funds over the last twenty years. Some economists argue that such programmes serve to increase the nation's stock of capital assets. Others, however, have queried such programmes, the chief reason being that, because of the time they take to complete, the government's economic circumstances may change drastically while they are still under way. In Britain, for instance, the road programme has been a major victim of cuts in public expenditure forced on the government by economic recession.

ing to increase its own expenditure to compensate for any shortfall in private sector spending. This type of compensatory expenditure is referred to as a counter-cyclical fiscal policy. Similarly when tax revenue exceeds expenditure the budget will be in surplus and such a situation is likely to arise when there is excess demand in the economy, so that a compensatory or counter-cyclical fiscal policy requires an overall reduction in aggregate demand.

Deficits on the budget increase the indebtedness of the public sector while surpluses help to reduce it. The cumulative total of deficits less surpluses over time, make up the current outstanding total of a nation's national debt.

A deficit-financed fiscal policy increases the national debt. During this century, the most significant occasions when such policies were introduced were during periods of war. The legacy of these wars are the very large national debts of many countries, especially, those of the US and the UK, and the only way in which their size can be reduced is by the various governments

achieving a surplus in their budgets. The likelihood of such surpluses in the public sector has decreased substantially in most countries in recent years, so that the net indebtedness of the public sectors in all countries has tended to increase.

Public expenditures can be grouped into two broad categories – exhaustive and non-exhaustive.

Exhaustive resources are allocated away from the private sector to the public sector in order to provide goods and services. These involve direct claims on goods and services which can be further sub-divided into current expenditure and capital formation. Current expenditure involves the provision of public sector services such as health and education, the bulk of whose budget goes on wages and salaries. Capital formation involves expenditure on buildings such as hospitals, schools, and roads, which increase the nation's stock of capital assets. In some countries, capital formation is undertaken either by nationalized industries or by public utilities.

Non-exhaustive expenditure does

One of Europe's largest hospitals, Northwick Park. **The British National Health service is still the envy of the world, but, according to some medical pressure groups, successive cuts forced on it have brought it close to collapse. Health illustrates the dilemma facing many governments today – how to provide the welfare services their people need and expect at a time of economic recession and determined attempts to control the money supply to stop ever-increasing inflation.**

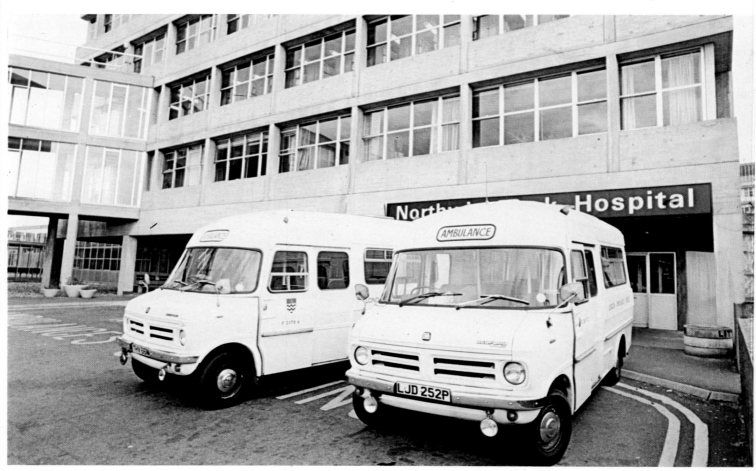

Right: In Britain, the Meals on Wheels service brings cooked food to those among the old who are no longer able to fend for themselves. **The philosophy of the welfare state is that no one should suffer want; but, according to some economists, the demands of modern economics may well mean that a limit on the amount of government spending may have to be set.**

not directly absorb goods and services, but consists of transfers of incomes from one consumer or producer to another. Included in this category are transfer payments such as pensions, national insurance benefits and student grants, which enable the government to achieve a more equitable distribution of income. Other forms of transfer payments are subsidies to producers. These may be aimed at keeping down prices of vital commodities like bread and milk; alternatively, they may act as an investment incentive. The final important transfer is the interest that has to be paid on the national debt, which transfers income from the general taxpayer to holders of existing government bonds.

Exhaustive and non-exhaustive public expenditures are undertaken by both central and local governments.

Paying for public services

During this century, government expenditure in all countries has increased considerably as a proportion of GNP. There are a number of reasons for this. Except during wars, the two most important have been government attempts to achieve certain social objectives such as better health and

education services, and their efforts to manage the economy in such a way as to achieve full employment and other economic objectives. Governments throughout the world now accept greater responsibility for the provision of social services. In the process they have moved away from the 19th century philosophy of 'laissez faire', when the view was that the government should confine itself to upholding law and order while letting the market system determine the allocation of re-

sources and the distribution of income. The result of this shift of emphasis was a rising share of public expenditure in GNP from about 5 per cent in 1900 to nearly 25 per cent in 1950. Since then, the growth of public expenditure has been even more rapid, partly because a better educated electorate has demanded better public services and a higher quality of life.

The more active role played by governments in the management of the nation's economic affairs stems

Current government expenditure as a percentage of Gross National Product in the USA, UK, France, West Germany, Japan and Australia in 1955 and 1975. **In all five countries, public expenditure has increased – most noticeably in West Germany – and this has created the problem of raising enough revenue to finance the growth. Increased taxation has provided the chief answer.**

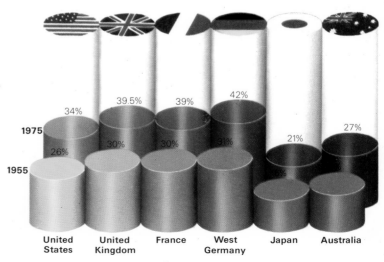

	1975	1955
United States	34%	26%
United Kingdom	39.5%	30%
France	39%	30%
West Germany	42%	31%
Japan	21%	
Australia	27%	

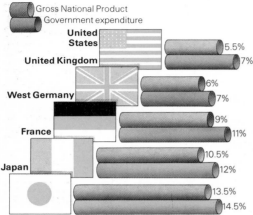

Gross National Product
Government expenditure

United States	5.5%	7%
United Kingdom	6%	7%
West Germany	9%	11%
France	10.5%	12%
Japan	13.5%	14.5%

Left: Growth of public expenditure and Gross National Product in the USA, UK, West Germany, France and Japan, based on the annual averages between 1955 and 1965. **In the last 25 years government spending has increased to over 60% of the GNP in some cases. This percentage includes both exhaustive and non-exhaustive expenditure, however, and the former has in fact been decreasing during the period.**

Below: Types of taxation **Taxation takes effect in two ways – either through direct taxation, frequently deducted from wages at source, or through indirect taxation, the amount of government tax included in the price of goods purchased by the consumer. Direct taxes are usually progressive, so that the lower paid pay less, but indirect taxes are regressive so that the lower paid pay proportionately more.**

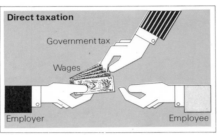

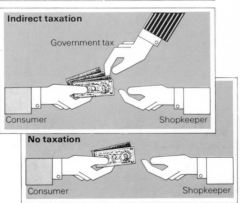

Direct taxation
Government tax
Wages
Employer — Employee

Indirect taxation
Government tax
Consumer — Shopkeeper

No taxation
Consumer — Shopkeeper

from the Keynesian revolution in economic thinking that began in the 1930s. Keynes's analysis of the Great Depression identified the main cause of mass unemployment as deficient aggregate demand, and suggested that governments could maintain full employment by regulating its level. But in practice, this has led to increased government expenditure during slumps while there has been no corresponding decrease in booms. Such asymmetric developments, known as 'ratchet effects', have contributed to the more rapid growth in public expenditure.

In attempting to achieve their social and economic objectives, general government expenditure in the last 25 years has increased to over 60 per cent of GNP in some countries but this figure includes both exhaustive and non-exhaustive expenditures. In all countries exhaustive expenditures have been a decreasing proportion of total government expenditure, and the greatest increases have been in the area of transfer payments.

In most countries, public expenditure has been rising faster than GNP and the excess is on average about 20 per cent each year. The main cause of this rise was the increased provisions of health, education, welfare services, and other transfer payments. Many of these payments are spent by the private sector largely on private sector goods and services. This means that a better measure of government influence on the economy is the share of exhaustive expenditures only.

Direct and indirect taxation
The increase in public sector expenditures create problems in that they require increased revenues to finance

them. The main source of finance for all governments is tax revenue which is obtained through three major sources:
(a) direct taxes on the incomes of households and firms;
(b) indirect taxes on the expenditures of households and firms;
(c) social security contributions levied on households and firms.

The distinction between direct and indirect taxation is partly administrative and partly economic. A direct tax is levied on the taxpayer and cannot be avoided, while an indirect tax is levied on particular goods; this can be avoided by not buying the taxed items. Indirect taxes affect the prices of particular goods and services while direct taxes do not. Direct taxes tend to be progressive in that the tax rate tends to increase faster than the level of taxable

income, so that the poor pay proportionately less. Indirect taxes tend to be regressive because the effective tax rate decreases as a proportion of income; therefore, the poor pay proportionately more in tax.

Social security contributions are levied on wages and salaries, sometimes as a fixed levy or as a percentage of income, but usually with a fixed maximum contribution. They are levied on both the employee and the employer, but the employer usually pays the greater proportion. It is, in effect, a direct payroll tax on employers.

Indirect taxes make a more important contribution to total revenue in countries such as France and Germany than in countries like the US and UK, where direct taxes are the most important source of revenue. Even so, during the last 20 years, indirect taxes

in all countries have tended to contribute a smaller proportion of the total. This is partly due to inflation – many indirect taxes are per unit taxes (expressed as a specific amount on each item), which means that the real value of the tax declines as the price of goods in general rises. Other indirect taxes are *ad valorem* taxes, which are expressed as a percentage of the value of the goods. An example is value-added tax (VAT) whose real value tends to keep pace with inflation.

Fiscal drag

Direct taxes in all countries over the last 20 years have thus accounted for a greater proportion of the total. A progressive income tax structure, at a time of inflation, means that the rapid rise in the nominal value of wages and salaries draws more and more tax-

Above: Tunnellers, one of the highest paid groups of British workers, and *right*, the percentages of their wages taken by the state in direct taxation, social security and indirect taxation. **Indirect taxes are more important in France and West Germany; direct taxes in the UK and the USA.**

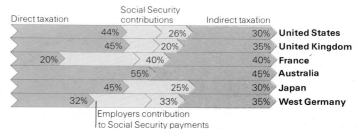

Direct taxation	Social Security contributions	Indirect taxation	
44%	26%	30%	**United States**
45%	20%	35%	**United Kingdom**
20%	40%	40%	**France**
55%		45%	**Australia**
45%	25%	30%	**Japan**
32%	33%	35%	**West Germany**

Employers contribution to Social Security payments

payers into the higher tax bands, causing a greater proportion of incomes to be paid in tax. When these higher tax bands are not raised to take account of inflation, the process has a depressing effect on consumers' real incomes. This is known as a fiscal drag.

The fastest growing revenue element in all countries other than Australia has been social security contributions, mainly because they are easy to collect and difficult to evade.

Countries which have difficulties in implementing effective income taxes because of widespread evasion tend to rely more on social security levies. In Italy nearly 50 per cent of tax revenue is raised in this way.

The debate over the merits of direct as against indirect taxes and proportional versus progressive taxation has been going on for centuries. It is often argued that direct taxes are a disincentive to work effort and labour

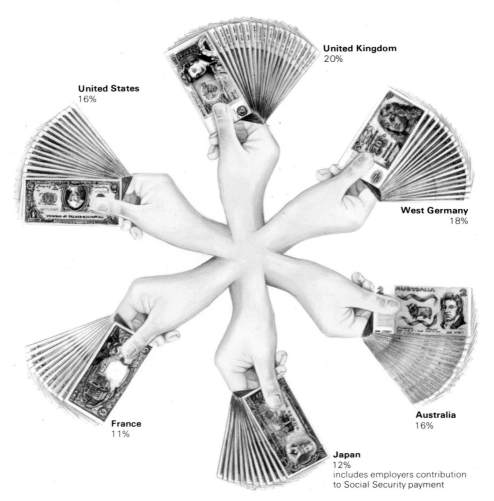

United Kingdom
20%

United States
16%

West Germany
18%

Australia
16%

France
11%

Japan
12%
includes employers contribution
to Social Security payment

The amount of personal income raised by tax and social security contributions in 1975 **The governments of the UK, France and West Germany raised tax revenue equal to more than 40% of the Gross National Product – near double the percentage of Japan.**

mobility and that they encourage tax evasion as well as avoidance through legal loopholes which are discovered by lawyers and accountants at a high cost to society.

It is also suggested that when taxation exceeds 25 per cent of GNP it becomes inflationary, because taxpayers, and trade unions, react against high taxes by either forcing up pre-tax incomes or reducing their saving to maintain their expenditure plans. This reaction, together with indirect taxes forces up industrial costs, and, with taxes already a high proportion of GNP, governments are forced to resort to raising additional revenue by printing money.

The revenue obtained from taxation is generally used to finance public expenditure. In addition to this main role, all three types of taxation are also altered for purposes of economic management. Taxes are an integral part of the government's fiscal policy so that taxes may be raised in a boom to curtail private sector demand, independently of the need to finance current government expenditure. Direct taxes may be increased as a proportion of total taxes independently of any revenue effects, simply to change the distribution of national income.

Financing public enterprise

There are important differences in national accounting practices. The UK is unique in including the borrowing of nationalized industries within the public sector accounts. In other countries, public enterprises raise finance on the capital markets in their own name, and their deficits do not directly affect the government's borrowing requirement. Thus sensible international comparisons need to be concentrated on the financial balance of individual countries rather than the borrowing requirement. In some countries, such as France and the US, intermediate bodies are set up to fin-

ance public housing independently of the government's coffers.

The public sectors in all countries had significant deficits between 1974 and 1975. Most of these were due to counter-cyclical fiscal policies implemented to help overcome the world recession initiated by the quadrupling of oil prices in 1973. But even in 1975, in most countries, the current accounts of their public sectors were in surplus and the deficits were largely due to capital expenditure.

Government debt incurred to finance capital expenditure is not necessarily a burden on a nation because it inherits both the capital assets and the interest liabilities on the loans incurred to finance current public consumption. But when public sector debt is incurred to finance current public sonsumption interest liabilities are generated which are not matched by capital assets. Since no extra wealth is created, there is no likelihood of government revenue increasing and in all prob-

Below Sheets of Japanese yen being cut into notes **Issuing banknotes is usually the sole prerogative of the government, as they are a form of government debt. Supply is therefore strictly controlled. Printing too much money, as in the Germany of the 1920s, can dramatically fuel the fires of inflation.**

Left: Weighing finished coins at the mint before they are packed for distribution to the clearing banks. **Like banknotes, coins are also issued by governments and their supply is also strictly controlled.**

ability the government will be forced into further borrowing, thus worsening the situation. In this type of case public sector debt is a burden on society.

In Italy, in recent years the financial balance has been consistently negative, ranging between 5 per cent and 10 per cent of GNP, with both the current and capital accounts in deficit. In such circumstances, it is increasingly difficult for government to continue borrowing without resorting to an inflationary increase in the money supply. Normally as long as the deficit is incurred to pay for fixed capital asssets and is financed by the issue of long-term bonds, the government is acting in a similar way to private sector corporations and no financial bank-

ruptcy is implied. But when current expenditure is financed by the creation of money, this causes inflationary pressures and general concern is often voiced about this type of public sector borrowing.

Public *vs.* private borrowing

The enormous size of recent public sector deficits has led to a more general fear that government borrowing will take place at the expense of other borrowing, and that the public sector borrowing will crowd out the private sector. This is particularly likely when profitability is low, making internal funds scarce, and when companies are forced to rely on borrowed funds. If the public sector borrowing require-

ments bids up financial interest rates, then private sector borrowings can be priced out of the market.

OECD misgivings

Recent large borrowing requirements provoked from the Organization for Economic Co-operation and Development (OECD) a summary of these concerns: "The fear has been expressed that the large budget deficits predicted for some countries could lead to excess demand conditions in which private expenditures would be displaced by government spending and public sector borrowing, due to rising prices and interest rates.

"There are apprehensions that, if monetary management were too cau-

tious, large-scale government borrowing operations could create tight conditions in financial markets and 'crowd out' private credit demand, even in the current situation of low pressure on resources.

"Unrestrained monetary accommodation of budget financing operations, on the other hand, is frequently thought to be inconsistent with present stabilization aims; there are fears that it would rekindle inflation at an early stage of recovery or result in a build-up of excess liquidity, complicating the task of monetary control once the upswing had gained momentum."

These fears about government borrowing requirements highlight the problem of deciding what proportion is borrowed from the banks. Although the banks are an important source of government finance, if they are relied on too heavily, it tends to increase the money supply and is likely to be inflationary. Most governments make sure they limit their dependence on the banking system.

How governments borrow

There are three main sources of finance for government borrowing – the banking system, other (non-bank) financial intermediaries, and private sector enterprises and households. The banking system includes the commercial banks, discount houses – and other financial institutions closely allied to the banks – and the central bank. Other financial intermediaries are mainly pension funds and insurance companies. Governments issue a variety of different borrowing instruments in order to make use of all these possible sources.

Most important of these is the issue of medium and long-term bonds. They are government securities with fairly long terms to maturity bearing fixed rates of interest. In the UK, they are referred to as 'gilt-edged securities' or simply 'gilts', and are broken down into 'shorts' and 'longs' depending on their term to maturity. In the US, these securities are referred to as Federal Notes when their term to maturity is less than five years, and as Federal Bonds when they mature in five years or more. All such bonds are traded on the stock market and are referred to as marketable debt. The price and yield of these securities are determined in a similar fashion to corporate

bonds as they are put out initially in the new issue market and their yield is determined largely by the secondary market where existing government bonds are traded.

There are various forms of non-marketable debt organized through national savings schemes. These offer savings accounts and were initially set up to provide a limited banking service to less well-off households. Also included in this category are lotteries and other savings bonds issued in small denominations to suit the needs of small savers. This source of finance is particularly important in Western Europe.

Short-term bills, usually called Treasury Bills, which usually have a term to maturity of three months and always less than a year, differ from bonds. They are traded on money markets rather than capital markets and new issues are sold at competitive auctions to the highest bidder. Treasury Bills do not yield interest in the form of a coupon rate but are sold at a discount.

Treasury Bills are very liquid assets and form part of the reserve base of a banking system. When the Treasury Bill issue is increased, banks' reserves rise and this can lead to an expansion of the money supply. In the modern financial world when a government resorts to excessive use of this means of finance it is accused of 'printing money'. The issue of short-term Treasury Bills has taken over from the printing press as the modern form of money creation.

Seigniorage

The money supply is made up of notes and coins and bank deposits with bank deposits accounting for over 80 per cent of the stock of money in most countries. When banks' reserves rise after an issue of Treasury Bills this leads to an expansion of deposits and is a way of printing money. But the printing of notes also remains a form of finance for governments, and these are a form of government debt. The difference between the money value of a note or a coin and its real value is referred to as seigniorage. In all countries the seigniorage from the issue of such money, which in the case of notes is almost 100 per cent, accrues directly to the government.

When governments borrow to fin-

Dividend day at the Bank – an 1850 view **Even today, British banknotes carry a "promise to pay the bearer"; strictly speaking, this means that the note would have to be redeemed on demand – in Victorian times, for gold.**

Gambling on the future

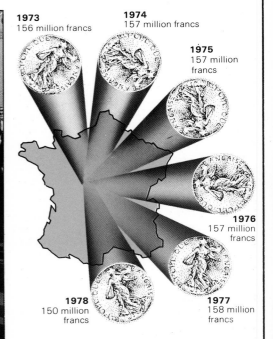

1973 156 million francs

1974 157 million francs

1975 157 million francs

1976 157 million francs

1977 158 million francs

1978 150 million francs

Lotteries, in which prizes are allocated by lot or chance, have helped finance a vast number of projects, including Sydney Opera House, London's Westminster Bridge and the British Museum.

The Roman emperors, Nero and Augustus, operated lotteries with houses, ships and slaves as prizes. But the present form of state lottery – in which a government organises the mass sale of lottery tickets, giving some of the proceeds as prizes, and retaining some for state purposes – originated in Italy as long ago as the Middle Ages.

In England, from 1569 onwards, lotteries paid for a number of public works until in 1832, they were banned for the encouragement they gave to gambling. In France the national lotteries, a royal prerogative since the 1500s, came into disrepute in the seventeenth century, when Louis XIV and his courtiers won the top prizes.

Lotteries have been revived in the last few decades, and are now permitted in most countries in the world, including the Eastern bloc. In countries with state lotteries, notably France, Italy and Spain, they are an important source of state revenue.

For example, the French Loterie Nationale, re-established in 1933, had a financial turnover of 700 million francs in 1977, including a net profit of 158 million francs for the treasury. The Republic of Ireland runs the Irish Hospitals Sweepstake, and three American states have reintroduced lotteries. But the real home of the lottery is Australia: in New South Wales alone, one million tickets are sold each week.

A variation on the lottery is operated by the UK government. Premium Savings Bonds were introduced in 1956 to supplement the national savings scheme. The bonds, which are in units of one pound, go into a draw each month and the prizes, derived from the total monthly interest at five and five eighths per cent on all bonds sold, is divided between prizewinners chosen by a computer known familiarly to the British as Ernie, which stands for Electronic Random Number Indicator. The top monthly prize so far is £100,000.

Above The profits from the French national lottery. *Left* Lottery tickets being sold on the streets of *top* Leningrad USSR and Paris, France.

ance a deficit (on capital account) by issuing long-term bonds it is regarded as quite acceptable, because long-term assets are created to match these long-term liabilities. When governments use the proceeds of their national savings to finance capital expenditure these too are part of the total. But when governments resort to the issue of short-term bills, which effectively means borrowing from the banks, and even if the proceeds are used for capital expenditures, this form of finance is often objected to because it triggers inflationary pressures.

Large public sector deficits are a problem if the government cannot easily obtain long-term finance. This is most likely when the current annual deficit is exceptionally large because the new issue of long-term bonds to cover a deficit may force the price of government bonds down to very low levels, and push up interest rates to very high levels. Governments are reluctant to use this form of finance, preferring usually to rely on the more inflationary issue of short-term bills.

National Debt structures
The total of all the debt instruments – long-term, marketable debt, non-marketable debt and short-term bills including notes and coins – make up a country's National Debt. There are marked differences between countries in the total of the National Debt and its size in relation to GNP. The composition of the debt in terms of its maturity structure also differs markedly between countries.

Part of a country's National Debt may be held by foreigners, and can be considered as more of a burden on domestic resources than domestically held debt, which simply redistributes resources, because interest payments on foreign holdings may drain official gold and dollar reserves. When a public sector raises loans abroad, either by central government, local authorities or nationalized industries, such borrowing is not to cover domestic expenditures, but is a way of financing a balance of payments deficit. When local authorities are encouraged to borrow abroad it is in order to strengthen the country's official reserves.

When a country has a balance of payments deficit, the private sector surrenders domestic currency to the

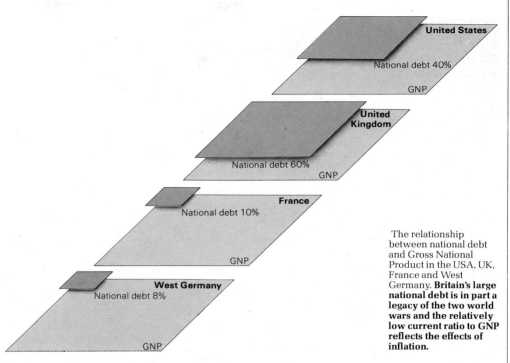

The relationship between national debt and Gross National Product in the USA, UK, France and West Germany. **Britain's large national debt is in part a legacy of the two world wars and the relatively low current ratio to GNP reflects the effects of inflation.**

central bank in exchange for foreign currency. The domestic currency can then be lent by the central bank to the government to help finance current expenditure.

Supplementing local taxes
In the US individual states have traditionally relied on sales taxation and municipal authorities have derived most of their revenue from taxes on property. These sources provided over 60 per cent of total revenues in the 1950s, but by 1975 they provided less than 50 per cent with the gap being filled largely by federal grants, and by some states introducing personal income tax in addition to federal income tax. A similar development has occurred in other countries where a decreasing share of total revenue has come from the local property taxes or rates, and an increasing share from the central government. When local revenues, including central government transfers, fall short of planned expenditures on both current and capital accounts, local authorities are forced to borrow money on the money and capital markets in similar fashion to central government.

Local government bonds
In most countries, provincial authorities make bond issues in their own name. In the US the State and Local Government Bond Market is a large and grow-

ing sector of the capital market. Interest payments on these bonds are exempt from federal income tax to encourage investors, but because many local authorities are not well known the costs are high and such bonds are often issued through banking syndicates which underwrite the issues. In France a collective organization arranges grouped bond issues on behalf of a number of local authorities. In Germany the Länder (state authorities) also issue their own bonds. But in all countries the provision of central government funds is providing an increasing share of total finance.

The sources of finance to public enterprises are similar to those of private corporations except that there is increased reliance on the central government, both in the form of borrowed funds and grants. The UK is unique in centralizing the borrowing of all public enterprises, while in France and many other countries public enterprises issue bonds in their own name. This implies less dependence on the government but no real difference is involved. There are also special public credit institutes which channel funds to public enterprises, but generally where public enterprises raise their own long-term finance, it is underwritten or guaranteed by the central government and is indistinguishable from government bonds except in name.

INTERNATIONAL TRADE AND INVESTMENT

As the world economy has expanded, so have the opportunities and the complexities of international trade. Two factors dominate the problems of financing international trade: credit risk and foreign exchange risk. Credit risk – the risk of not being paid for goods – arises since it is difficult to repossess them when they are outside your own country. Foreign exchange risk arises out of possible changes in the exchange rate between the time when the contract is negotiated and the time when payment is made.

Export finance

For the exporter of goods, the banking system provides several methods of receiving payment, and to the importer several ways of making payment.

Before any goods are shipped, the importer and exporter will agree on the terms of the transaction, such as price, insurance, freight and dates of shipment. There are three methods of payment – cash with order, open account,

Right: A cartoon attempt to convince the British public of the dangers of Free Trade, in the face of growing German competion. **Free traders** believed that the abolition of trading restrictions between nations, would lead to prosperity for all, as traders would have complete freedom to buy and sell in the best possible markets. Protectionists, on the other hand, feared that an open market could lead to "dumping" of cut-price goods by industrial competitors and so put the native labour force out of work. In Britain, they pointed in particular to the recession which hit farmers, unable to compete with cheap grain from Canada and the USA and cheap meat from South America. The conflict between the two philosophies was resolved in protection's favour in the world slump of the late 1920s and 1930s, and, now, the problems of world trade are so complex and interwoven that it would be impossible for governments to refrain from intervening. However, many economists now believe that excessive protectionism brings its own dangers.

The Export Revolution

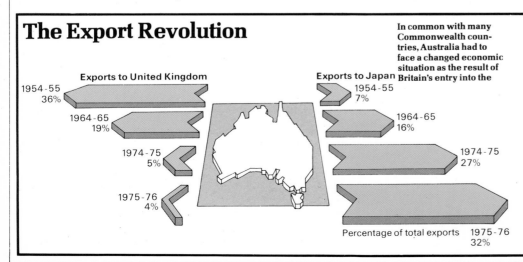

Exports to United Kingdom

1954-55 36%

1964-65 19%

1974-75 5%

1975-76 4%

Exports to Japan

1954-55 7%

1964-65 16%

1974-75 27%

Percentage of total exports 1975-76 32%

In common with many Commonwealth countries, Australia had to face a changed economic situation as the result of Britain's entry into the European Economic Community in 1973. Previously, a high percentage of Australia's exports – some 36.8% in 1954-55 – had gone to Britain. Though this percentage had been gradually falling over the years, the restrictions imposed by the Treaty of Rome accelerated the process and new markets had to be found.

New Zealand, with an economy based firmly on agriculture, was even harder hit. Its exports of butter and meat, for instance, which had chiefly been exported to the UK, were drama-tically affected by the quotas imposed by the treaty.

Australia, on the other hand, had already begun the switch from an agriculture-based economy to one in which manufactured goods played an increasingly important part. This change aided the drive to find new markets.

One of the most important of these was Japan. In 1975-76, out of a total of \$A9,600,748 in exports, just over \$A 3 million went to fuel the Japanese economic miracle. The total for the UK was \$A 406.083.

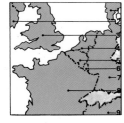

The EEC (left) consists of Belgium (5), Denmark (1), France (8), Federal Republic of Germany (7), Irish Republic (2), Italy (9), Luxembourg (6), Netherlands (4), and the United Kingdom (3), EFTA (right) consists of Austria (6), Faroe Islands (4), Finland (1), Iceland (2), Norway (3), Portugal (8), Sweden (5) and Switzerland (7).

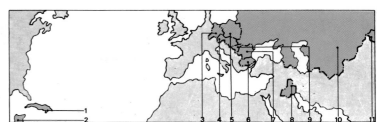

COM-ECON (above) the Communist equivalent of the EEC – has Bulgaria (6), Czechoslovakia (4), Poland (5), Cuba (1), German Democratic Republic (3), Hungary (9), Iraq (8), USSR (10), Mexico (2), Mongolia (11), and Romania (7).

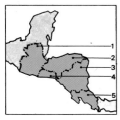

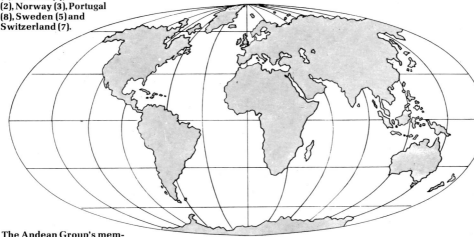

CACM (the Central American Common Market, (above) consists of Costa Rica (5), EL Salvador (4), Guatemala (1), Honduras (2), and Nicaragua (3).

ASEAN (the Association of South East Asian Nations, (above) has Indonesia (3), Malaysia (4), Philippines (5), Thailand (1), and Singapore (2). The Arab League (left) consists of Jordan (4), Iraq (6), Kuwait (7), Lebanon (3), Libya (2), Morocco (1), Saudi Arabia (8), Sudan (10), Syria (5), UAR (9), and Yemen (11).

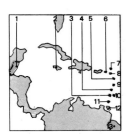

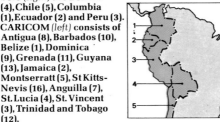

The Andean Group's members (right) are Bolivia (4), Chile (5), Columbia (1), Ecuador (2) and Peru (3). CARICOM (left) consists of Antigua (8), Barbados (10), Belize (1), Dominica (9), Grenada (11), Guyana (13), Jamaica (2), Montserratt (5), St Kitts-Nevis (16), Anguilla (7), St. Lucia (4), St. Vincent (3), Trinidad and Tobago (12).

Trading Blocks. The complexity of international trade today has led to the development of trading blocs – nations linked together in a common economic policy. These blocs usually take two forms: in customs unions, such as the European Economic Community, the member states remove all internal tariffs and quotas on each others goods and establish a common tarriff against outsiders; in free trade areas, such as the European Free Trade Association, each member controls its own tariffs as far as non-members are concerned. Major trading blocs now cover many areas of the world. Frequently membership of these blocs entails more than economic obligations. For instance, the Treaty of Rome, which links the members of the EEC, binds them to work towards an eventual political union.

and bills of exchange.

Cash with the order is the most desirable system of payment for the exporter, although in international trade it is customary to give some sort of credit to the importer. If the seller receives cash with the order, this means that he has both the goods and the money – a means of payment that can be used only when the buyer completely trusts the seller. The buyer must also be sure that the country from which the goods originate is not likely to prohibit their export, due to some unforeseen trade regulation, after he has paid for them. The buyer must also be sure that advance payments are permitted by the exchange control regulations in his own country, and he must have enough working capital to finance the transaction.

With an open account system, the importer and the exporter agree that the debt will be settled at a future predetermined date and the goods and shipping documents are sent to the buyer before payment is made. This system has risks for the exporter if payment is not forthcoming. Trading under open account usually only takes place when there is a strong business relationship between the two parties, and the exporter is satisfied as to the creditworthiness of the importer.

There are four basic ways of paying by open account. The quickest method is the telegraphic transfer, in which an instruction is sent from the importer's bank to the exporter's bank. Payment can also be made by mail transfer which is a similar process, except that it is affected by delays in the postal system and takes longer. The third method is for a bankers' draft to be used in which a cheque is drawn by one bank on another and lastly, payment can be made by a bill of exchange. This is an unconditional order in writing requiring the purchaser to pay on demand, or at a fixed date in the future.

Bills of exchange can be of various types. Firstly there are clean bills. When

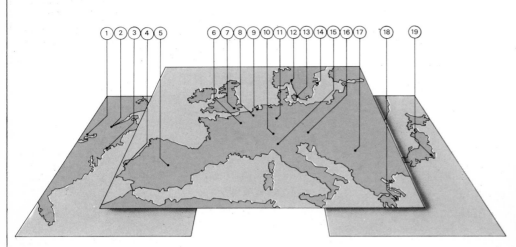

Left: Leading foreign exchange centres. **Across the world foreign currency transactions are the backbone of world trade and a network of exchange centres stretches across oceans to finance such operations. One of their most important functions is to provide companies with credit to finance foreign trade, and also to help them avoid some of the risks involved in foreign exchange dealings.**
Leading exchange centres are: Toronto (1), Montreal (2), New York (3), Lisbon (4), Madrid (5), Paris (6), London (7), Brussels (8), Amsterdam (9), Zurich (10), Frankfurt (11), Oslo (12), Copenhagen (13), Stockholm (14), Milan (15), Vienna (16), Belgrade (17), Athens (18) and Tokyo (19).

the exporter and the importer know each other well, the exporter may be willing to send the documents of ownership direct to the importer and draw a clean bill – that is, one without documents attached, which he will pass to his bank for collection. This method is similar to an open account except that the onus of settling lies with the buyer on open account terms, and with the seller under a clean collection. Secondly, there are documentary bills, which are bills of exchange accompanied by documents of title to the goods which the exporter sends through the bank for delivery to the importer. If the bill is a sight or demand bill, the documents will only be handed over once payment has been made. If the bill is a usance bill, some credit is given to the importer, and the documents are normally handed over when the bill has been agreed.

Thirdly, payment may be made by a bank bill. A bank bill is one which has been accepted by a bank, and as it carries little risk it can be issued at the lowest rate of discount. Fourthly, payment can be made by trade bills, which are drawn up and accepted by commercial companies. If they bear the signature of a company of repute, they can be discounted at rates only fractionally higher than those for bank bills.

Bills of exchange

The advantages to the exporter of using bills of exchange are that they are cheaper than documentary credits and they open the way to several sources of finance.

For example, a bank may buy its customers' foreign currency proceeds of an export, at the time when the goods are sent abroad. This provides the exporter with working capital and the bank may also give an advance.

With a bill of exchange, the exporter can use accepting house credits. Under this scheme, documentary drafts drawn by the exporter are handled as documentary collections by the accepting house. These documents, normally with a government guarantee, are pledged to the accepting house. The exporter is then able to draw a draft on the merchant bank. After acceptance this draft, known as an accommodation bill, is discounted, usually by a discount house, and the proceeds paid to the exporter. Another way bills of exchange may provide finance is if there is a government guarantee which enables the company to obtain a bank loan. Bills of exchange confer a major benefit in that where title documents are to be released only against payment, the exporter's position is more secure than on open account terms.

Bills of exchange do have disadvantages for exporters. The exporter cannot be paid until the money is received by the bank, and this may be expensive. The security of payment is not as good as that offered by cash in advance or of a letter of credit, for the importer may refuse to pay. There may be a sudden imposition of exchange controls or political problems may arise preventing payment. This would involve the exporter in the costs of storage, legal fees, and finding a new buyer.

From the importer's point of view, a bill of exchange has the advantage of providing a period of credit. Also, the importer can check before paying and, in general, this method is more

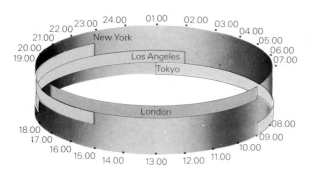

Left: Twenty-four hour market. **Modern foreign exchange markets span the world – and modern communications, principally the telex and satellite telephone, mean that these markets can operate throughout the day and night. A dealer in London, for instance, can arrange a foreign exchange transaction with his counterpart in Tokyo, even** though the London market has closed. *Below:* The foreign exchange dealing room of a major Swiss bank in Zurich. **The clocks on the boards above the telex machines are linked to the times in other major financial centres, while the boards (above and right) are constantly updated with information to give the dealers a global view. Switzerland is one of the** world's leading foreign exchange centres; the Swiss control vast deposits of foreign exchange, while the "holy franc," as their currency is nicknamed, is one of the strongest – and one of the safest – in the world.

convenient and cheaper than a letter of credit. But there can be some disadvantages to the importer. Documents against acceptance collections make the importer legally liable on an accepted bill of exchange. This enables the exporter to sue without having to go to the trouble of proving the contract of sale. Then, too, documents against payment collections may result in the buyer having to pay for goods which he did not order from the exporter in any case.

Bills of exchange increase the degree of certainty of payment in international operations, although they are more costly than cash in advance and open accounts.

Documentary credits

A documentary credit is a formal instruction by a buyer's bank that any withdrawals made by a seller for goods supplied will, subject to the conditions laid down, be honoured. For the seller, a documentary credit is the next best thing to obtaining cash with order, and an exporter may insist on payment in this form. If the terms of the contract are agreed, the importer's bank can open a documentary credit in favour of the exporter in which the bank will stipulate all the documents which the exporter must present before he

receives payment, and draw up a letter of credit addressed to the seller. It is in the interests of the exporter to insist that the importer opens an irrevocable credit, so that the terms of the credit cannot be altered without agreement. A revocable credit offers no such protection to the exporter, as it can be modified or cancelled at any time without notice.

The main advantage of a documentary letter of credit, under which a bank

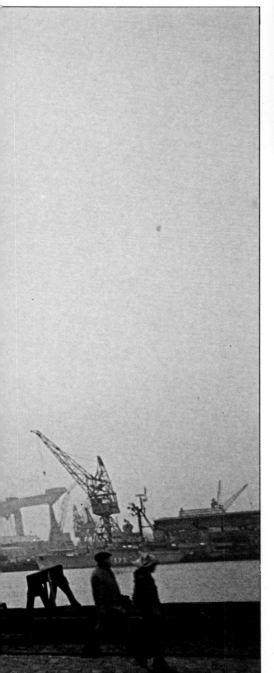

Economic lifeblood. The nuts and bolts of world trade are the exports and imports each country depends on for economic survival – either by sea (left) or air (above). These are shown in economic terms in the balance of payments statistics produced by practically every nation in the world. These statistics are usually divided into three categories. The balance of imports and exports, as well as the effects of "invisible earnings" – such as the money earned from banking, shipping and tourism – are shown as current account. Capital account itemizes the effects of long and short term capital investment and state loans, while a third section details changes in the nation's gold and foreign currency reserves. All these figures are a barometer of the economic health of the nation concerned.

undertakes to pay a seller for his goods, is that it guarantees prompt payment to the exporter while assuring the buyer that no payments will be made until documents stipulated by him (normally a bill of lading, invoices and insurance documents) have been produced by the exporter. Letters of credit are of greatest benefit when the parties involved are relative strangers, or where one of them is in a country where trade and political difficulties increase the risk of non-payment.

In recent years, an increasing proportion of world trade has been conducted between giant multinational companies, subsidiaries and associates of the same company, and long-established trading partners. In virtually all these cases, the risk of non-payment is so greatly reduced that trading on open account is considered quite satisfactory.

Apart from the changing pattern of international trade, letters of credit themselves have certain drawbacks which have brought alternative methods into favour. A small importer wishing to open a letter of credit may be called on by his bank to provide partial, or occasionally even full, cash cover. The effect this has on companies' cash flows can be sufficiently serious to encourage them to find other ways of arranging payment. They may turn to a confirming house (also known as international trade finance companies), or to an international credit union to arrange extended payment terms. Suppliers will be happy to deal with the confirming house, which makes payment on behalf of the importer; this renders the security of a letter of credit unnecessary. Exporters can improve cash flows by selling their debtors' books to a factoring house. The functions of a factoring house are to give the seller 100 per cent credit insurance by taking over invoices as the goods are supplied, and providing cash either immediately, or at an agreed future date for the full value of the invoices, less charges.

The foreign exchange market

The foreign exchange market provides the framework for individuals, firms, banks and brokers to buy and sell foreign currencies and it exists wherever one currency is bought and sold for others.

The foreign exchange market provides three major functions. Firstly, it provides a mechanism for transferring the money of one currency into the money of another. For example, a US exporter to the UK requires payment in his own currency, the dollar, and the importer, whose currency is the pound sterling, uses the market to convert sterling into dollars. So long as different currencies exist, a foreign exchange market will be necessary for trade. Secondly, the foreign exchange market provides a way for companies to obtain short-term credits to finance trade. In this case, if an exporter is willing to be paid in three months, an arrangement made possible by the forward exchange market, he is effectively granting credit to the importer. Thirdly, the market provides facilities for companies to avoid foreign exchange risks. The existence of the forward market enables a company with a future asset or liability to sell or buy it forward to minimize the exchange risks.

Foreign exchange markets tend to be located in national financial centres near the related financial markets. The more important exchange markets are found in New York, Toronto, Paris, Frankfurt, Amsterdam, Milan, Zurich, London, Brussels and Tokyo.

The market that never closes

The foreign exchange market is a market only in an abstract sense since, unlike a Stock Exchange, it does not exist in one specific place. It is a communications system for business, and consists of a network of telephones and telexes that connect exchange markets all over the world. The communication system is so good that the market, despite time differences, is a single world market. As the market in Europe is closing, the market in the United States is opening for business, and when the United States finishes, the market in Tokyo is beginning its day.

There are two basic exchange rate systems – fixed and floating – although there are many variants of these. With a fixed exchange rate system, the monetary authorities accept an obliga-tion to maintain the foreign exchange value of the home currency within very narrow limits of a par value, and are committed to intervene in the foreign exchange market whenever these limits threaten to be exceeded. Within the narrow range above and below the par value, the foreign exchange rate is usually free to vary under the influence of market forces, so that rates are not rigidly fixed. The world monetary system operated a fixed rate system from 1946 until 1971.

Under a floating rate system, the authorities no longer have an obligation to intervene in the foreign exchange market and, in principle, there is no reason why the equilibrium exchange rate should not be established by the operation of market forces. But even under a floating rate system, the exchange rate is such an important variable that governments still sometimes intervene.

The present world monetary system is a combination of fixed and floating rate systems. Some currencies are floating, such as the US dollar, the Swiss franc and the pound sterling, and some currencies are fixed together, such as the guilder, the Deutschemark, and the Belgian franc.

Since an exchange rate is the price of one currency quoted against another, it will respond to the supply of, and the demand for, a particular currency. Importers sell their native currency to buy foreign currency to pay for their purchases abroad.

Speeding the flow. **The container warehouse at Tilbury docks, London, is one of Britain's answers to the chief problem facing exporters and importers all over the world – how to cut the time involved in the delivery of goods so that they can be paid speedily. This problem also affects governments; delayed delivery of imported machine tools, for instance, means that an unfavourable balance can occur on the balance of payments months after the initial order. As far as shipping is concerned, the modern answer is containerisation, transporting goods from factory to dock to factory in containers specifically designed to carry the largest volume possible with the minimum labour cost.**

Balance of payments

When a country's imports exceed its exports, the nation's currency falls in relation to other currencies. The difference between foreign exchange inflows and outflows is recorded in the balance of payments. In most countries, this is divided into several categories. Under the current account heading, the balance of imports and exports are shown as well as the net effect of services such as shipping, tourism and banking. The capital account itemises the effect of long and short term capital investments and official loans. Any signs that reserves are falling rapidly is a good indication of a fall in the value of a currency.

Short term capital investments can occur in response to higher interest rates in one centre when compared with those of another. The centre with the highest interest rates tends to attract capital inflows and a correspondingly higher demand for its currency.

But capital movements to a financial centre only occur if there is confidence in the currency concerned. If a currency has high interest rates, but investors fear a currency devaluation, they will be reluctant to invest. Similarly, if a currency has low interest rates, investors expect a currency revaluation and this will increase their demand for the currency. To protect their reserves, many countries have exchange controls which restrict the freedom to buy and sell currencies.

A basic determinant of the exchange rate in the long run is the relative purchasing power of currencies. The value of money is the volume of goods and services it will buy; this relationship is called purchasing power parity. Deviations from purchasing power parity invariably lead to exchange rate movements.

There are three types of transactions undertaken in a foreign exchange market. These are transactions in the spot, forward and deposit markets. In the spot market currencies are bought or sold for immediate delivery, although in practice, two working days are allowed for the currency to be delivered. In the forward market, currencies are bought or sold now for future delivery. This market enables payment to be made in the future, but at an exchange rate agreed upon at the time of the transaction. In the deposit market, currencies are borrowed or lent

Deutche Mark

Swiss Francs

Italian Lire

UK Pound

Others

Figures in US $ millions

2650

2060

1538

1212

1135

827

376 378 403 333

1965 1966 1967 1968 1969 1970 1971 1972 1973 1974

Foreign bonds. **A major part of the flourishing foreign exchange market is the part concerned with the issue of foreign bonds – a bond sold by a borrower of one nationality, guaranteed by brokers and sold in the currency of another country. International organisations are probably the biggest investors. In the period between 1965 and 1974, foreign bond issues reached their peak in 1973; the largest part of the total in that year was the $1,526 million invested in the Swiss franc.**

and a bank will have to repay or will itself be repaid. Deposit market trading can take place within one country.

In a foreign exchange market, there are both individuals, and institutions, such as companies, requiring foreign currency. They may want a currency other than their own to travel, or to finance trade or investment abroad. There are also the commercial banks which operate through their foreign exchange dealing rooms.

Apart from commercial banks, merchant banks are also very active in the market. The third major participant in the market is a country's central bank. Under a fixed rate system, a central bank may intervene to keep rates within agreed limits.

The Euromarkets

The Euromarkets consist of Euro-currencies and Eurobonds. Euro-currencies are monies traded outside the country of their origin. Thus Eurodollars are financial assets and liabilities denominated in dollars but traded outside the United States, although no matter how often they are transferred from one owner to another, they never actually leave the US. The difference between a Eurodollar deposit and any other dollar deposit is that the original owner of the dollars looks not to the US for repayment, but to a foreign bank. Eurocurrency markets exist in all the major trading currencies. The importance of Eurodollars can be seen by the fact that they averaged 80 per cent of the Eurocurrencies market between 1970 and 1977.

The Eurocurrency markets exist because of government regulations. The Eurodollar market provides the opportunity for trading dollars outside the control of government regulations imposed on residents within the boundaries of the US. When these regulations start to constrain the dollar money market in the United States, then companies' requirements are satisfied by creating another dollar money market with Eurodollars.

The international bond market can be divided into foreign bonds and Eurobonds. A foreign bond is an international bond sold by a foreign borrower, but denominated in the currency of the country in which it is placed. It is underwritten and sold by a national underwriting syndicate in the lending country. For example, a US company can float a bond issue in the Swiss capital market, underwritten by a Swiss syndicate and denominated in Swiss francs. The bond issue is sold to investors in the Swiss capital market, where it will be quoted and traded.

In comparison with the Eurobond market, US companies have not dominated the foreign bond market. Instead, for the period between 1965 and 1974, international organizations such as the World Bank have been major participants in this market accounting for approximately half of the foreign bonds. Foreign governments are now major borrowers in the foreign bond market.

Eurobond and Eurocurrency

The Eurobond is an international bond which is underwritten by an international syndicate and sold in countries other than the country of the currency in which the issue is denominated. The Eurobond market has emerged as the most important segment of the international capital market. The dominant

US $

Deutche Mark

Other currencies

Figures in US $ billions

17.5

14.3

8.4

4.2

2.1

1973   1974   1975   1976   1977

Eurobonds. **A fairly recent entry on the bond scene is the Eurobond, which is gradually replacing foreign bond issues in importance. The bond, sold internationally, except in the country in which it is denominated, and underwritten by an international syndicate, has greatly attracted governments, international institutions and multi-** **national companies. One of the reasons for this is the relative speed and attractiveness of the yield from investment; another has been the relative availability of Eurodollars – dollars held by individuals, insititutions and governments outside the USA – compared to more strictly-controlled currencies.**

form of international new issue activity has moved from foreign bonds to Eurobonds.

The role of official borrowers and foreign corporations and the role of the dollar are the Eurobond market's striking characteristics.

The Eurocurrency markets provide substantial benefits to multinational companies. The market can supply or absorb very large quantities of capital, some of which may only be available temporarily. Finance can often be raised more cheaply than on any national market.

In 1969-70 British companies used the Eurodollar market extensively to avoid domestic bank credit controls. This practice was blocked by Bank of England controls in 1971. Judicious use of the market can be a protection against currency movements. In the US multinational dollars are available when it might not be possible, due to controls, to move funds from the country. The market can aborb the spare funds of multinational companies over periods varying from a day to five or more years. The market can also be used to reduce financial dependence on any other sources.

Governments also recognize some of these benefits in using the markets themselves.

Eurocurrency borrowing has a disadvantage, however, when there are changes in the exchange rate. This is in addition to such problems as the status of borrowers, or the viability of the project financed, which may have to be accepted but must never be ignored by the industrial or commercial borrower of Eurocurrencies.

Repayment of loans will normally come out of the earnings of the project financed, or more rarely, from the general funds of the parent company. The exchange rate risk lies in the possibility of the borrowed currency's being upvalued (after it has been received and before it is repaid) in comparison with the currency in which earnings are expected, or with the currency in which the shortfall of earnings will be paid from central reserves. Equally, a devaluation of the currency to be received against the currency owed, during the period of the loan, will mean an extra cost to the borrower. These risks can be eliminated, if exchange controls permit, by use of the forward market.

Unemployed in a square
of Berlin in June 1919, the
aftermath of defeat in
war and run-away
inflation.

5.

MONETARY POLICY

With the total dependence of the world on money, the efficiency of the financial system that supplies and controls it is a matter of vital concern for all. Without the existence of specialised financial institutions, such as banks, the whole business of lending, borrowing and saving would soon become so complex that economic activity would stagnate, if it did not become impossible to maintain. Yet, the system as it exists, is often criticised on two main counts. The first favours greater competition in the system and attacks monopoly; the second, however, fears that over-competitiveness, without tight controls, can lead to inflation and slump.

BUDGETS, TAXATION AND DEMAND

Since the Second World War, the governments of most of the developed nations have made the maintenance of a high level of employment a major objective of their economic policies.

The key to achieving full employment, according to Keynesian economic theory, is to maintain a high level of demand for goods and services in the economy. Firms produce to meet demand, and if demand is high, firms will produce more, and in the process take on more workers and make full use of their capital equipment. Keynes saw the problem of the Great Depression of the 1930s, when unemployment reached over 20 per cent of the labour force in many countries, as one of a deficiency of demand. Without the demand for goods, production was stagnant, machinery was left idle, and men thrown out of work. The cure for unemployment, according to Keynes, is to stimulate the demand for goods and services, to expand production and increase employment.

Just as demand can be deficient and lead to unemployment, as in the Great Depression, it can also be excessive. If the demand for goods and services is greater than the productive capacity of the economy, shortages and bottlenecks will appear, demand will be unsatisfied and inflation will probably follow. The idea, then, is that the government should try to manage demand, to maintain a high level to avoid recession and unemployment but not so high as to create shortages and inflation.

The most obvious way for a government to affect the level of demand in the economy is for it to spend more – say on building more roads or schools. This means that more people will be employed – in the first instance in the construction industry and allied trades. But that is not the end of the story. For the people who find jobs on the new projects will earn more and will therefore spend more, too. There will be a 'second-round' effect of higher spending – probably on a wide range of

consumer goods. This in turn will boost output and hence employment in the consumer goods industries, providing additional income for those working in them. This further round of additional income will lead to further increases in spending, and so on. Thus the original government expenditure is multiplied several times over in terms of its final effect on demand. This process is known as the 'multiplier effect'.

In practice, in modern conditions, the second and subsequent effects of the multiplier process are likely to be quite small. The reasons are taxes and social security benefits. If the government spends a million on wages for some new project, the effect on the net take-home pay of those finding jobs on the project taking into account their loss of unemployment pay and other benefits, and the taxes they pay on their earnings, will be very much smaller than a million. The second round of the multiplier process will, of course, be very much smaller than the first, and subsequent rounds correspondingly smaller still.

Increasingly, in many countries governments spend money not on the purchase of goods and services but on transfer payments – cash payments such as old age pensions and social security benefits. An increase in transfer payments also boosts demand by increasing the purchasing power of the people receiving them. Governments too, make transfer payments to industry in the form of such items as investment grants and employment subsidies. Again demand is boosted, though in this case it is more likely to be demand for new machinery, rather than for consumer goods, that is increased.

Governments can influence demand

The multiplier effect. **Government spending on projects such as housing, roads and schools, does not just create jobs for those employed on such undertakings. It stimulates demand in other parts of the economy and this creates further employment in other sectors. Those who earn more money as a result of the first round of government spending, themselves spend more – usually on consumer goods. These industries expand, taking on more staff to cope with the increased demand. The extra money these people earn stimulates** **more demand and more employment, and so the process, known as the multiplier effect, continues.**

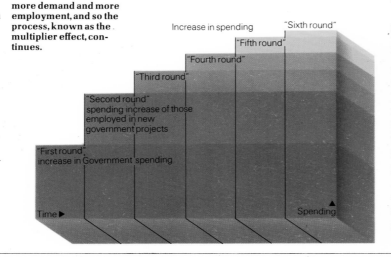

John Maynard Keynes, drawn by David Low for the *New Statesman*, London, in 1933. **In the early 1930s Keynes developed his hugely influential theory of aggregate demand. This implied that governments could take specific actions to remedy unemployment, instead of simply relying on time and the action of free market forces.**

The Great Depression. Triggered by the Wall Street crash in 1929, the Great Depression in the United States convinced governments of the need to plan their economies along Keynesian lines. The Pontiac factory (top left) was one of thousands which remained idle for months on end. In agriculture the crisis was exacerbated by the wind which carried away the topsoil from a large area of the Great Plains creating the dust bowl, and innumerable farms were abandoned (left). In the cities people resorted to any means they could find to obtain money. One of these was marathon dancing (top), where a prize was awarded to those who could stay on their feet the longest. Thousands queued for free soup (above, centre), and depression was rife in more than the economic sense; many had nothing to do but sit on park benches (above).

not only through their spending, but also through the other aspect of their budget – taxation. A tax cut leaves people with more purchasing power and so demand will be increased. Or government can cut taxes on industry in the hope of stimulating more new investment.

Balancing the budget

The level of demand can be increased or reduced through changes in government fiscal policy – that is, spending or taxation operated through the government budget. In most countries, the government introduces its budget at the beginning of each tax year, setting out the tax rates for that year. In presenting the budget, the Finance Minister will usually start by outlining the economic

prospects for the coming year. If the main worry is a high level of unemployment, it is likely that the Finance Minister will want to introduce an expansionary budget involving increased government spending or tax cuts. If the worries are more concerned with excess demand or inflation, it is likely that government spending will be cut, or taxes increased. Of course, the budget judgment is not always as simple as this suggests – problems like 'cost-push' inflation or the effect of the recent oil price increases cannot be dealt with in this way.

If fiscal policy is expansionary, so that government spending is greater than its tax receipts, the government will have a financial deficit. Essentially, the govern-

ment can borrow either from the public by the issue of long-term debt from national savings, or from the banking system. Any of these will affect interest rates, credit conditions, and so government monetary policy. A tight money policy is one in which interest rates are high and credit is both expensive and difficult to come by. The consequence is that some spending is either discouraged (because of the high cost of borrowing) or becomes impossible (because no source of credit can be found). The opposite is an easy money policy, when credit is cheap and easy to come by. This may encourage spending and thus increase demand.

There are basically three possible mechanisms in which a government

A 'New Deal' for a nation

"I pledge you, I pledge myself, to a new deal for the American people" proclaimed Franklin D. Roosevelt in 1932, at the beginning of his campaign for the presidency of the United States. The economic situation of the country – then in the grip of the Great Depression – was desperate. Some 14 million people were unemployed; poor relief was below subsistence level; a million people roamed the country in search of work; the banking system was paralysed and agriculture was in chaos.

Elected by a vast majority, Roosevelt set about implementing his New Deal. In his first 100 days of office, he established an emergency relief and recovery programme which resolved the banking crisis, he allocated five billion dollars to poor relief, created thousands of jobs by initiating a construction programme of public works and utilities, and set up codes of fair competition between business and labour. The New Deal aimed to cure the economy by spreading work and increasing purchasing power; however, his critics claim that the measures were not radical enough, and that the depression ended only as the American war machine swung into full production in 1939-40.
Above Roosevelt making a campaign speech *right* Fontana Dam built by the Tennessee Valley Authority 1942-44.

Right: British Chancellor of the Exchequer, Denis Healey leaving Downing Street with the budget box on his way to deliver the annual budget speech. **Most countries have annual budgets to determine the tax rates for the coming year. In Britain the budget proposals come into force almost immediately – only very occasionally does parliament vote against, and therefore reverse, the Chancellor's intentions. In other countries, notably the United States and West Germany, the constitution makes the implementation of tax changes more difficult and lengthy.**

can influence credit conditions: open-market operations, controls on the banking system and selective credit controls.

Monetary policy

Open-markets are the most fundamental mechanism of monetary policy. If the government wishes to create tight money conditions, it increases sales of its own debt. In order to persuade people to buy the additional stock, it may well have to offer a higher interest rate, and this will lead to a general increase in interest rates in the economy as a whole.

But the effects of open-market operations go further than this suggests. Normally, when people buy or sell

stocks, money is paid from one person to another and the total quantity of money in the economy is unaffected. But, with open-market operations, people buying the additional government stock hand over money to the government, and the total stock of money in the economy is reduced. People take money out of their bank accounts to pay for the government stock, and in consequence banks' cash reserves are reduced. In these circumstances the banks will have to call in loans, advances and overdrafts, or at least reduce the rate of new lending. The reduction in the money supply brought about by the open-market operation, working through the banking system, creates a general tightening of credit conditions.

The second mechanism of monetary control works directly through the banking system. The government may, for example, through the central banks increase the amount of cash reserves that banks need to hold. Then again, banks will need to call in existing loans, or reduce their rate of new lending in order to find the additional cash required. Similarly, the government may institute limits on the amount of bank lending. If banks are not allowed to lend money, again their reserves (or holdings of short-term government debt) will increase. But in either case bank lending will be reduced and credit will become tighter.

Traditionally, banks have lent primarily to firms rather than to households. Thus, the main impact of monetary policy has been on firms affecting, for example, their ability to raise finance for the purchase of new capital equipment. The personal sector has escaped relatively lightly and this has produced the third mechanism of monetary policy – selective credit controls.

A major source of credit for personal spending has been for purchase by instalments. While the cost of instalment purchase depends on the interest rate, more important to most buyers is the size of the down-payment. Many governments have regulated the minimum down-payment in hire purchase contracts for purposes of monetary policy. The objection to this policy is that the whole of its impact is concentrated in a few sectors – cars, televisions, household appliances – while other sectors remain unaffected. Repayment conditions for credit cards can also be

regulated by government, while the other major source of personal finance – mortgages for house purchase – has come under increasing scrutiny from the viewpoint of monetary policy.

Selective controls may divert credit rather than reduce its total. If instalment purchase credit is held back by higher minimum down-payments, the finance companies which provided the credit will now have surplus funds which they may lend elsewhere. The total of demand in the economy may not be reduced.

Sensitivity of interest rates

A major issue in monetary policy has been how 'easy' or 'tight' monetary policy should be measured. There is no obvious way of measuring the ease with which credit can be obtained. One approach is to use interest rates – tight money being associated with high interest rates and easy money with low interest rates. The difficulty is that interest rates can be affected by many other factors – business confidence, inflation and interest rates in other countries – as well as by monetary policy. Interest rates are therefore not always a good indicator of whether monetary policy is expansionary or restrictive.

An alternative measure is the quantity of money itself. A contraction in bank lending will have, as its counterpart, a contraction in bank deposits which means a reduction in the stock of money. The difficulty is that there are many different types of bank deposits, and correspondingly many different definitions of the money supply according to which types of deposits are included or excluded. The definitions commonly used are 'narrow' or 'transactions' money – often called M1 – which includes cash and current accounts (accounts from which money can be withdrawn by cheque) at banks, and 'broad' money – called M3 – which includes cash and all types of bank deposit. It is the broad money indicator, M3, that is now most commonly used as an indicator of the stance of monetary policy.

Demand management: the post war record

The years between the end of the Second World War and the oil crisis of 1973, marked a period of unprecedented economic prosperity. Throughout the

developed world, standards of living improved steadily and rapidly and, by historical standards, the level of unemployment was low. The contrast with the inter-war years of the Great Depression could not have been more marked. It is tempting to attribute the new-found prosperity to the fact that governments were now taking responsibility for maintaining full employment.

But the reasons may be more complex, since the conversion to Keynesian ideas in several countries has been less than wholehearted. Britain, and other Commonwealth countries such as Australia, took to the Keynesian philosophy with no reservations. The countries of Western Europe, particularly West Germany, were much more cautious, and Keynesian ideas did not dominate government policy in the United States until the early 1960s. But even if the Americans, or West Germans, had been more enthusiastic about Keynesian ideas in principle, they would have found difficulty in applying them in practice.

In America, tax changes have to pass

The Stock Exchange, London. **Governments frequently reduce the money supply by issuing and selling government stock through the channels which are used for the buying and selling of commercial stock. The money supply is reduced by the amount the government receives for its stock. Such manoeuvres are known as "open market operations". In Britain government stock is handled by the Government Broker, who is traditionally the senior partner in the stockbroking firm of Mullens and Co. Nowadays only the Government Broker and a few others wear top hats on the floor of the stock exchange.**

through the legislative arm of Congress, which asserts its independence of the executive (the Government) so there is no guarantee that fiscal policy changes can be legislated at all or achieved at the time the President wants. A further limitation on the Government's ability to control demand in the United States, is caused by the federal system, when states and municipalities possess the sovereign power to impose income and expenditure taxes. This means that in the US taxation is a much less precise tool for regulating demand management. By contrast, the British Parliament will only very rarely oppose major tax changes. The British system of government facilitates interventionary fiscal policy while the American system obstructs it, while in West Germany, the constitution actually prevents the government running large budget deficits.

West Germany, with the least help from Keynesian policies, has had one of the most successful records of economic progress since the Second World War. Britain, where Keyne-

sianism has flourished, has had one of the worst. One explanation is, that Keynesian policies were superfluous for much of the period, since the world economy was buoyed up by a massive investment boom. This began with post-war reconstruction boosted by great technological advances and the rapid growth of international trade. Keynesian policies are designed for times when demand is deficient and economies depressed, not for times when demand is buoyant and jobs already plentiful.

It has been claimed that demand management policies in these circumstances are not just unnecessary, but may be positively harmful.

Often, deflationary policies have been taken at times when the level of demand was already falling and their result can only have been to exacerbate the subsequent recession. Similarly, expansionary measures have often been taken when demand is already growing too fast. One reason is that the course of the economy is often difficult to chart and always difficult to predict.

In a recession, the government may stimulate demand, not realising that a recovery is already under way and that inflation, rather than unemployment, is the major threat.

Monetary targets

For these reasons a strong case can be made for avoiding interventionary demand management policies in 'normal' times, and instead pursuing fiscal and monetary policies that are conducive to long-term stability. The first to set out such a programme, back in 1950, was Milton Friedman in Chicago. Experience with demand management policies has led to increasing support for his views in recent years. The programme involves, in fiscal policy, setting such tax rates in relation to government spending, that the government budget would balance at full employment (with an allowance for those changing jobs or unable to work). If the level of economic activity falls below full employment, tax revenues will fall, and the budget would go into deficit, but on this programme tax rates should be held constant. (By

Prosperity for all

MACMILLAND

You've never had it so good!

GOVERNMENT OF THE TORIES, BY THE TORIES, FOR THE TORIES

FRANKLIN

Britain belongs to — guess who?

The booming sixties – *above left* The space race in progress at Cape Canaveral, Florida, US *top* Theatre programme of the times, 1959 *Above* Harold MacMillan at the Tory Party conference and *left* as one British cartoonist saw it.

"You've never had it so good!" was Harold Macmillan's proud summing up of Conservative achievement as the British went to the polls in 1959. The phrase was an affirmation of the public mood. After the war, and the years of austerity that followed there now came unprecedented economic prosperity. This was true for all the developed countries. The standard of living rose steadily; full employment was the norm; luxury foods and goods filled the shops. Between 1948 and 1965, the number of private cars on European roads rose from 5 million to 44 million.

Macmillan's government was returned to power, but in fact the UK, with an annual average growth in gross domestic product of 2.5 per cent from 1948-63, was lagging behind the rest of the developed world.

The boom – a remarkable recovery from wartime chaos – was due in part to the US. It injected capital into Europe and Japan, and helped to introduce a new monetary exchange system tied to the dollar. Other important factors were the wartime expansion industrial capacity, a new spirit of international economic co-operation and, above all, the exploitation of new technology.

As the sixties progressed, however, it became obvious that there were problems attendant on the boom. Inflation, accepted as necessary in some measure as a corollary to full employment, began to get out of control. The dollar became overvalued against the Japanese yen and the German mark, giving rise to currency speculation.

Rates of unemployment, growth and inflation of six major nations. **Growth is measured over the period 1960 to 1977. The unemployment figure is for the year 1977. The inflation rate is measured between 1976 and 1977. It is significant that Japan and West Germany, who have the best overall records, have made very little use of Keynesian policies of demand management. Many economists now feel that the Keynesian approach is only useful in periods of recession and may even be harmful when there is an investment boom of the type experienced worldwide in the post-war period.**

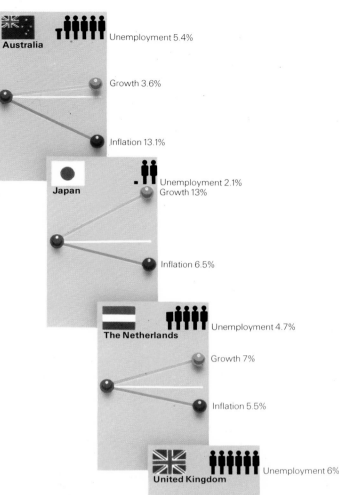

Australia
Unemployment 5.4%
Growth 3.6%
Inflation 13.1%

Japan
Unemployment 2.1%
Growth 13%
Inflation 6.5%

The Netherlands
Unemployment 4.7%
Growth 7%
Inflation 5.5%

United Kingdom
Unemployment 6%
Growth 3%
Inflation 14.2%

United States
Unemployment 7%
Growth 4.5%
Inflation 6.7%

West Germany
Unemployment 4.2%
Growth 6%
Inflation 3.7%

Unemployment figures, 1977
Growth figures, 1960–77
Inflation figures 1976–77

contrast, an orthodox classical economist would want to increase tax rates so as to balance the budget, while a Keynesian would want to cut tax rates to stimulate demand.) For monetary policy, the idea would be a steady rate of expansion of the money supply at the average rate of growth of the economy. The quantity of money is a major factor in determining the availability of credit in the economy, and if it grows at the same rate as the economy credit conditions, will remain reasonably stable. The benefit of the programme is that it creates stability and removes the uncertainty brought about by frequent changes in policy.

Restoring stability in the '70s
The economic upheavals of the early 1970s, starting with the collapse of the post-war system of fixed exchange rates in 1971, followed by the oil price increases of 1973 and later, unprecedented rates of inflation combined with a deep recession, have led to a renewed emphasis in policy on restoring stability. One component of this policy has been

to aim for a steady growth in the money supply, with the aim of restoring confidence in financial markets. West Germany, France, the United States and Britain have all adopted monetary targets in recent years for this reason.

But the adoption of monetary targets has run into two immediate problems. If the monetary target is set low, credit conditions may become very tight, and interest rates may rise sharply. This would not only be disruptive in financial markets but could severely affect housebuilding and industrial investment. On the other hand, if the target is set high it may give the impression that the government is prepared to tolerate a more rapid rate of inflation. In West Germany, the monetary target has been set at 8 per cent growth each year, and each year the actual growth rate of the money supply has been slightly faster. But the target cannot be increased for fear that this would be taken as a sign of more rapid inflation to come.

A related question is whether the monetary target should be changed if circumstances change. Monetary targets that are frequently revised to take into account changes in circumstances are known as 'rolling targets'. These are operated in the United States, and their introduction is being considered in Britain. Though such flexibility may have its advantages in the short run, it may be difficult to reconcile it with long-term stability in the growth of money stock.

INFLATION AND UNEMPLOYMENT

Inflation is defined as a sustained increase in the general level of prices. Historically, most periods of inflation have had an obvious cause – a rapid increase in the quantity of money in an economy. Inflation is often described as a process of 'too much money chasing too few goods'. In recent years, though, inflation has often become deeply entrenched in many economies and attributable to different causes. The 'new' inflation is said to result from the power of organised labour to force wage increases, or the power of big business, or international cartels like OPEC, to increase their prices.

During inflation the prices of all the different goods and services will not rise at the same rate. For a great variety of reasons, some prices will rise faster and some slower than others. To measure a change in the general level of prices we need some average or index of prices. The measure most often used is the retail price index – or consumer price index – which is a weighted average of the prices of goods bought by a typical household.

Inflation is then defined as the rise in a general price index such as the retail price index. A one-off event, such as a drought, which can ruin the harvest of many crops in a number of countries, leads to sharp, but temporary, price increases. The increase in the retail price index resulting from the drought would not be inflation by this definition, for the price increases would be temporary and specific to particular crops, rather than sustained and general throughout the economy.

In the days of metallic currencies, there were two basic causes of inflation. The first was the discovery of new

Right The French fleet returns to Brest at the height of the Napoleonic Wars. **Napoleon I's France was the first nation in world history to gear its economy totally for war. But this, combined with the British naval blockade of overseas trade, led to economic stagnation, inflation and slump.**

supplies of the precious metals which formed the basis of the currency. An early example is the inflation in sixteenth century Spain (which spread into the rest of Europe) resulting from the discoveries of gold and silver in South America. The second, and more common, method of increasing the money supply was by debasing the currency – that is, reducing the precious metal content of the coinage and replacing it by base metals such as copper. The Roman Empire, for example, suffered a continual debasement and inflation with conditions approaching hyperinflation in the third-century.

In England there was a major debasement of the currency in the early part of the sixteenth century, combined with an increase in the coin issue from precious metals gained from plate looted from the monasteries. Prices rose by 65 per cent during this period in less than ten years – a record unsurpassed in peacetime until the 1970s. These periods apart, the price level has tended to be static or even descending. The fourteenth and fifteenth centuries – before the Spanish gold discoveries – were times of price stability, and in Britain the price level at the outbreak of the First World War in 1914 was scarcely higher than it had been in the time of Oliver Cromwell over two and a half centuries earlier.

One factor behind this stability is that the supply of precious metals increased very little. By the eighteenth century, paper and credit money had appeared, and by the twentieth century it had completely replaced the precious metals. With the introduction of paper money, the physical constraint on the growth of the money supply has disappeared. With paper money, there is no limit to the quantity of money that can be created, nor the rate at which the money supply can be increased.

The paper crises
There is one historical characteristic common to all periods of currency debasement or of rapid growth of paper money issue. All were periods of fiscal crisis, where the government was unable to raise the tax revenues to

Right: The looting of the monasteries in Henry VIII's England. **When money was represented by precious metal, inflation rarely occurred. However, in England in the early sixteenth century the currency was debased, meaning that a higher proportion of base metals was included in the coins, and at the same time new coins were issued, made from gold looted from monasteries. As a result prices rose by 65 per cent in less than ten years.**

Left: Spanish ships unloading South American gold. **In the sixteenth century the Spanish brought back large quantities of gold from South America. In a short time almost the whole of Europe was suffering from inflation.**

finance its spending. Sometimes the reason was extravagance. Sometimes it was political instability – a weak government without the authority to collect taxes. But most often it was war. In wartime, governments find their spending rising more rapidly than the taxes they can raise, and part of the deficit is met by printing money.

But why should an increase in the quantity of money cause prices to rise? What is the 'transmission mechanism' between the increase in the money supply and the increase in prices? The process was spelt out by David Hume in his essay "Of Money", as early as 1752.

He saw the process in three steps. Firstly, an increase in the quantity of money increases the demand for goods. The government creates new money to buy goods. The people selling the goods and receiving the money spend some of it on other goods and services which directly increases the demand. They might save the remainder, but saving money implies lending it to someone else who wishes to borrow it, who will in turn either buy goods or lend it. The increased availability of funds is likely to lead to a reduction of interest rates, which may encourage additional spending. Directly or indirectly, the demand for goods and for money too, will rise.

The second part of the process entails an increase in the demand for goods which leads to an increase in prices. For some goods, increased demand tends to raise prices immediately – for example, fresh foods whose prices are set every day according to market conditions. But in the case of manufactured goods the process can take much longer. To begin with, producers may be able to meet the higher demand from stocks, or by increasing production. As production increases, so firms will require more raw materials and additional capital and labour. The prices of raw materials are likely to rise since their prices reflect market demand. If shortages of labour develop wages are also likely to increase. These price increases then feed through (as cost increases) to the prices of the manufactured goods.

The third part of the process described by Hume is that an increase in prices eliminates the excess demand for goods. The demand for goods rose, originally, because people had more money than they needed so, rather than hoard the excess, they spent it or lent it to others to spend. But as prices rise people need more money to finance their everyday transactions. If prices rise, on average, by the amount of the increase in the money supply, the whole of the extra money will be absorbed in the higher prices and none will be left over to allow an increase in the quantity of

Below: How increased demand leads to increased prices. **In normal circumstances** (*upper diagram*) **customers, 1, go to a shop, 2, and pay a fixed amount for cigarettes, 7. The shopkeeper places a regular order with the factory, 3, and pays a certain price for them. The factory orders sufficient tobacco for its needs from a farmer, 4, and pays an agreed price. If demand for cigarettes increases** (*lower diagram*)**, the shop will at first supply its customers from its stocks, but it will then need to send extra orders to the factory. Stocks at the factory will meet the increased demand at first, but it too will send extra orders to the farmer. However, the farmer cannot meet all the additional orders from his tobacco harvest, and this causes a rise in prices. When demand** exceeds supply, the supplier will endeavour to raise his prices to a point at which some of the demand falls away – customers who do not think the tobacco is worth the new price – so that supply can meet demand once again. The factory therefore receives the same amount of tobacco, but has to pay more for it, and passes the price rise on to the shop which receives the same number of cigarettes as before, which is not enough to meet the increased demand which triggered the whole process. However, the shop will also pass on the increased price to its customers, some of whom will now find the cigarettes too expensive; they will cease to demand them, and – in a perfect economy – demand will once again equal supply.

goods people wish to buy. As the extra monetary purchasing power is mopped up by the higher prices, production falls back to its original level. Therefore, the ultimate effect of an increase in the quantity of money is an increase in prices, though the intermediate or transitional effect is a higher level of economic activity, production and employment. Monetarists would now normally expect the transition period to last for a year to eighteen months, with the major effect on prices slowing up about two years after a monetary expansion.

The process can work in reverse, but periods of rapid contraction in the money supply are very rare – and there is no symmetry between the creation and the destruction of money. Apart from currency reforms after hyperinflations, the most severe monetary contraction was that in the United States after the Wall Street crash of 1929. The crash led to a wave of bankruptcies and bank closures as people who had

Left: David Hume. **In 1752, in an essay entitled "Of Money", the Scottish philosopher David Hume explained why an increase in the money supply causes an increase in prices. Hume's analysis still forms the basis of inflation theory.**

Queuing for bread during the Great Depression. **Although an increase in the money supply causes a rise in prices, the converse has not been observed to be true. After the Wall Street crash, the banks that survived became very cautious and built up their reserves; this meant that throughout the 1930s the money supply in the United States was 40 to 50 per cent smaller than in the previous decade. This led to a drop in the demand for goods, with many people only concerned with obtaining essentials like bread, but it did not bring about a comparable drop in prices.**

From boom to bust

The United States' most disastrous economic era began with the Wall Street Crash of 1929 when share prices on the New York stock exchange suddenly plummetted. The Crash was the fearful end to a decade of bounding business confidence and dizzy speculation in which prices of securities reached unprecedented heights. One piece of land in Florida, sold initially for 25 dollars, was resold eventually for 150,000 dollars. Although the land was found to be useless swamp, or even non-existence, speculation fever continued, much of it financed by loans to brokers, which totalled over five billion dollars at the beginning of 1929. By the autumn, confidence was waning and the stock market becoming more and more uncertain; then, on Tuesday, October 29, panic set in. Some 16 million shares were sold that day and the days following, mostly at immense losses. Unable to repay their loans, many speculators went bankrupt and in turn the banks that had made the loans, failed. The business world went into paralysis. There was no effective government intervention and in the next few years, 5,000 banks and 85,000 businesses went bankrupt. New investment fell from 10 billion dollars to one billion, and the number of unemployed rose to 14 million – over one quarter of the labour force. Economic recovery started only after 1933 when the effect of Roosevelt's 'New Deal' policies began to be felt in the worst hit areas.

Left Clerks study the ticker after the night of October 29th *right* and *below* brokers and bankers can only stand and wait for further news after the panic of the previous day.

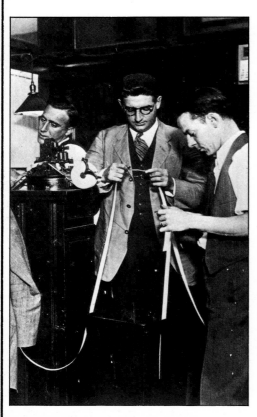

borrowed to buy securities that had become worthless found themselves unable to repay their loans. The banks that survived naturally became very cautious and substantially increased their holdings of reserves. While government policy was passive, the collapse of bank lending led to a very sharp reduction in the money supply in the early 1930s which persisted throughout that decade. The Great Depression of the 1930s can be explained in terms of the first step of the monetarist argument – the reduced quantity of money leading to a fall in the demand for goods. But the second step – the fall in prices – clearly did not materialize. Though wages fell slightly – cuts of 40 per cent to 50 per cent, roughly equalling the fall in the money supply, did not materialize.

The new inflation
While there are many new theories of inflation, their common thread is that inflation is caused not by excessive money creation but by the ability of organised labour, or of business cartels, to raise their prices irrespective of the demand for their products. For example, the balance of power in a wage bargain has been shifted towards the trade unions. A strike may lead to substantial losses for a firm, though if it gives in, it can pass on the higher costs to its customers, providing that its competitors are likely to be facing – and conceding – the same wage demands.

This source of inflationary pressure in the economy seems plausible, but two major criticisms can be levelled against these new theories. The first is that they are incomplete. That is, wage claims differ very substantially from one year to the next, and often from one industry to another. In some years, firms seem prepared to meet wage claims, or to reach a negotiated settlement, in other years they are not – and this can lead to many industrial disputes and strikes. A theory based on bargaining power should give some indication as to why the outcome of the wage bargain should average, say, seven per cent in one year and 27 per cent a few years later. Attempts to relate the size of wage settlements to some factor connected with the bargaining process – for example, the growth of trade union membership – have not proved very successful.

The second criticism concerns the role of money in the inflationary process. If prices rise, people will need more money to finance their everyday transactions. If the money supply is not increased, credit conditions will become tight, interest rates rise, demand for goods fall, and production cut back. Wage inflation, in the absence of monetary expansion, will lead to a recession and unemployment. To avoid unemployment, the government may therefore expand the money supply in response to wage inflation, thereby 'validating' the price increases. In this case, the new theory of inflation merges into the old – wage increases become just one of the many possible factors that may lead to increases in the money supply. But the evidence is not favourable to this view. A recent example is the very rapid monetary expansion in the UK in 1972/73, when by mid-1972, the money supply was growing at a rate of almost 30 per cent per year, though the rate of wage increases at the time was still in single figures. Wage increases of the order of 25 - 30 per cent did not appear until two years later – in 1974/75 – though the growth of the money supply at that time – and subsequently – has been kept close to 10 per cent.

Policies to control inflation
The different theories of the cause of inflation suggest different policies to control it. If inflation is blamed on excessive wage claims by trade unions, it follows that an effective counter-inflationary policy must reduce such claims – most obviously through some form of wage controls. Governments in the United States, Britain and many Western European countries have introduced various types of incomes policies on a number of occasions in recent years. The rationale for an incomes policy is that, while no individual trade union or group of workers can afford to get left behind in the scramble for higher wages, all realise that the scramble itself is futile since the only effect is higher prices. No one union will be prepared to moderate its wage claim unless it knows others will do so as well.

The record of incomes policies has not been a very successful one. Where the limit is clear and simple, such as a flat rate increase across the board, its inflexibility creates anomalies. Where flexibility is allowed, the policy rapidly becomes ineffective. Powerful unions whose members might hope for above average wage increases will oppose the policy and will often be able to defy it

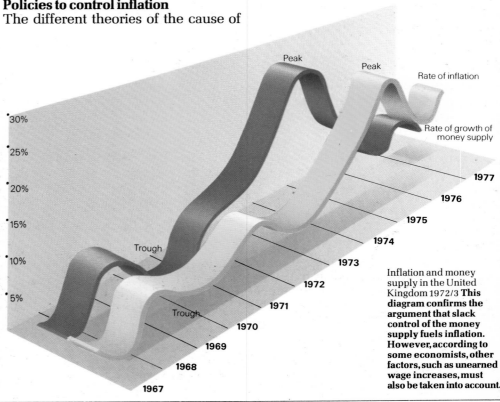

Inflation and money supply in the United Kingdom 1972/3 **This diagram confirms the argument that slack control of the money supply fuels inflation. However, according to some economists, other factors, such as unearned wage increases, must also be taken into account.**

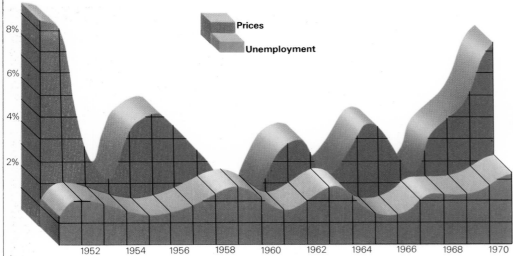

8%

6%

4%

2%

Prices

Unemployment

1952 1954 1956 1958 1960 1962 1964 1966 1968 1970

Right: Japanese miners on strike. **The potential influence of organised labour within an economy is now well recognized. A firm is likely to give in to the threat of a strike if it feels its competitors are facing the same wage demands. This causes a rise in prices throughout the industry concerned. To meet this price rise the consumer is likely to seek a rise in his own wages.**

Fluctuations in the levels of unemployment and prices in the United Kingdom. **It is well established that when the rate of inflation (here represented by prices) falls, unemployment is likely to rise. This happens when the government reduces inflation by restricting the growth of the money supply; when there is less money available, demand for goods and services falls and unemployment rises. However, the trends shown here bear out the theory that there are two kinds of inflation, one of which can occur at the same time as rising unemployment. After 1967 prices and unemployment began to rise together. An explanation of this is that cost-push inflation replaced the earlier demand-pull inflation. Instead of prices rising because of a growing demand for goods and services, the theory suggests that, after 1967, prices rose because the costs of production rose. Certainly, the higher costs of imports after the 1967 devaluation of the pound, higher indirect taxes and higher wage demands all contributed to a large increase in costs of production.**

successfully. Analysis of the effects in practice of incomes policies show that they have a temporary effect in holding down wage increases, but usually by the second or third year the policy has either collapsed or become largely ineffective.

If inflation is blamed on excessive money creation, the remedy is obviously for government to control the growth of the money supply more firmly. But the immediate effect of such a policy is to reduce demand and create recession and unemployment. While the policy may well slow down inflation, it does so only at the cost of high unemployment which is economically wasteful and may be socially disruptive (particularly if it is concentrated among certain groups or in specific areas). But the relatively high unemployment rates of the 1970s are usually accepted as a lesser social evil than rapidly accelerating inflation.

There is a third possibility. If incomes policies are ineffective and monetary policies excessively costly, it is possible to make no effort to reduce the inflation rate. It would be perfectly possible for an economy to have a permanent, moderate rate of inflation of around 5 per cent or 10 per cent (or even 20 per cent or more). Many of the worst aspects of inflation occur when it is sudden and unanticipated – particularly the arbitrary redistribution of income and wealth and the uncertainty and insecurity that it creates. If inflation is anticipated, people will take it into account and, for example, hold their savings in forms which offer protection against inflation. A more general scheme for protecting people from the

effects of inflation – called indexation – involves linking the monetary value of savings, and other contracts also, to an index of prices so their real value is unaffected by inflation. But, even so, indexation cannot remove all the costs of inflation. The main objective of policy is likely to be to reduce the inflation rate rather than educating the population to live with it.

Hyperinflation

A major fear of allowing even a moderate rate of inflation is that it may accelerate out of control. Episodes of spiralling inflation when money has become worthless, and the financial and economic system of a country devastated by war or revolution, are known as 'hyperinflations'. Best-known is the German hyperinflation of 1922-23, but there have been a number of similar episodes in other countries – especially in the periods immediately following the two World Wars.

All hyperinflations are characterized by a phenomenal increase in the quantity of money. In Germany in 1922-23, prices were rising by over 300 per cent in each month – that is, doubling in a week – for a period of almost a year and a half. Even this is dwarfed by the terrifying Hungarian inflation of 1945-46 when prices rose on average 200 times each month for almost a year. But more devastating even than the average inflation rate is its acceleration. The German inflation accelerated from an average of 300 per cent to a peak rate of 32,000 per cent per month by October 1923. In Hungary, prices were increasing three thousandfold per

week by July 1946 in the wake of war.

A rapid inflation is turned into uncontrollable hyperinflation by a flight from money – itself the result of rapid inflation. As soon as workers get paid they rush to the shops to buy goods rather than hold money whose value is always falling. The shopkeepers, rather than hold cash, immediately go back to their suppliers to replenish their stocks. The frantic rush to buy goods simply pushes their prices up faster still. Meantime, the high price of goods forces the government to print still more money to finance expenditure.

In the German inflation in 1923, the government had to enlist no less than 30 paper mills and 100 private printing firms to cope with the increase in the note issue. Bank notes had to be dispatched from Berlin to banks in some distant parts of Germany by air; otherwise they would have been valueless by the time they arrived. At the same time, workers were paid with baskets, sacks and suitcases full of money. By November 1923, a loaf of bread in Germany cost over 400 billion marks. Bank notes were denominated in larger and larger units though no German note ever equalled the dizzy record set by Hungary. There, in July 1946, a banknote was issued with the face value of 100 million billion pengo.

In these circumstances, work and saving count for nothing: all that matters is holding goods and assets whose value keeps ahead of the general inflation. Hyperinflations are characterized by frenzied speculation in all sorts of

Above: Hyperinflation in Germany. **In 1922–3 prices rose by over 300 per cent every month for almost 18 months. Employees were forced to collect their wages armed with suitable containers.**

Below: Hyperinflation in Central Europe 1921–4. **The phenomenal monthly increases in money supply and prices in Germany dwarfed the rates of inflation in the other countries.**

Period of Hyperinflation

Quantity of money increases

314%

72.7%

49.3%

30.9%

32.7%

Germany
Poland
Russia
Austria
Hungary

1921   1922   1923   1924

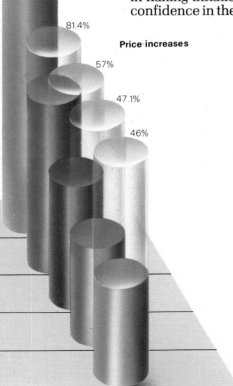

322%

81.4%

57%

47.1%

46%

Price increases

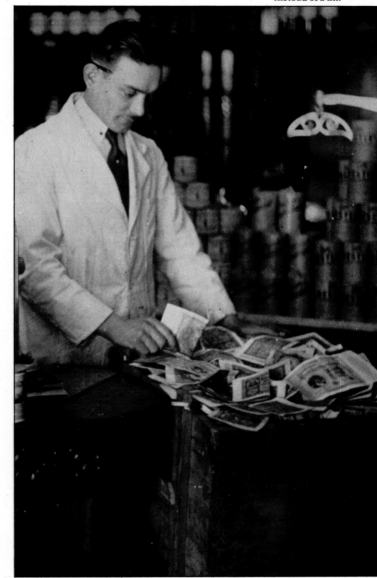

goods, foreign exchange and industrial shares. Similarly, firms buy capital equipment or stocks not for use in production but as a hedge against inflation.

While speculators flourish in a hyperinflation, ordinary people are reduced to poverty or destitution. Many people find their savings worthless, or their income reduced to nothing if they are not in the position to force increases that will keep up with prices. Quite apart from the economic hardship created, such unjust redistribution of wealth brings about political conflict and social disorder. Although hyperinflations often pave the way to political dictatorship, they have always arisen from a combination of political instability and economic weakness in the aftermath of war. In fact, Hitler's accession to power in Germany in 1933 was more directly a consequence of the mass unemployment of the Great Depression than of the hyperinflation ten years earlier.

Hyperinflations are always ended by a currency reform essentially replacing the old currency by a new one whose quantity can be controlled. At the same time, wages and salaries are revalued in terms of the new currency. Though often inequitable such currency reforms are generally successful in halting inflation and quickly restore confidence in the financial system.

Below: Banknote over-printed 1,000,000 marks. **By the end of 1923 even this note was worthless.**

THE BALANCE OF PAYMENTS

The two major objectives of monetary policy are full employment and price stability. But a government cannot conduct its economic policy in isolation from the rest of the world. Many of the goods produced in the economy are destined for markets overseas and many industries are dependent on imported fuel or raw materials. A nation has to pay its way in the world by earning, through sales of exports or from receipts from services provided to foreigners, enough foreign exchange to cover its import bill. A nation not paying its way in the world – selling fewer exports than it buys imports – has a deficit in its balance of payments. Often the primary objective of government policy is to remove a balance of payments deficit (or sometimes surplus), and this can take precedence over other policy objectives such as full employment.

Balance of payments problems, the form they take, and how they can be solved, depend very much on the arrangements governing the finance of international trade through the international monetary system. The first system to be established, towards the end of the nineteenth-century, was the gold standard. Historically, it was short-lived – it collapsed at the outbreak of the First World War – but many regard it as an ideal system and many reforms have been, and still are, attempts to get back to its principles.

The gold standard
The principle of the gold standard is that the same currency should be used for international trade as for ordinary domestic transactions. Gold was therefore accepted as a means of payment both domestically and internationally. Foreign trade consisted of private transactions between the parties involved, with no place for governments or central banks in its finance.

A balance of payments deficit could arise in these circumstances if people living in one country were, on balance, buying more goods from foreigners than they were selling abroad. In so doing they would be paying out more gold than they were earning from abroad, and, as an automatic consequence, the amount of gold in the country would fall. The fall in the amount of gold would, in principle, cause prices to fall, enabling the country with a deficit to sell more goods abroad, so getting rid of its deficit. Similarly, a surplus country would have an inflow of gold and its prices would rise, thereby removing its surplus. Through this mechanism the balance of payments

British Chancellor of the Exchequer, Winston Churchill on his way to deliver his budget speech, 1925. **This was the year in which Churchill restored the gold standard with, according to Keynes, disastrous consequences.**

In theory the gold standard has the advantage of providing a common base for international transactions, but ever since the upsurge in paper money during World War I it has proved difficult to operate.

Current Account

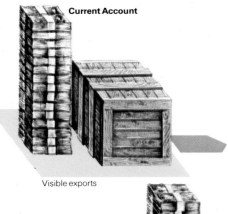

Visible exports

Visible imports

Invisible Trade

Invisible receipts

Invisible payments

Total Exports and receipts

Current Balance of Payments

Total Imports and payments

Left: The balance of payments. **A country's balance of payments consists of its balance on current account added to its balance on invisible trade. Current account is made up of visible exports and imports, visible in that they are actual goods or raw materials which have to be transported in or out of the country. Invisible trade consists of receipts or payments for such items as insurance and tourism. A prolonged deficit in the balance indicates that a country is not paying its way.**

became self-correcting, and no intervention from governments or central banks was required.

In practice, the gold standard did not operate quite as simply as this, for by the end of the nineteenth-century, paper money and bank deposits had largely replaced gold in domestic transactions. But the paper currencies of the various nations were all convertible into gold, at a price fixed by the central bank of each country. Central banks had to ensure that their issues of paper currency were limited by the extent of their gold reserves so as to maintain the convertibility of the paper currency into gold. The domestic money supply was determined primarily by the gold

Below: The Bretton Woods pacts. **The Earl of Halifax signs on behalf of the United Kingdom at the State Department in Washington in 1946. 29 nations signed the pacts.**

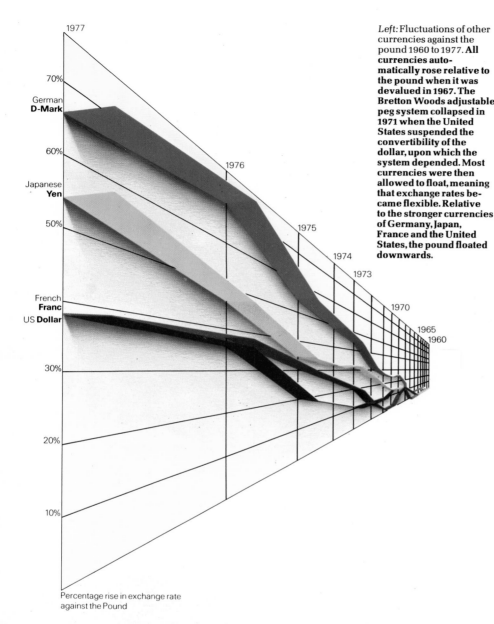

Percentage rise in exchange rate against the Pound

Left: Fluctuations of other currencies against the pound 1960 to 1977. **All currencies automatically rose relative to the pound when it was devalued in 1967. The Bretton Woods adjustable peg system collapsed in 1971 when the United States suspended the convertibility of the dollar, upon which the system depended. Most currencies were then allowed to float, meaning that exchange rates became flexible. Relative to the stronger currencies of Germany, Japan, France and the United States, the pound floated downwards.**

Planning a world economy

The Mount Washington Hotel, Bretton Woods, New Hampshire, USA *above,* **was the scene of the international conference held in July 1944 to plan the world's financial future after the ravages of the Second World War. The chief aim of the delegates, representing 44 nations, was to avoid repeating the mistakes which had led to the world slump of** **the 1930s. The dominant figure was the British economist J. M. Keynes, but his plan was considered too radical to be adopted. Instead, the delegates decided to establish the International Monetary Fund and, in addition, pledged to keep their exchange rates fixed to within 10% of parity, though larger changes were to be allowed in special cases.**

reserves, so the system operated according to gold standard principles.

During the First World War, the supply of paper currencies increased rapidly to enable governments to finance war expenditure, and the convertibility of paper currencies to gold was suspended. In the inter-war period, there were many attempts to restore the gold standard but none survived the collapse of trade during the Great Depression of the 1930s. It was only after the Second World War that a viable new international monetary system was created. It was based on principles laid down at a conference at Bretton Woods (in New Hampshire, US) in July, 1944. This system survived about twenty-five years of exceptionally rapid growth

in world trade and capital movements.

The Bretton Woods system

The Bretton Woods system sought to retain what had been seen as the major benefit of the gold standard – that the value of one country's currency in terms of another (the exchange rate) should be fixed. It was believed that international trade could develop fully only if exchange rates were stable, and that if exchange rates were not fixed by governments, fluctuations might be so severe as to inhibit international business.

Under the gold standard, exchange rates were fixed, because all paper currencies were convertible into gold. Under the Bretton Woods system, it was

for central banks to ensure that exchange rates remained fixed. With the gold standard, the correction of a balance of payments deficit (or surplus) was automatic, operating through changes in the money supply. The Bretton Woods system provided for governments to pursue economic policies to balance their international trade at the fixed exchange rate. Had these principles been rigidly enforced, economic policies would have been as much dominated by the balance of payments under the Bretton Woods system as they had been under the gold standard.

But, in practice, in the years following the Second World War, nations were more concerned with domestic policies. In some countries – Britain and France – the main policy objective was full employment. In others – West Germany or Switzerland – it was price stability. In consequence, the first group – the expansionist countries – found their balance of payments frequently in deficit, while those aiming for price stability found their export markets expanding and their balance of payments in surplus. The Bretton Woods system did provide an escape clause. When a country's balance of payments was in 'fundamental disequilibrium', it could alter the value of its currency. A deficit country could devalue its currency (or a surplus country revalue), attempting thereafter to maintain the new value. This system is known as the 'adjustable peg' – at all times the value of the currency is fixed, but the rate at which it is fixed can, in certain circumstances, be changed. Under these arrangements there were devaluations in the UK (1949, 1967) and France (1957, 1958, 1967), and revaluations in West Germany (1961, 1969) and the Netherlands (1961).

Currency speculation

Whatever the merits of the adjustable peg mechanism, in principle its main practical impact was to create massive speculation in the different currencies. As currencies became more freely convertible in the 1950s, and with the upsurge of international and multinational business, there was a tremendous growth in the amount of money that could be held in different currencies, and rapidly transferred from one to another. This money, which might, for example, be the working balances of a multinational company or international trader, was not covered by any exchange control regulations. Because of the ease, and speed, with which it could be, and was, switched from one currency to another, these funds became known as 'hot money'. No one would want to hold their funds in a currency where there was a risk of devaluation, so, if any country was running a balance of payments deficit, it would be vulnerable to a speculative outflow of hot money. Unless its reserves were very large, or it could mobilize a large amount of borrowing, the speculative outflow might itself precipitate a devaluation, which would profit the speculators who had sold the currency in the first place. Similarly, a country with a balance of payments surplus might experience an inflow of hot money, forcing it to revalue its exchange rate.

In 1971, the US balance of payments was in 'fundamental disequilibrium' and the US dollar overvalued. But by this stage the US dollar had achieved a pivotal role in the system, and its value could not be adjusted in the same way as could other currencies. This came about through the provision of international liquidity, another aspect of the Bretton Woods system.

Right: The adjustable peg. **The adjustable peg system of fixing exchange rates was adopted at the Bretton Woods conference and may well be readopted at some time in the future. The principle is that each currency is fixed in terms of all the others and only a small percentage of fluctuation is permitted. However, allowance is made for any currency's peg to be moved down by devaluation or up by revaluation. The small margin of fluctuation is again imposed.**

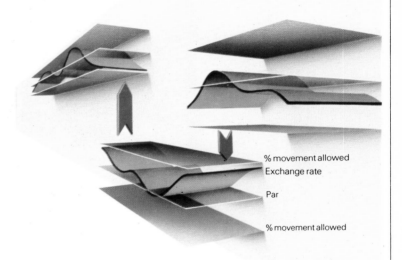

% movement allowed
Exchange rate

Par

% movement allowed

Below: The delegates to the Bretton Woods conference. **Its success ushered in the era of international cooperation in monetary policy.**

Birth of the IMF

International liquidity is the currency used by central banks to settle their debts – arising from balance of payments deficits – with other central banks. Under the gold standard, international liquidity consisted simply of the gold held by central banks. The growth of international trade in this period was, by chance, matched by a growth in international liquidity resulting from gold discoveries in California and elsewhere. Under the Bretton Woods system, the aim was to replace gold as a source of inter national liquidity by a central bank – the International Monetary Fund (IMF). Just as bank accounts have replaced gold in everyday transactions, the IMF was planned to replace gold for transactions between central banks. Each central bank was to have an account at the IMF, and the IMF would transfer funds between central bank deposits in settlement of balance of payments deficits. Central banks are permitted overdrafts – or loans – from the IMF, but such loans are conditional on the pursuit of economic policies which, in the view of the IMF, will remove the country's balance of payments deficit.

The total of deposits with the IMF when it was set up in 1947 was about $9 billion, as compared to central banks' gold holdings, at that time valued at about $35 billion. The idea was that the IMF deposits would be increased as world trade expanded and eventually take over from gold as the main component of international liquidity. In fact, world trade expanded very rapidly, and nations came increasingly to use a different source of international liquidity – the United States dollar. The US emerged from the Second World War with a strong economy and a strong balance of payments, and its currency was valued 'as good as gold' by other countries. The US dollar became the usual means of payment between central banks, and the values of other currencies were fixed in terms of US dollars.

During the 1960s, particularly as a consequence of the Vietnam War, the US balance of payments moved from a position of surplus to one of very substantial deficit. Initially, the outflow of dollars was welcomed as it enabled other central banks to strengthen their reserves, but eventually the persistent deficit undermined confidence in the value of the dollar. In 1968, the US Government suspended the convertibility of the dollar into gold for private holders, while retaining convertibility for central banks. This created two markets for gold (the two-tier system). There was a market for private holders where the price of gold would be established by market principles of supply and demand, and an official market was set up where central banks could use gold to settle debts between themselves at the official price (then $35 per ounce). The two markets were completely separate because central banks undertook neither to sell nor to buy gold on the free market.

With the continuing US balance of payments deficit, central banks became increasingly unwilling to hold US dollars. At the end of the Second World War, the US gold stock was worth about three times its outstanding dollar liabilities. By the end of the 1960s, the figure was less than half. If the other

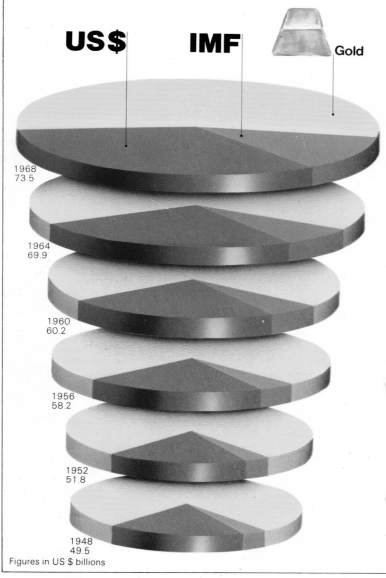

US$ **IMF**   Gold

1968
73.5

1964
69.9

1960
60.2

1956
58.2

1952
51.8

1948
49.5

Figures in US $ billions

Left: The world's international reserves. **Central banks use international reserves to balance their accounts with other central banks. The reserves are held in gold or U.S. dollars, and a smaller proportion is made up of payments made by central banks to the International Monetary Fund.**

Below: International reserves and external liabilities of the United States. **During the 1960s the U.S. balance of payments moved into deficit. Its international reserves of gold fell while its external liquid liabilities (dollars held by foreign banks and convertible into gold) grew. In 1971 the U.S. suspended convertibility of the dollar.**

International reserves (Gold stock)

External liquid liabilities ($)

Figures in US $ billions

1950   1955   1960   1965   1967

The IMF

The International Monetary Fund (IMF) was set up in March 1947 with two major functions:
1 To supervise the operation of the international monetary system, according to the arrangements and code of conduct agreed at Bretton Woods.
2 To provide a new source of international liquidity.

A major objective of the post-war international monetary system has been to encourage the rapid development of world trade. Under the General Agreement of Tariffs and Trade (GATT), tariffs have been reduced and trade controls dismantled. Nations in balance of payments difficulties have been discouraged from resorting to protectionist measures such as import controls. Parallel to the expansion of world trade has been a liberalisation of world capital.

Under the Bretton Woods agreement, exchange rates were to be fixed. Nations in balance of payments difficulties were to borrow to finance temporary deficits, or make a once and for all adjustment in the case of permanent or 'fundamental' deficits.

To enable nations to finance temporary deficits, there would need to be an expansion in international liquidity; this was to be the second function of the IMF. Countries were given 'quotas'– roughly in proportion to their economic importance – which they would deposit with the IMF. Of this, 25 per cent had to be in gold, and 75 per cent in their own national currency. They were then allowed to borrow the full amount of their quota, but in the currencies of other countries. Such loans were unconditional, except that they had to be repaid within five years. Further borrowing was permitted at the discretion of the IMF. In agreeing to further loans, the IMF officials must satisfy themselves that the country's balance of payments deficit will indeed be temporary. In practice, they have often taken the view that deficits are the result of excessive government spending or monetary growth, and have made their loans conditional on a government commitment ('Letter of Intent'), to reduce spending or to control the money supply. Governments seeking IMF loans may seem to surrender control over domestic economic policies to the IMF, though in reality, it is the exchange rate commitment which is the constraint.

The receipt of an IMF, loan has now come to be seen as an endorsement of a government's financial policies, and as a means of strengthening confidence in a country's currency. Even after the collapse of the fixed exchange rate system, in 1976, countries such as Britain and Italy have sought IMF loans to ward off confidence crises in their currencies.

Two managing directors of the IMF – P. Schweitzer *(above)* and J. Witteveen *(below)*

central banks had wished to convert their holdings of dollars into gold, even at the official price, the US had only a fraction of the gold required. In August 1971, the US formally suspended the convertibility of the dollar. With the lynchpin removed from the system, there was no official policy to determine exchange rates. Most currencies were allowed to 'float', thus having their values determined by supply and demand in the market rather than by official policy.

Flexible exchange rates

The adoption of floating or flexible exchange rates in the early 1970s was a response to the collapse of the Bretton Woods system, rather than part of any deliberate policy. But there has always been an argument that floating exchange rates are, in principle, the best way of organizing the international monetary system. The argument is that a change in the exchange rate is the most efficient means of dealing with a balance of payments deficit or surplus. If a country has a balance of payments deficit and a fixed exchange rate, it has to deflate its economy, causing recession and unemployment. It may be able to reduce its inflation rate below that of its competitors and thereby improve the competitiveness of its goods in international markets, but that can be achieved more quickly and effectively,

and without the cost of an intervening recession, by a depreciation of the exchange rate. With fixed exchange rates, as under the gold standard, a surplus country can be forced to 'import' inflation from the rest of the world. Under flexible exchange rates, it can instead allow its exchange rates to appreciate.

However, experience of floating exchange rates in the 1970s has shown up some weaknesses in the system. The fluctuations in the exchange rates have themselves been quite substantial, and certainly greater than can be justified in terms of relative costs and prices. Such fluctuations can have a disruptive effect on international trade by continually altering the competitive position of companies in different countries. Exchange rate movements can also have a grave impact on economic policy objectives. If the exchange rate is pushed down too low, import prices rise to generate inflation, while if it is too high, exports become uncompetitive which can lead to unemployment. To avoid such problems, governments may still have to give the balance of payment priority over domestic policy objectives.

The European Economic Community

One group of countries which have been particularly anxious to avoid the effects of exchange rate uncertainties

on their trade with one another are those of the European Economic Community (EEC). The EEC countries formed a currency 'snake', an arrangement limiting the extent to which the currency of any one member country can move relative to the others. Now, a number of EEC countries have dropped out of the snake (France, Italy, UK and Ireland), while two non-EEC countries have joined (Norway and Sweden). Countries remaining in the snake have also not maintained rigidly fixed exchange rates. The currency values within the snake can be changed, though these adjustments in practice have been quite small. The snake started life in a 'tunnel', in that there was a limit to how far the snake currencies could float up or down against the US dollar. The tunnel was removed in March 1973, since when snake currencies have been floating freely against all others.

The snake was formed by the EEC countries as the first stage in the process towards a European Monetary Union (EMU). EMU has always been a longer-term objective of the EEC. It would mean not only that member countries would subordinate their national policies to the exchange rate, as required by any fixed exchange rate system, or by the snake, but that they would surrender the control over all monetary matters to some supranational EEC authority. EMU would

Free floating rate **Managed exchange rate** **Absolutely rigid**

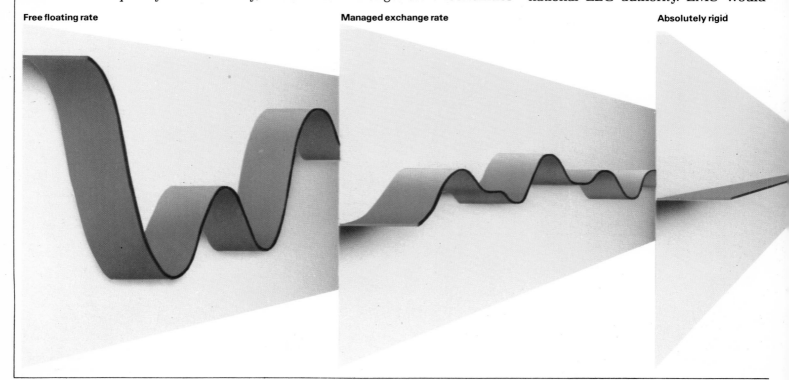

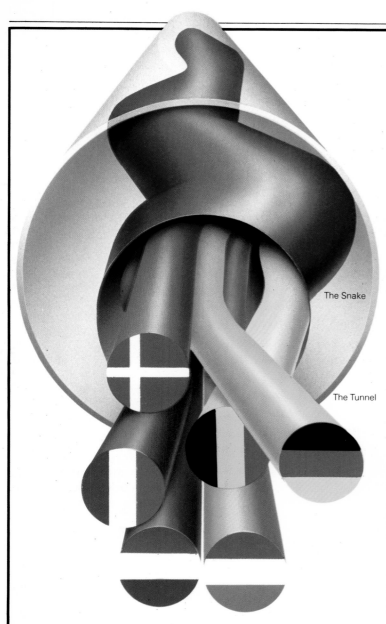

The Snake

The Tunnel

The currency snake

The snake was born in the aftermath of the collapse of the fixed exchange rate system in August 1971. Since this collapse did not lead immediately to a system of freely floating exchange rates, there was, in December 1971, a new attempt to fix their value. This became known as the 'Smithsonian Agreement' (after the Smithsonian building in Washington where the negotiations took place). Values of currencies were pegged in terms of US dollars but, in view of the increased instability, currencies were allowed to fluctuate relative to the dollar by a wider margin (up to 2¼ per cent either way, instead of the 1 per cent previously permitted). In the Smithsonian Agreement, each country was required to keep its currency within this 'tunnel', with a ceiling 2¼ per cent above, and a floor 2¼ per cent below, its dollar parity.

Even this limited degree of flexibility was thought excessive by the Common Market countries. In February 1971, the EEC Council of Ministers had accepted the recommendation of the Werner Report for monetary union, which envisaged a transitional phase of narrowing the range of permissible exchange rate fluctuations. The snake was intended to keep the EEC currencies closer together. The idea was that the weaker EEC currencies would be supported and the stronger held down, to limit the movements in EEC currencies relative to one another. The EEC currencies would continue to be loosely pegged to the dollar in the 'tunnel', but they would tend to move together relative to it.

In March 1973, after another foreign exchange crisis, the Smithsonian Agreement was abandoned, and exchange rates became fully flexible. The EEC countries decided to maintain the snake, which was now to float freely against other currencies and no longer confined to the tunnel.

In the meantime, however, three EEC countries had dropped out of the snake as a result of foreign exchange crises (UK and Eire in June 1972, and Italy in February 1973). France was also to leave the snake in January. Two non-EEC Scandinavian countries, on the other hand, have joined the snake (Norway in May 1972 and Sweden in March 1973). France rejoined in 1975 but left again in March 1976.

Fixed peg with small fluctuations

Crawling peg

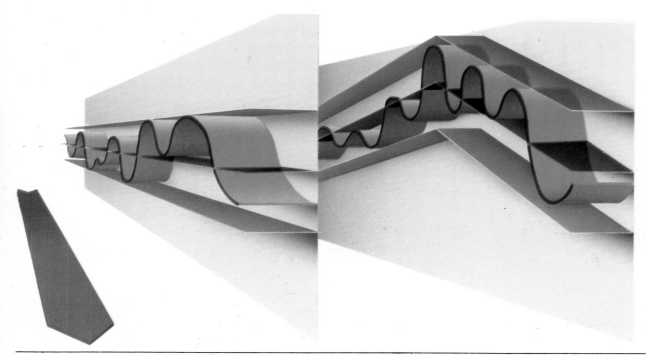

Left: Methods of establishing exchange rates. **Free floating exchange rates have been in force since the early 1970s. The rate simply floats up or down depending on the balance of payments surplus or deficit of the country concerned. The argument against this is that the competitive positions of companies in different countries become unpredictable. Alternatives are: a managed exchange rate where a government intervenes by buying or selling its own currency in order to keep the rate relatively constant; absolutely rigid rates which have never been tried; fixed peg with small fluctuations which would be similar to the gold standard; and the crawling peg whereby relative rates might change, but only by small fixed amounts each year.**

mean that, for most economic and monetary purposes, the EEC would become a single country.

The impact of the oil crisis

Towards the end of 1973, the oil exporting countries (OPEC) quadrupled the price of oil. This was generally seen as a political response to the Middle East War, but the price of oil had been set by long-term agreements which had not been adjusted to the inflation of the early 1970s. Oil prices had risen less than most other commodities.

The significance of the oil price increase, was that it created massive increases in revenues for a number of states, such as Saudi Arabia, Kuwait and the United Arab Emirates, which had no means of spending that money. In consequence, most countries of the world would inevitably have balance of trade deficits, while some of the OPEC states would have huge surpluses. The main fear was that the trade deficits would lead to a series of foreign exchange crises which in turn, might lead to competitive devaluations or protectionist measures. The end result could be a slump in world trade on the scale of the great recession of the 1930s.

But the OPEC surpluses had to be invested somewhere, and, despite the huge sums involved, the bulk was invested through commercial markets in New York and London. Most of the money was then lent to other countries, with the result that the majority found little difficulty in attracting ordinary commercial loans to even out their trade deficits. There were also official arrangements to 'recycle' funds from countries which had received a large volume of the OPEC surpluses to those which had received little or none.

While these commercial and official recycling arrangements have been regarded as quite successful, the OPEC surpluses themselves have added massively to the amount of volatile short-term capital (hot money) in the system. All currencies are more vulnerable to speculation as a result, chief among them the US dollar and the UK pound, because New York and London initially attracted most of the oil surpluses. The sharp fall of the pound in 1976, and of the US dollar in 1977, can be very largely attributed to a change in OPEC investment policies.

1. Saudi Arabia
2. Venezuela
3. Iran
4. Kuwait
5. Libya
6. Nigeria
7. Iraq
8. Abu Dhabi
9. Indonesia
10. Algeria
11. Ecuador
12. Gabon
13. Qatar
14. United Arab Emirates

The OPEC countries **Most of the member countries are concentrated around the Persian Gulf.**

Left: Meeting of OPEC representatives, Stockholm. **OPEC is a cartel formed by the oil exporting countries to fix oil prices. Competition has been removed, prices are high and consumption has dropped.**

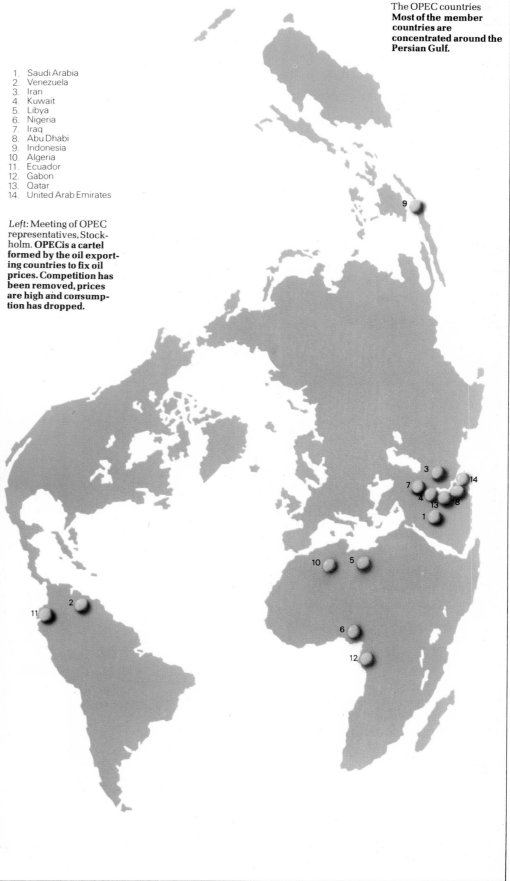

Oil was first produced in Pennsylvania in the 1860s from finds that were to form the beginnings of the immense Rockefeller Standard Oil empire. There were many subsequent discoveries in the United States (particulary in Texas) which, by the time of the Second World War, dominated the world oil industry, accounting for about two-thirds of total world production. Five of the seven major oil companies that dominate the world oil industry originated in the United States in this early period.

Oil was known to exist in Venezuela and in the Middle East before the war, but by 1940 these sources were producing only 9 per cent and 5 per cent respectively of world production. Since the Second World War, there have been discoveries of immense quantities of oil all over the world. Most important have been the enormous oil finds in the Middle East, but there have also been significant discoveries in Africa (Libya, Algeria and Nigeria), Indonesia and many other places including, most recently, the North Sea. During the 1950s, new oil fields were being discovered at a rate exceeding the current level of production by about five times, so that the known reserves of oil were increasing rapidly (known oil reserves were about seven times as great in 1960 as in 1945).

During this period, with existing oil fields being developed and new producers entering the market, there was a persistent over-supply of oil, and competition between producer countries and between oil companies led to low prices and a continual pressure for price cutting. A consequence of the low prices was a very rapid expansion in the consumption of oil which, for

Right: Water towers in Kuwait. **Always one of the richest of the oil-producing countries, Kuwait has now embarked on extravagent and delightful new building programmes.**

Below: Oil consumption and reserves in the ground (excluding communist countries). **Since oil is not manufactured, but merely sucked out of the ground, its production equals its consumption. Oil will begin to run out when consumption becomes greater than the average rate of new discoveries. Projections suggest that this would soon have happened if the price had not risen in 1973.**

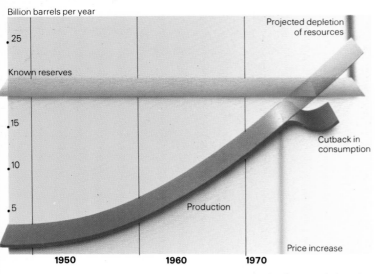

Billion barrels per year

Projected depletion of resources

Known reserves

Cutback in consumption

Production

Price increase

1950　　1960　　1970

1973
2.59 US $

1974
11.65 US $

Left: The cost of a barrel of oil. **At the end of 1973 OPEC raised the price of oil to four and a half times its former price.**

Below: Major oil importers, 1977. **Following the massive price rise, all countries except the United States and Japan, spent less on oil in 1975 than in the previous year. In 1977 Italy, West Germany and the United Kingdom still spent less on imported oil than they did in 1974.**

France
382.84

Italy
247.37

United States
583.83

United Kingdom
151.50

West Germany
161.89

Japan
584.10　　Figures in US $ millions (monthly averages)

example, replaced coal as the major fuel for electricity generation. World oil consumption has increased by about 7 per cent per year in the post-war period, equivalent to a doubling of consumption every ten years.

But even this rapid growth has not kept up with the increase in the industry's productive capacity. In 1960, OPEC, the Organisation of Petroleum Exporting Countries, was formed in the attempt to prevent competitive price cutting by producer nations. Its original members were Iran, Iraq, Kuwait, Saudi Arabia and Venezuela, but new oil producers such as Indonesia, Libya, Algeria and Nigeria have joined since. OPEC is a cartel – a producers' agreement to charge higher prices than would prevail under competitive conditions – and like all cartels it can sustain a higher price

only if it can persuade its members to hold back their production. In the 1960s, with many new oil producers, this proved difficult.

In the 1970s, the balance of supply and demand began to change. While new discoveries continued, the rate of consumption had caught up, and known oil reserves were no longer increasing. If consumption continues to grow in excess of the rate of new discoveries, reserves will be run down. From this viewpoint, oil is a finite stock to be conserved, rather than a free commodity of which there is a plentiful supply each year. Producers might think it is sensible to reduce their production and conserve their supplies in anticipation of higher prices as shortages develop, rather than selling their oil as quickly as possible.

There were pressures for oil price increases

from some of the producer nations before the Middle East War of October 1973, though the price increase actually materialised as a result of oil being used as a political weapon during that war. The economies of many Western European nations, and of Japan, had become dependent on Middle East oil and the Arab producers placed an embargo on deliveries to discourage these countries from supporting Israel. As a result of the embargo, oil prices rose very rapidly, and in December 1973, the oil producers decided to relax the embargo, but maintain the higher prices. This led to an approximate quadrupling of producer nations' oil revenues.

There are few ready substitutes for oil, and consumers have had little alternative but to pay the higher prices. But if oil, and all the many oil-

Below: Fertilizer factory in Saudi Arabia. **OPEC states invest some of their money in their own countries, although much of it has been used to** speculate in the foreign exchange markets to the detriment of the U.S. dollar and the pound sterling.

based products cost more, people can afford to purchase less. The immediate effect of the oil price increase was a world recession on a scale unknown since the 1930s. As a result of the recession and the high price, oil consumption

which had been growing at 7 per cent per year up to 1973 has been falling since. The industry has again been facing the problems of over-supply and competitive price cutting, and the real price of oil has been falling since 1974.

Left: Sheik Yamani. **The Secretary General of OPEC and Saudi Arabian representative.**

Below: Queues for petrol in London, 1973. **The politics of the Middle East War caused petrol shortages and price rises.**

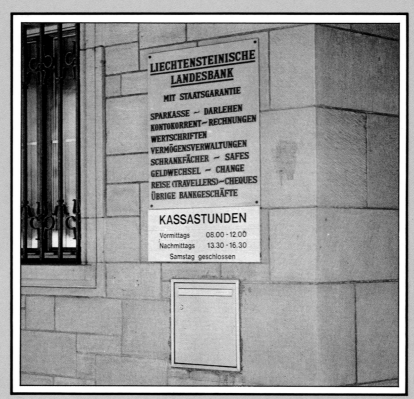

A plaque outside the
Liechtensteinisches
Landesbank, Liechtenstein,
lists a comprehensive range
of banking services.

AN EFFICIENT MONETARY SYSTEM?

Throughout money's history, economic systems have been transformed as social conditions have altered. Many economists would argue that the world today is entering another such period of change, as the economic balance swings away from the industrialised nations of the west towards the new nations of the third world – the rise in oil prices in recent years being a classic example of this shift in operation. There are many differing arguments about how such a change could or should be dealt with. Some economists urge reliance on basic market forces, with the minimum amount of intervention; others, on the other hand, call for more and more intervention and control to ensure economic stability.

COMPETITION OR CONTROL?

The chief purpose of most financial institutions is to ease the transfer of money from those who have some and wish to lend, to those who have none, and wish to borrow. True, such transactions can be accomplished without an intermediary, simply by one person lending money to another, but once complications set in, there is no doubt that specialized financial institutions do have their uses.

To begin with, they provide a common meeting ground for lender and borrower and, in addition, can change the whole nature of the transaction. Most private lenders want to get their money back, plus a reasonable interest, as quickly as possible, and are therefore reluctant to lend on the long term. But many borrowers – a couple setting up home, or a businessman who needs to retool his factory – often require a loan that will be extended over a long period. This conflict can be resolved by a financial house – in the case of a businessman, a bank. The bank can offer him a five or ten year loan because, even though most of its funds are in the form of deposits repayable on demand, it knows that not all its customers will be wanting all their money back at the same time. It will therefore have large sums available for judicious investment, which it hopes, will provide a return both for the bank and its depositors.

The funds of most financial institutions are made up of deposits from many thousands of individuals, and this pooling of resources allows them to take a more relaxed view of the needs of the borrower than a private lender could sensibly afford on his own.

The market for stocks and shares is another example of a device that enables borrowers to have the long term use of funds, while lenders retain the option of being able to realize their investment at any time.

Financial institutions do not necessarily exercise a beneficial effect on the economy by transferring funds from lender to borrower. The economy, in fact, is only as good or as bad as its financial structure.

Restrictive practices may be in operation, for example, impeding the effectiveness of the system, or the funds available might not be channelled towards those projects which offer the best return for the risk involved.

Something for nothing?

Financial institutions compete with each other for funds. Commercial banks and savings organizations build up extensive networks of branch offices, hoping to attract custom by making it very convenient for clients to use the facilities offered. Banks may offer 'free' cheques to customers and stockbrokers offer 'free' research and investment advice to clients. The basic price for facilities remains the same,

Below: the Hamburg Kommerzbank and *right* the Bank Suisse. **Banks today compete fiercely for custom, but, under the surface, the differences between them are not great. Some economists attack this on the grounds of monopoly; others argue that over competitiveness might bring all the dangers of speculation, recreating the conditions that led to the boom and crash of 1929.**

but institutions compete by offering various supplementary services. In many instances, it pays the buyer to shop around.

Such practices may result in an uneconomic allocation of resources. To attract business, financial institutions are probably providing a level of supplementary frills far beyond the level clients would actually want if they had to pay for them. Many clients would no doubt prefer a cheaper service without frills, but this choice is seldom offered.

There is little evidence that these benefits have much effect on the customer, and indeed, it is hard to ascertain exactly why a particular individual takes business to a particular institution. Yet if borrowers are not motivated solely by where they can obtain the best bargain and if potential lenders do not put their funds into investments offering the highest return for

the risk taken, the incentive for financial institutions to minimize costs and to allocate resources efficiently is reduced.

The trouble is that people do not always act in a strictly rational way. Social factors – such as choosing a firm recommended by family or friends – unwillingness to make a change and a general lack of knowledge about the range of services offered by different institutions tend to militate against good decision making by potential private customers. Big companies, on the other hand, do shop around and take a deep interest in the subsidiary services offered by different financial institutions.

The newcomers

Competitiveness in the financial world is also apparent in the degree of ease or difficulty a new company experiences in gaining access to the market, and in

how much opposition an established institution faces when expanding into new areas.

As in any major industry with well-entrenched existing companies, newcomers encounter considerable difficulties. For instance, it is difficult to conceive of a major new commercial banking network springing into existence in the industrialized Western world.

However, since the 1960s, there have been enormous changes in the world's financial structure. One important development was the growth of the new money markets outside the traditional systems which were primarily concerned with short-term funds. In these, the main lenders were large companies, and the principal borrowers local governments and finance houses. The stimulus to growth stemmed, at least in part, from the established banks' lack of competitiveness on interest rates, which created opportunities for other institutions to attract customers by offering higher rates on deposits and lower rates on loans.

Sharper competition still was provided by major foreign banks that set up branches in Europe during the last decade or so. The effect was a healthy one that led to a much greater flexibility in the system. This was reflected in the growth of the interbank system, the incursion of merchant and investment banks into traditional banking areas, the growth of the Certificate of Deposit market and the increasing use of fixed term lending by the old major banks.

When the system goes wrong

Though a degree of competition is desirable, uncontrolled activity in the financial structure can and sometimes does, lead to inflation, though the precise causes of this are obscure. But what happens, and how inflation affects the economy, is perhaps best illustrated by the example of a manager of a large factory.

It is the manager's job to produce and sell his product, but this process takes time. First, there is the time between purchasing raw materials and the day when the finished article rolls off the production line; then, there are delays between selling the product and the receipt of income. Because of the time factor, the manager must make decisions about the allocation of resources that will have implications for the future.

One decision is how much raw material to buy; another is when to invest in new plant or machinery that may have a potential economic life of 20 years or more. Then he must decide when to take on labour, a decision which in many countries now involves the company in a legal commitment to provide continuous employment or make expensive redundancy payments.

These decisions, and many others, have to be taken in the face of an uncertain future – which, however, can be made less uncertain through careful study of the financial information available. The most useful source of such information is the vast array of prices facing the company – prices of raw materials and labour costs in different locations, of capital equipment, and of the prices charged by the

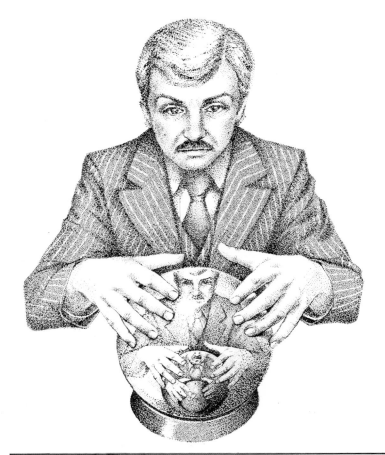

The crystal ball. **Accurate predication of economic trends and possibilities is vital in planning the future of a firm, industry or country. All the factors involved must be carefully weighed before any decision is made.**

Left: Belgian workers returning home and *above* workers leaving a Volkswagen car factory in West Germany.

Industrial relations are one of the more difficult factors to be taken into account when predicting economic trends.

competitors in the particular field.

These provide vital signals for future profitability. Though it is true that prices change, and that planning for the future has to be based on projections that differ from current prices, they usually provide a good indicator of future trends. But inflation adds considerably to the company's difficulties. The course of future prices, never certain, becomes much less so as inflation bites, and past decisions prove costly when the price assumption on which they were based turns out to be false. **Under** inflation, prices change frequently, not only in response to the general rise, but in their relationship to each other as well. In consequence, they become less reliable as signals for the decision-maker; he is no longer able to make the distinction between relative and absolute price movements that usually decides how he will allocate his resources.

Inflation and government

Governments are the main beneficiaries from changes in the distribution of income that arise from inflation.

One reason is because they are almost invariably the major debtors in an economy, and they traditionally borrow long term and at fixed rates of interest. Originally, such borrowing was limited to times of war, but recently it has become more widespread. Keynes provided an economic rationale for this activity. This rationale permitted governments to achieve a desired level of aggregate demand by running budget deficits, borrowing and then spending funds which would otherwise be saved and remain unspent.

Debt financing has become an important part of counter-cyclical policies. Its widespread adoption is associated with periods of accelerating inflation; it is argued that as debt financing leads to an excessive level of aggregate demand, it directly causes inflation.

Governments also benefit because taxation of incomes is progressive, and tax rates and income tax bonds are fixed in money terms. Since inflation raises nominal income, the lower income groups who would not normally pay tax find themselves paying it, and the upper groups are charged at progressively higher rates.

Another advantage to governments is that they control the supply of money. The more money they issue, the higher inflation becomes and government income rises in proportion. In a sense, inflation is a form of taxation, that enables governments to maintain higher levels of public expenditure than would have been the case if each item of expenditure had been individually agreed. Much of the profit, of course, goes to those members of society who benefit from government contracts.

But as people become aware of the means by which governments benefit from inflation, pressures develop to limit them. An obvious means is to index tax rates and tax bonds; governments may also find that it becomes progressively more difficult to borrow from the private sector.

Inflation and private companies

The difficulties that inflation sets for companies considering investment stem from the uncertainty of future planning. Even if the investment is based on a 'realistic' view of the infla-

Below A North Sea oil rig takes shape in a British shipyard **The British economy in particular has benefited from the discovery of North Sea oil, but pessimists wonder what happens when it runs out.**

tionary rise, the costs to the company of being wrong – if there is a fall in inflation, for example, – can be catastrophic. Although companies may have benefited from previous increases, if they are heavily committed, they can lose if inflation falls.

The costs of a fall in inflation, which might include bankruptcy, will be greater than any potential benefits that they might derive from inflationary price rises. Although companies benefit from higher inflation as debtors, they also suffer greatly from the increased uncertainty that inflation induces in consumers, who provide the demand for their products. The evidence of the last few years has emphasized the extent to which rising inflation raises companies' demand for cash. They receive a much higher level of financing, forcing them to take on more debt than would normally be prudent.

Inflation makes accounting particularly difficult. A company's accounts are intended to provide a true statement of its affairs, but inflation greatly complicates matters, especially for large companies. For example, companies make

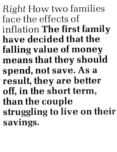

Left: Logs floating down a Norwegian river to a lumber mill and *below* loading paper and timber in British Columbia, Canada **Another problem facing the world today is the gradual exhaustion of natural resources. In Canada, for instance, an intense reforestation programme is under way to repair the damage done by earlier ruthless over-exploitation.**

provision for depreciation that covers the extent to which capital equipment wears out in the course of a year, so that when the plant needs to be replaced, finance is available. This ensures that profits are not inflated by ignoring the cost of capital services, which are embodied in all existing plant. But with inflation, depreciation needs to be based on the present cost of installing similar equipment rather than on the historic cost when the original plant was installed.

Another problem is presented by stocks. Stocks of raw materials are an essential requirement for most companies, and if they rise in value after being bought as a consequence of inflation, this might be regarded as profit. But such profits are of a different nature than true profits. Inflation accounting deals with them differently, though the treatment remains arbitrary.

Then there is the matter of debts. Debts and loans should, if possible, be measured in real terms and take account of the effect of inflation on the real value of future interest payments and receipts. But in practice, it has proved almost impossible to do so.

Inflation hits companies hard, and as they are the productive backbone of any capitalist system, the effects they feel are rapidly passed on to the entire national economy.

Inflation and the public

The effect of inflation eventually reaches down to embrace the entire population.

Virtually all sections of the community dislike inflation although some sections benefit temporarily. The uncertainties affect everyone, from the housewife buying her weekly shopping to the company director.

Inflation forces people to behave defensively. Though it would not appear to be a particularly rational response, savings rose in all countries during the period following the high inflation of 1974. Probably, people were endeavouring to restore the confidence in themselves and their assets that they had temporarily lost; such problems are common during inflationary periods. Suspicions flare, warranted or not, about government efficiency and the vast profits that big companies may be making. Always too, there is the nagging fear of redundancy, unemployment and debt. This perhaps, is the greatest price we pay for inflation.

Right How two families face the effects of inflation **The first family have decided that the falling value of money means that they should spend, not save. As a result, they are better off, in the short term, than the couple struggling to live on their savings.**

Computer at work. Computers
today have an essential role in all
banking transactions, and
their importance will
grow in the future.

7.

AFTERWORD

This book has traced the story of money from
prehistoric times to the present day. Over these
centuries, there have been many changes—some the
natural result of social and technological advance,
but others a result of deliberate choice—and, now,
many would argue that mankind must make
perhaps the most crucial choice in its entire history.
Can today's advanced society survive in its present
form? Or will such factors as the dwindling supply
of natural resources ensure that the growth we all
have come to expect will have to stop? Some
experts predict that it will; others, however, believe
that man's natural ingenuity will enable him to
overcome all such problems. Whatever happens,
money—the life blood of the world—will have its part
to play.

AFTERWORD

Inflation and unemployment

It seems reasonable to expect that the problems of inflation and unemployment that have dominated economic policy since the Second World War will continue to do so.

The steady increase in unemployment in recent years has been a worldwide phenomenon. One explanation is that since unemployment pay is now much more generous than it was, people are prepared to spend more time searching for a suitable new job. If the average rate of job turnover is unchanged, but people take longer seeking employment, then the recorded level of unemployment will rise. So far as this explanation may be correct, governments need not be too concerned about the increase in unemployment.

Another reason offered is that technological change is causing severe levels of unemployment in some industries and trades. This is potentially much more ominous as it raises the possibility that a percentage of the population will be unemployed for very long periods of time or that whole areas – associated with declining industries – may become permanently depressed. As far as can be seen, there has been no tendency for this type of unemployment – 'structural unemployment' – to become any more severe in recent years, though it may do so in the future.

Unemployment will also be affected by a country's trade performance. An increasing level of imports reduces the potential demand for goods produced internally.

It seems fairly clear that as long as there is a worldwide tendency for unemployment to rise, it will become increasingly more difficult for individual nations to reduce their own level of unemployment significantly.

The future of money

The future of money will largely depend on the kind of changes that may arise in its traditional role as a means of payment. There may also be alterations in the international management of the monetary system.

Bank deposits of one kind and another represent the vast proportion of money while notes and coins represent only a small part. The importance of cash in transactions has steadily diminished since the Second World War, and will presumably continue to do so.

Bank accounts are an outstandingly convenient form of keeping money and it is most unlikely that their role will lessen in the future. But the techniques of payment will almost certainly change. A cheque is an instruction to a bank to transfer funds to someone else. The person accepting the cheque normally considers it as representing immediate payment, even though there may be some delay before the sum is credited to his account. Similarly, the payer regards himself as having discharged his debt, even though it may be several days before his account is debited.

The process appears ideally suited for computerisation and indeed, computers have already taken over much of the work at different stages. However, the process can be improved. If all the details of bank accounts are recorded on a computer (as they normally are), and if the computers could be linked, instantaneous transfer would be achieved. All that is needed is a computer terminal, say, a press-button telephone at the point where the transaction is made, with some kind of built-in security system to ensure that no money is stolen through recording a transfer from someone else's account.

First evidences of such a system are apparent in cash points and similar services, that use computer access to individual bank accounts. In the United States, some banks provide computer terminals in stores which transfer funds immediately from the customers' account when a purchase is made.

There seems little doubt that the use of computer money will grow and that cheque books will become progressively less important until finally, they disappear. Notes and coins would be used only for the smallest transactions.

A change to computer money would not in any way change the economic status quo. Transfers would still depend on the account containing sufficient funds or overdraft facilities.

But if such a system was put into action it would lose the flexibility that only human intervention can provide. Banks would still have discretion over bank loans, but the computer would be incapable of deciding whether overdrawn cheques should be honoured or not. It is possible, however, that the traditional 'discretion' afforded to bank managers, might one day be replaced by a simple set of rules which might be fed into a computer.

Such a change would dramatically accelerate the circulation of money – and reduce compulsory credit balances as well. Under the present system it is costly, in terms of time, to pay cheques into a bank. The longer the gap between such visits the higher an average balance has to be. Also, since there is no time limit to the presentation of cheques, no one can be quite sure at any given moment exactly what their bank balance is. Though delays in presentation may benefit large firms, they are highly inconvenient to private depositors.

Through electronic transfer, payments would be debited instantly, and true bank balances determined in moments. Credits would also be instantly registered, and the present cost of paying in cheques would virtually disappear.

The switch to computer money would not affect the basic nature of the monetary system. What might affect it, however, would be any further major extension of the use of credit cards.

At the moment, credit cards are a convenient way of saving time and money by allowing a large number of transactions to be settled at once. This also permits the holder of a credit card to reduce his average bank balance since he need only build-up immediately before the bill has to be paid. For the rest of the month he could, for example, keep his funds in some form of savings. But on the whole, credit cards tend to increase the velocity of circulation of money.

But there is also the element of credit. All users of credit cards get some credit, even if they settle the account promptly. There must always be a delay between buying goods from a shop and paying the company that issued the card. The shop, however, is paid immediately by the company less a small fee.

In terms of the behaviour of the monetary system, it is as if the credit card company (usually a bank or a group of banks), made a free loan to the cardholder which is used to pay the shop. The entries do not appear against the customer's bank account, but they do appear in the customer's credit card account.

Once the customer becomes liable for interest payments, the nature of the loan becomes more obvious although it is still not recorded against his bank account. Thus credit cards, because they provide a readily available source of credit from the banking system, are likely to put extra pressure on the money supply and will in fact cause an increase, unless governments take some action to offset this. Nevertheless, it is already true that credit cards reduce the need for cash.

The national and international control of money

The most important question about the future of money is whether nations will preserve a system of flexible exchange rates, or whether they will move back to the system of fixed exchange, with occasional adjustments, which ruled the world economy from the end of the Second World War until 1971-2. One solution, that of a common currency system, has already been proposed by the partners in the European Economic Community.

Under a system of fixed exchange rates, the authorities have to intervene as soon as there is either an excess supply of or an excess demand for a currency at agreed limits. To prevent a rise, currency is sold and to protect a fall it is purchased, possibly with international assistance.

Fixed exchange rate systems have limits agreed and they are known internationally. If a country abandons fixed exchange rates there may still be a considerable amount of intervention, but the limits for fixed exchange rate movements are set by government who can change them whenever necessary.

It was hoped that by abandoning the fixed exchange rate system, it would be possible to gain greater freedom of economic policy. Experience since 1972 suggests that this freedom has only resulted in very high inflation and that the performance of many major economies has deteriorated considerably, even considering that problems were very much exacerbated by the huge increases in oil prices.

There is now an increasing awareness that flexible exchange rates are not necessarily a solution. It has been argued that fixed exchange rates impose an important discipline on governments which forces them to adopt monetary and fiscal policies consistent with a low rate of inflation. The correct policies could be enforced without the need to join a fixed currency system, but it is feared that governments need the external constraints which fixed exchange rates provide.

Although a common currency is only a special case of fixed exchange rates, it is a big jump from one to the other, since a common currency virtually rules out any possibility of flexibility once the system is established.

In the past, the major objection to such a system in the EEC was that parts of the Community would become permanently depressed. Under flexible exchange rates, it is possible in principle to change relative costs so that an area of poor productivity can still compete with other areas. But in a common currency area, whole countries or large areas, such as the Appalachian region in the United States, experience prolonged high unemployment. More recent history suggests that flexible exchange rates do not solve the problem either, so that particular objection to a common currency is no longer valid.

In the end, the major difficulties over a common currency are likely to be political ones. Members of the EEC, for example, are reluctant to accept the loss of sovereignty that membership of a common currency would entail. It is likely therefore that there will be some return to fixed exchange rates possibly with wider margins, and more frequent changes than in the past. These decisions will have important implications for international monetary policies and will restore some of the restraints that existed before 1972.

ekonomi

economía

wirtschaften

economy

économie

zuinigheid

8.

THE GLOSSARIES

This section charts the key dates and people involved in the history of money over the ages, together with an A-Z listing of commonly used economic terms. Through using these pages, it is possible to see how, like building blocks, one event or idea led to another, while the section provides an instant source of reference and additional information on the lives of many of the personalities mentioned in the other sections of this book.

ECONOMIC EVENTS AND PERSONALITIES

○ *c.*4000 BC   City of Susa founded. Sumerian civilization begins in "Fertile Crescent"

● 2000-1501 Trade routes spre

● 3000-2501   Sumerians begin to use metal coins which replace barley as legal tender

○ *c.*3000 BC   First Egyptian dynasty

Aristo

Adelman, Irma (1930-) Of Romanian birth, Professor Adelman was educated in the US, gaining a PhD in economics in 1955. She lectured both at Stanford and the University of Maryland before publishing her empirical work, 'Theories of economical growth and development.' In this, she emphasises that under-development needs to be explained in terms of many inter-related factors rather than isolating one single cause. She also sug-

gests that, in the early stages of development, the majority of the population tends to become poorer as the economy grows. She argues too, that there is a trade-off between growth in gross national product and depauperization, and that depauperization should take priority.

Allen, Sir Roy George Douglas (1906-) Statistician, economist and mathematician, Professor Allen studied at Sydney, Sussex, Cambridge, before being appointed as a lecturer in the London School of Economics in 1928. During the Second World War, he was made Director of Records and Statistics of the British Supply Council in Washington, and later, Director of the combined Production and Resources Board. In 1944, he was appoin-

ted Professor of Statistics at London University. During the 60s he was chairman of a famous government committee inquiring into the impact of rates on households. The Allen Report, issued in 1965, concluded that the impact was regressive. Sir Roy's published works include: *Mathematical Analysis for Economists* (1938), *Statistics for Economists* (1949), *Mathematical Economics* (1956), and *Macro-Economic Theory – a Mathematical treatment* (1967).

Aquinas, Saint Thomas (1225-1274). Perhaps the most remarkable of medieval theologians, Thomas, a native of Naples, gained his doctorate at Paris under Alberthus Magnus and later taught at various European universities. His most famous work was his 20 volume *Summa Theologica.* In this, he expresses his concern with the concept of justice in the distribution of income and stresses the importance of a 'just wage' and 'just prices.' He believed that interest should only be taken if it was earned; unearned interest was tantamount to 'The Sin of Usury.' However, he also preached that it was immoral to attempt to alter the distribution of income in spite of its inequalities. St. Thomas was canonised in 1323.

Arrow, Kenneth Joseph (1921-) The 1972 Nobel Prize-winner in economics, Kenneth Arrow began his academic career on the research staff of the Comles Commission in Chicago and later taught at Stanford and Harvard.

He has done much important work on economic equilibrium analysis, applying the mathematical theory of convex sets and has contributed to the theories of growth and decision. His best known work is his analysis of voting processes, *Social Choice and Individual Values* (1951) in which he tried to mathematically demonstrate that voting processes would result in a 'socially desirable' composition of government. However, the 'Arrow Possibility Theorem' concludes that perfectly responsive representative

government of this kind is not possible. Arrow's other publications includes *General Competitive Analysis* with F H Hahn (1971) and *Essays in the Theory of Risk Bearing* (1971).

Bagehot, Walter (1826-1877). This famous British commentator on economic affairs was editor of *The Economist* from 1861 to 1877. *Lombard Street*, his work analysing the role of the Bank of England, was published in 1873.

Bator, Francis (1925-). Hungarian-born

00BC	1000BC	500BC	0	500AD	1000AD

Earliest forms of paper money : Tang dynasty (China) 650-800 ●

○ 753 BC Rome founded

Paper money in China leads to inflation and state bankruptcy 845 ●

● 600-501 First Persian coin with picture of ruler

Sung dynasty founded in China 960 ●

○ 490 BC Battle of Marathon : Athenians defeat Persians

Carthage destroyed by Romans. Rome becomes dominant Mediterranean power 146 BC ○

Commercial treaties between Kiev & Constantinople 907 ●

○ c.1400 BC Knossos burnt. Temple of Luxor built in Egypt

● 350-301 Jewish trading centres in Egypt and Cyrene

○ AD c.30 Jesus Christ crucified

Hadrian becomes Roman Emperor. Roman Empire reaches greatest extent 117 ○

First Arab coinage 695 ●

m Eastern Mediterranean through Europe

● 500-451 Coins used as legal tender Direct commercial relations between Egypt and Italy 973 ○

Magdeburg becomes important trade centre at the Slav frontier 804 ●

● 268 First appearance of Roman silver coin (denarius)

● 600-501 Banking business practised in Babylon Otto grants Bremen the authority to hold markets 966 ○

● 700-601 Coins in Lydia made of electrum (gold-silver alloy)

Gold treasure of the Anglo-Saxon king Ethelhere 645 ●

● 700-601 Nineveh becomes trading centre Working of silver and copper mines in the Harz, Germany 964 ●

Corinth becomes trading centre 350-301 ● ○ 44 BC Julius Caesar Murdered

Trade agreement between Rome and Carthage 348 ● "Burning water" (Petroleum) used in Japan 615 ●

Silk industry becomes state monopoly in Byzantine Empire 553 ●

First Roman coins 350-301 ● In Italy the monetary system is replaced by barter 600 ●

Cordoba becomes the seat of Arab science, learning, commerce and industry in Spain 930 ●

Venice and Genoa carry on flourishing trade between Asia and Western Europe 983 ●

○ 960 BC Solomon succeeds David, builds Yahweh temple in Jerusalem Tea tax introduced in China 793 ●

gards money as a medium of exchange only ; interest considered as unacceptable 322 ● Kiev becomes well known as trading centre 750 ●

Population explosion in China, the first large urban developments 700 ○

● 500-451 Soldiers and judges of Athens receive regular salaries

○ 214 BC Construction of Great Wall of China begins

Alexander the Great becomes King of Macedon 336 BC ○ Charlemagne becomes first Holy Roman Emperor 800 ○

---

graduate of MIT, Bator became Special Assistant for National Security to the President of the United States, a member of the senior staff of the National Security Council, and Senior Economics Adviser to the State Department. He is now Professor of Political Economy at Harvard.

His deep concern regarding insufficient US Government spending on defence, foreign aid, education, urban renewal and medical services is reflected in his major publications: *The Simple Analytics of Welfare Maximisation*, (American Economic Review, 1957) and *The Anatomy of Market Failure* (Quarterly Journal of Economics, 1958).

Bentham, Jeremy (1748-1832). British economist, philosopher, eccentric and founder of University College, London; educated at Westminster School and Queen's College, Oxford. His books, *Defence of Usury* (1787), *Principles and Morals of Legislation* (1823) and *Manual of Political Economy* (1825) all extol the classical liberal tradition of laissez-faire.

Bentham is best known for his utilitarianism, especially in his calculus of pleasure and pain.

Beveridge, William Henry, Lord Beveridge (1876-1963). British economist and Director of the London School of Economics from 1919 to 1937, Beveridge was particularly concerned about the problem of unemployment. His most important work on the subject, *Unemployment*, was published in 1931. In 1942, Beveridge prepared the report *Social Insurance and Allied Services* at the request of the Government. The Beveridge Report, as it was popularly known, set out a plan for a system of child allowances, a comprehensive health service, and full employment. The Family Allowances Act of 1945 and the National Health Service and National Insurance Acts of 1946 were based on the Beveridge Report's recommendations.

Böhm-Bawerk, Eugen von (1851-1914). Austrian economist and Professor of Economics at Vienna. His most important contribution to economic theory was his analysis of capital and interest in which he argued that people were prepared to pay interest in order to borrow, because they expected to be better off in the future and put a higher valuation on present, rather than future goods. Böhm-Bawerk said that capital bought with borrowed money would increase productivity until, in equilibrium, productivity became equated with the rate of interest. He expounded these ideas in *Capital and Interest* (1884) and *The Positive Theory of Capital* (1889).

Boulding, Kenneth E (1910-). Born in Liverpool, England, but educated partly in the US, of which he became a citizen in 1948. He has taught at Edinburgh, Colgate, Fisk, Iowa State, Ames, and the University of Michigan. He is now Professor of Economics and Director of the Program on General, Social and Economic Dynamics at the University of Colorado. For a long time Boulding has seen economics as a tool to achieve optimal efficiency in production and distribution, but believes that the present means of measuring economic welfare are at fault. Recently published work includes *Disarmament* and *World Economic Interdependence* (1967) and *The Economy of Love and Fear* (1973).

Bowley, Sir Arthur Lyon (1869-1957). British statistician and mathematical economist. Among the distinguished posts he held were those of Professor of Mathematics, Economics and Statistics at the Universities of Reading and London, and Director of the University of Oxford Institute of Statistics. His major works were *Three Studies on the National Income* with J Stamp, published in 1938, and *Wages and Income in the UK since 1860*, published in 1937.

Buchanan, James (1919-) American economist. Having served on the faculties of Florida State University, the University of Virginia, and UCLA, James Buchanan is now Director of the Center for the Study of Public Choice, which concentrates on exploring

1000AD   **1050**   **1100**   **1150**   **1200**

○ 1225 Cott◀

● 1053 Danegeld abolished

● 1189 Third Crusade launched

● 1081 Commercial treaty between Venice and Byzantium

○ 1233 Co◀

● 1000 Danegeld – general tax in England

○ 1189 First paper mill in Europe

● 1170 "Inquest of sheriffs", financia◀

○ 1066 William of Normandy conquers England, becomes king

○ 1200 60,000 merchants li◀

○ 1095 Urban II initiates First Crusade

○ 1147 Second Crusade launched

○ 1132 Henry I grants charters of corporate towns

○ 1150 Arabs in Spain manufacture paper

○ 1193 Indigo and brazilwood

● 1124 First Scottish coinage struck

● 1158 Munich becomes centre of salt trade

○ 1206 Genghis Khan becom◀

● 1054 Expansion of commercial relations between Italy and Egypt

● 1189 First silver florins minted

Mongol hordes invade Europe 1241○

○ 1215 King John sig◀

---

common ground between economics and political science. In 1962 he wrote *Calculus of Consent* with Gordon Tullock, which argues that the rational pursuit of self-interest on the part of individuals is applicable to political institutions as well as to the marketplace. In 1968, *Demand and Supply of Public Goods* was published. In this, Buchanan attempts to analyse how output decisions are reached about public goods.

Burns, Arthur (1904-). Australian born American economist. Taught at Rutgers University and at Columbia. In 1959, he became President of the American Economic Association having built a considerable reputation for his work on business cycles. He chaired the Council of Economic Advisers

under Eisenhower, and later advised Nixon in his 1960 and 1968 Presidential campaigns. After election, Nixon appointed Burns as Counselor to the President. He became Chairman of the Federal Reserve's Board of Governors in 1970, a period of great economic instability. His chairmanship was been characterised by attempts to steer a middle course between 'Monetarist' and 'Keynesian' policies.

Cantillon, Richard (1680-1734). Irish international banker. His work *Essai sur la nature du commerce en général* was published in 1755. Cantillon was one of the first writers to see the fault in the mercantilists' contention that the wealth of a country was determined by the amount of gold or money it

had. Cantillon argued that money can only be a measure of wealth while wealth itself is actually derived from production. He believed that only agriculture yielded a surplus, and to this extent he anticipated the Physiocrats. His view of 'pure rent,' and the circulation of wealth may also have influenced the Physiocrats.

Cassels, Gustav (1866-1945). Swedish economist. Professor of Political Economy at the University of Stockholm. His most important contribution to economics was an analysis of interest rates and trade cycles, dealt with in *Grundriss einer Elementaren Preislehre* (1899) and *The Nature and Necessity of Interest* (1903). His main work *Theory of Social Economy* was published in 1918.

Cassels' writing shows the influence of Alfred Marshall. He gained a considerable reputation for his contribution to the monetary policy debate during the First World War.

Chamberlin, Edward H.(1867-1967). American economist. His book *The Theory of Monopolistic Competition*, was an attempt to make economic theory more relevant to the real world. Chamberlin tried to devise a model in which elements of both competition and monopoly were present.

Clark, Colin (1905-). British economist, educated at Winchester and Oxford and Lecturer in Statistics at Cambridge from 1931 to 1937. Among his works are *The National Income, 1924-31*, published in

1932, *National Income and Outlay*, 1937, *The Conditions for Economic Progress*, 1940, and *The Economics of 1960* in 1942. During the fifties his book *Welfare and Taxation* challenged the economic rationale behind the Welfare State.

Has written many other important books and articles and has lectured in universities round the world, as well as acting as advisor to several governments.

One of his chief contributions to economic theory was his discovery of a correlation between taxation and inflation.

Clark, John Bates (1847-1938). American economist, educated at Brown University and Amherst College; later, he became a famous Professor of economics at Columbia University. He passionately

believed in the importance of economics, but was dissatisfied with the economic theory of his time. His answer to the problem was to reformulate the propositions of classical economics (*Philosophy of Wealth* [1885]). In his *Distribution of Wealth* (1899) he applied the marginal principle to production and distribution (Marginal Productivity Theory).

Clark, John Maurice (1884-1963). American economist, son of J B Clark. Educated at Amherst and Columbia where he gained his Ph.D. Lectured at Colorado College, Amherst, the University of Chicago, and Columbia where he was given the J B Clark chair created in his father's honour. Clark's work is characterised by his attempt to transform the static models of

50	1300	1350	1400	1450	1500

nufactured in Spain
○1384 Incorporation of Fishmongers' Co, London

250 Commercial and industrial boom in northern and central Italian cities
Vasco da Gama finds sea route to India 1498○

ned for the first time in Newcastle
●1345 Bankruptcy of the great Florentine banking houses of Bardi and Peruzzi

○1294 Kublai Khan, Mongol Emperor of China, dies

quiry results in strengthening the exchequer
First printing from movable type, at Gutenberg's works 1453 ○

○1274 Thomas Aquinas, Italian philosopher, dies

Ferdinand of Aragon marries Isabella of Castile, creating unified kingdom of Spain 1469 ○

○1269 First toll roads in England
○1363 Tamerlane, Mongol Conqueror, begins conquest of Asia

d work in Constantinople
○1331 First record of weaving in England
Columbus makes first voyage to New World 1492 ○

First printing from movable type in Europe 1454 ○

1253 Linen first manufactured in England
○1348 Black death sweeps through Europe

otecting commerce and industry
○1338 Hundred Years War between England and France begins

○1315 Lyons silk industry developed by Italian immigrants

The Fuggers of Augsburg begin business dealing with the Habsurgs 1473 ●

ported from India to Britain for dyeing purposes
○1378 Disputed papal election : Great Schism begins

Mocha in South-western Arabia becomes main port for coffee export 1450●

●1282 Florence is the leading European city in commerce and finance

252 Golden florins minted at Florence
Richard III reforms law, trade and tax collection 1484●

Constantinople taken by Turks : Byzantine Empire ends 1453 ●

ongol Emperor
●1360 The first francs coined in France
Columbus discovers the "New World" 1492 ○

○1280 Rebellion of the textile workers of Flanders

○1368 Ming dynasty established in China

rence
1st German pawnshop at Nuremberg 1498○

●1300 Trade fairs at Bruges, Antwerp, Lyons, Geneva

●1274 AD Thomas Aquinas philosopher about economics ; Regards interest rates as unacceptable exploiters

gna Carta
○1366 The Fuggers come as weavers to Augsburg

○ 1321 Dante, Italian poet, dies
●1414 The Medici of Florence become bankers to the papacy

---

economic theory into dynamic models which would correspond more closely to the real world. His book *Economics of Overhead Costs* took economic theory a step closer to dynamic analysis.

Introduced the 'acceleration principle.' According to this principle, investment is dependent on the rate of change of output or consumption spending.

Coase, Donald (1910-   ) British economist. Intellectual founder of the 'new institutional economics.' In 1934, he published an analysis of the British postal system in *Economica*. In 1937, a paper on the Nature of the Company was published. He went to the US in 1951 and taught at the Universities of Buffalo, Virginia, and Chicago. His most famous article – *The Problem of Social Cost* – appeared in the *Journal of Law and Economics* in 1961. The method of institutional economics which Coase has pioneered is to select institutions, examine their effect on resource allocation, and then account for their continued existence in the light of the analysis of their effect on the allocation of resources.

Cournot, Antoine Augustin (1801-1877). French mathematician and economist. Probably the first economist to be competent in both sciences. Professor of Mathematics at the University of Lyons before becoming Rector of Dijon Academy. His most important writings are *Recherches sur les principes*

mathematiques de la theorie des richesses (1838) and *Revue sommaire des doctrines economiques* (1863). Much of this work was a restatement of previously postulated economic relationships in a mathematical form. However, he was the first economist to have a theory of monopoly, and he made important contributions to duopoly and oligopoly theory.

Dobb, Maurice H. (1900-   ). British economist. Educated at Charterhouse and Cambridge. Taught at Cambridge, Emeritus Reader in Economics and a Fellow of Trinity College. His writing shows a clear Marxist influence. In *Capitalist Enterprise and Social Progress*, published in 1925, Dobb developed the relationship between 'pure' profit and economic

uncertainty. Other important books were *Russian Economic Development since the Revolution* (1928), *An Essay on Economic Growth and Planning* (1960), and *Welfare Economics and the Economics of Socialism* (1969). Dobb has also worked closely with Straffa over the interpretation of Ricardo's writings.

Douglas, Paul (1892-1976) American economist. His early publications include *Theory of Wages* (1934), *Real Wages in the US* (1930), and *American in the Market Place* (1952).

In his statistical work, he tested Clark's marginal productivity theory of distribution. Best remembered for the development of the Cobb-Douglas production function with Charles E Cobb.

Duesenberry, James (1920-   ). American

economist. Professor of Economics at Harvard since 1957. His most important books are *Income, saving and the Theory of Consumer Behaviour* (1949), and *Money and Credit, Impact and Control* (1964), Duesenberry's *Relative Income Hypothesis* explained people's fixed expenditure patterns in terms of status.

Dupuit, Arsene Jules Etienne Juvenal (1804-1866). French civil engineer. His writings on the pricing policy for public services, such as *De la mésure de l'utilité des travaux publics* (1844) and *De l'influence des péages sur l'utilité des voies de communication* (1849). Laid the foundation for the development of the concepts of consumers' and producers' surplus.

Edgeworth, Francis Ysidro (1845-1926). British economist, who held the Chair of Political Economy at Oxford between 1891 and 1922. His most important published writings were *Mathematical Psychics* (1881), *Theory of Monoply* (1897), *Theory of Distribution* (1904), and *Papers relating to Political Economy* (1925). Edited the *Economic Journal* from 1891 to 1926.

Edgeworth developed indifference curve analysis and is famous for the 'Edgeworth Box diagram.'

Fisher, Irving (1867-1967). American economist. Professor of Political Economy at Yale University from 1898 to 1935. Fisher's most important work in economics was *The Making of Index Number*, published in

1500   **1510**   **1520**   **1530**   **1540**

○1513 Balboa discovers Pacific Ocean   ○1533 Ivan IV ("the Terrible") becomes Tsar of Russ

○ 1517 Martin Luther formulates 95 Theses : Protestant Reformation begins

○ 1542 Portuguese are fi

● 1500-1001 Extensive export and import trade in Egypt   ○1521 Hernando Cortez conquers Aztecs, becomes ruler of Mexico

● 1530 Antwerp exchange founded

● 1500-1501 Phonecians import tin from mines in England   ○1545 Coun

○1519 Magellan begins first circumnavigation of world. Leonardo da Vinci, Italian artist, philosoph

○1504 Postal service between Vienna and Brussels extended to Madrid   ○1532 Francisco Pizarro conquers Incas in Peru

● 1512 Public resistance to trading monopolies in Germany

● 1500 Silver guilders introduced in Germany (remain in use in Austria till 1892)

● 1532 Discoveries of gold and silver in South America

○ 1500 First regular postal service between Vienna and Brussels

○1529 Turks besiege Vienna   ●   1542 Heavy taxes

● 1515 First nationalized factories (weapons, tapestries) open in France

○ 1520 Suleiman the Magnificent becomes Sultan of Turkey : Ottoman power reaches its heigh

●   1540 Antwerp becomes

○1524 Peasants' War in Germany

○ 1534 Henry VIII becomes supreme head of Engli

● 1535 Beginning of the London Exchange

○1526 Battle of Mohacs : Turks, under Suleiman, defeat Hungarians

---

1922, in which he developed the theory of index numbers and established conditions that an index should satisfy. Fisher also introduced the famous 'quantity of money' equation. His other important economic writings were *Mathematical Investigations in the Theory of Value and Prices* (1892) *Nature of Capital and Income* (1906), *Rate of Interest* (1907), *Purchasing Power of Money* (1911) and *Theory of Interest* (1930).

Friedman, Milton (1912-   ) American economist. Professor of Economics at the University of Chicago and spokesman of the 'Chicago School' which believes in a free market economy. Friedman is the most influential exponent of the monetarist school of economic thought. The monetarists maintain that the economic cycle is primarily determined by the money supply and the interest rate. The impact of fiscal policy is confined to its effect on the supply of money. His best-known book, *A Monetary History of the United States, 1867-1960* (1963), written with Anna Schwartz, traces changes in the supply of money and assesses the impact of these changes on economic events. In 1976, Friedman won the Nobel Memorial Prize in economics. He has written many books, pamphlets and articles expounding his ideas. He frequently acts as advisor to the US Government on matters of economic policy. Today more and more countries adopt monetarist policies.

Frisch, Ragner A K (1895-1973). Norwegian economist and Professor of Economics and Statistics at Oslo University. In 1969, Frisch shared the Nobel Prize for Economics with the Dutchman Jan Tinbengen. His most important work was the paper *Propogation and Impulse Problems* in which he developed the mathematical potential of J M Clark's acceleration principle. The terms 'isoquant' and 'macro-dynamics orginates from Frisch.

Galbraith, John Kenneth (1908-   ). Canadian economist who moved to the United States where he taught at Harvard. Galbraith's books are often to be found in the best-seller lists. His most important works are *A Theory of Price Control* (1952), *American Capitalism* (1952), *The Affluent Society* (1958), *The New Industrial State* (1967) and *Economics and the Public Purpose* (1974). Galbraith is characterised by his critical attitude towards conventional economics. He believes that many assumptions upon which economists reason are no more than 'conventional wisdom.' He challenges the assumptions that firms are 'profit maximising' and that demand and supply determine the allocation of resources. Galbraith believes that free enterprise tends to lead to monopoly, that economic growth does not imply growth in the quality of life, and that decision-making over resource allocation is primarily in the hands of the 'technostructure' managers and professionals in the big corporations and Government departments.

George, Henry (1839-97). American economist and politician. Famous for his campaign for a single tax on the land values derived from rent. He believed that rents were received by landlords at the expense of workers and business interests, and that this caused poverty and reduced the level of investment in the economy, repressing potential economic progress. His most important work was *Progress and Poverty* (1879). Was a newspaper editor in California and stood for election as Mayor of New York for the 'single tax' party.

50   1560   1570   1580   1590   1600

In Marseilles first chamber of commerce founded 1599 ●

○ 1564 Shakespeare, English dramatist and poet, born. Michelangelo, Italian artist, dies

ropeans in Japan

○1572 Huguenots massacred on St Bartholomew's Day, France

Trent : Catholic Counter Reformation begins

○1571 Battle of Lepanto : Christian league defeats Turks

d engineer, dies

Coal mining begins in the Ruhr.1590 ○

● 1558 Hamburg Exchange founded

○ 1588 English defeat Spanish Armada

○1562 First religious war in France : Huguenots massacred at Vassy

● 1562 Milled coins introduced in England

inks in Bavaria

Edict of Nantes ends French religious wars 1594 ○

● 1558 Sir Thomas Gresham asserts that bad money drives out good

portant commercial city

In Marseilles first chamber of commerce founded 1599 ●

Windmills used in Holland to drive mechanical saws 1592 ○

urch

○1582 Pope Gregory XIII introduces Gregorian Calendar

● 1565 Sir Thomas Gresham founds the Royal Exchange, London

Union of Utrecht organizes resistance to Spain in Netherlands 1579 ○

Gresham, Sir Thomas
(1519-79) English
merchant and
financier, Financial
Adviser to Queen
Elizabeth I. In 1566-68
he devoted some of
his wealth to founding
the Royal Exchange.
He is still remembered
for Gresham's Law,
the statement that,
"Bad money drives
out good."

**Hansen, Alvin
Harvey** (1887-)
American economist.
Taught at the
University of
Minnesota from 1919
to 1937 and at Harvard
from 1937-1960. He
worked for the
Economic State
Department in
Washington from
1934-35, and was
special adviser to the
Federal Reserve
System between 1940
and 1945.

His published work
includes *Cycles of
Prosperity and
Depression* (1921),
Business Cycle Theory
(1927), *Fiscal Policy
and Business Cycles*
(1941), *America's Role
in the World Economy*
(1945), *Monetary
Theory and Fiscal
Policy* (1949), *Business
Cycles and National
Income* (1951), *A
Guide to Keynes*
(1953), *The American
Economy* (1957),
*Economic Issues of the
1960s* (1965), *The
Dollar and the Inter-
national Monetary
System* (1965).

Developed the
secular stagnation
hypothesis which
suggested that interest
rates could in times of
severe depression not
fall low enough to
induce investment.

**Harrod, Sir Roy
Forbes** (1900-1978)
British economist,
educated at New
College, Oxford.

Taught at Christ
Church, Oxford, from
1922 to 1952. Harrod
served under Lord
Charwell and in the
Prime Minister's office
between 1940 and
1942. Was statistical
adviser to the
Admiralty between
1942 and 1945. One of
his most important
works is *Essay in
Dynamic Theory*
(1939) in which he
synthesized the
accelerator and multi-
plier principles in a
mathematical
framework. Sir Roy is
most famous for his
contribution to the
'Harrod-Domar
Growth Model.'

**Hayek, Friedrich
August von** (1899-
) Austrian
economist. Came to
Britain in 1931,
teaching at the
London School of
Economics until 1950.
Moved to the
University of Chicago,
becoming Professor of
Social and Moral
Science. Currently
Professor Emeritus at
the University of
Freiburg in Germany.
In 1974, he won the
Nobel Prize for
Economics.

His most important
work is *The Road to
Serfdom* (1944) in
which he argues that
the trend towards
economic planning
and strong central
government could
lead to a curtailment
of liberty. Other
important writings are
*Monetary Theory and
the Trade Cycle*
(1929), *Prices and
Production* (1931),
*Profits, Interest,
Investment* (1939), *The
Pure Theory of Capital*
(1941), *Individualism
and Economic Order*
(1948), *The Constitu-
tion of Liberty* (1961),
and *Studies in
Philosophy, Politics
and Economics* (1967).
Von Hayek advocates
the minimum of
Government interven-
tion in the economic
process.

**Heller, Walter
Wolfgang** (1915-)
American economist.
Served as a fiscal
economist for the
Treasury, as director
and chairman of the
National Bureau of
Economic Research,
and as a Presidential
adviser. He has been a
consultant to the
Minnesota Depart-
ment of Taxation, to
the Governor of
Minnesota, and to the
United Nations
Commission on
Economic Develop-
ment. Heller's most
important books are
*Monetary vs. Fiscal
Policy* (1968), written
in conjunction with
Milton Friedman,
*Revenue Sharing and
the City* (1966), written
with Richard Ruggles,
and *New Dimensions
of Political Economy*
(1966).

The Glossaries

Hicks, Sir John Richard (1904-   ) British economist, educated at Balliol, Oxford. He taught at the University of Manchester, the London School of Economics, and at Oxford. His most important book is *Value and Capital* (1939), in which he investigated the general equilibrium proceeding from the subjective theory of value.

Other important works are *The Theory of Wages* (1932), *A Contribution to the Theory of the Trade Cycle* (1950), *A Remission of Demand Theory* (1956). In 1972 Sir John shared the Nobel Prize for Economics with the American Kenneth J Arrow for their pioneering contributions to general economic equilibrium theory.

Hotelling, Harold

(1895-   ) American economist. Professor of Economics at Columbia University, and Professor of Mathematical Statistics at the University of North Carolina. Hotelling established the case for marginal cost-pricing in public utilities in his article *The General Welfare in Relation to Problems of Taxation and of Railway and Utility Rates* published in 1938 in the journal *Econometrica*.

Hume, David (1711-76) Scottish philosopher, interested in economics. His *Political Discourses* (1752) contained several chapters devoted to economic analysis, the best known being his essay *Of Money*.

Hume dismissed mercantilist fears of free trade, pointing out that money movements respond

to rises and falls in prices which prevent permanent balance of payments surpluses or deficits. Hume's views on paper money anticipated the quantity theory of money.

Jevons, William Stanley (1835-1882) British natural scientist turned economist, educated at University College, London. Taught at Manchester and London. Wrote many books and papers, but by far the most important is his *Theory of Political Economy* (1871). Generally given credit for initiating the 'Marginal Revolution' (the Marginal utility theory). Also one of the founders of Econometrics.

Johnson, Harry Gordon (1923-1977) Canadian economist and influential academic. Had the unusual distinction of

being Professor of Economics at two major universities simultaneously, since from 1966 to 1974 he taught at both the London School of Economics and the University of Chicago. A prolific writer of books and articles. Johnson specialized in the areas of monetary theory, growth and international trade.

It is probably in this latter area that his theoretical writings have had their major policy impact. A strong supporter of free trade, he argued the case for freely floating exchange rates in an era of fixed exchange rates.

Kaldor, Nicholas (1908-   ) Hungarian-born economist, spent all his adult life in Britain. He graduated from the London School of Economics in 1930 and later lectured there until being

appointed to the Economics Commission for Europe in 1947. In 1952, he went to Cambridge where, in 1966, was appointed Professor of Economics. He is an established academic economist who has published major theoretical works, particularly in the field of economic growth. Kaldor is best known for his role as economic adviser to the Wilson Governments in the sixties.

Kantorovich, Leonid V (1912-   ) Russian mathematician and

economist. As a young professor of mathematics he developed what is now known as linear programming. In 1939 he published *Mathematical Methods for the Organization and Planning of Production*, the first paper in this field. Kantorovich's early applications of this theory to such basic economic problems as maximizing output subject to input constraints were not taken seriously in Stalin's Russia. After Stalin, the use of mathematics to solve economic problems gained approval, and Kantorovich was elected to membership of the Soviet Academy of Science and was awarded the Lenin Prize. In 1975, Kantorovich and Tjalling C Coopmans, of Yale University, shared the Nobel

50	1660	1670	1680	1690	1700

manufactured in Manchester   Peter I ("the Great") becomes Tsar of Russia 1696 ○

x introduced in England   ○1673   Moliere, French dramatist, dies

●1658   Swedish financier Johann Palmstruck devises 1st bank note, issued by the Swedish state bank

49   Free enterprise in England receives state support   ●   1681   First cheques in England

nasty established in China

○1661   Mazarin dies : Louis XIV begins rule in France   Bank of England founded 1694 ●

●1685   All Chinese ports opened to foreign Trade

○1652   Dutch colony founded at Cape of Good Hope, South Africa

W. Petty: *Political Arithmetic* 1691 ●

●   1664   Paper money as we know it issued in Britain

ace of Westphalia ends Thirty Years War   ○1672   William of Orange leads Dutch against French invaders

●   1661   First gold guinea pieces coined in England

649   Charles I of England tried and executed   Salt tax doubled in England   1694 ●

○1664   English take New York from Dutch

"Glorious Revolution" in England 1688○

○1653   Cromwell becomes Lord Protector of England   National Debt begins in England 1693 ●

gins. Cardinal Mazarin succeeds Richelieu   First bank notes from Bank of England 1695 ●

ttle of Lutzen   ○1669   Rembrandt, Dutch artist, dies

●1662   Last silver pennies minted in London

anish at Rocroiz   William (of Orange) and Mary crowned 1689 ●

of Austria and murdered

●1661   First paper money in Europe (Stockholm)

●1668   Samuel Pepys makes a payment to his father, using a banknote

illiam of Brandenburg, defeats Swedes. Rise of Prussian military power. 1675 ○   ○   1683   Turks besiege Vienna but are repulsed

First Canadian paper money ('playing card' notes) 1685 ●

Prize for economics. The citation for Kantorovich said he 'applied the analytical technique of linear programming to demonstrate how economic planning in his country could be improved.'

Keynes, John Maynard (1883-1946) British economist who revolutionized economic thought. The son of a Cambridge don, Keynes was educated at Eton and Cambridge where his first degree was in mathematics.

Encouraged by Alfred Marshall, he turned to the study of economics and in 1908, after briefly working as a Civil Servant, and was offered a lectureship in economics at Cambridge. Keynes' major work, the *General Theory of Employment, Interest and Money* was published in 1936. In this, he stressed the possibility of less than full employment equilibrium (the dominant feature of the thirties) and the need for government intervention. The *General Theory* confirmed Keynes as the outstanding economist of his generation and he has greatly influenced economists and economic policy ever since. At the 1944 Bretton Woods Conference, Keynes played a leading role in the creation of the International Monetary Fund. Apart

from numerous economic achievements, Keynes was a highly success-ful investor on the Stock Exchange on behalf of both himself, and his college. He was also a member of the literary-artistic Bloomsbury Set. His passion for the arts was reflected in his marriage, in 1925, to the Russian ballerina Lydia Lopokovia.

Kondratieff, N D (1892-) Russian economist who studied fluctuations in economic activity. His major contribution was the identification of long cycles of economic activity lasting some fifty to sixty years. These cycles, or 'long waves' as Schumpeter refers to them, are called 'Kondratieff Cycles.' The cycle begins with a long general upswing in the economy followed by a similar long decline.

The first Industrial Revolution, 1780-1840, encompasses one such cycle, as do the periods 1840-1890, and 1890-1950. Arrested and charged with sedition, Kondratieff was deported to Siberia in 1930 and has not been heard of since.

Koopmans, Tjalling C (1910-) Dutch-born economist and econometrician who became a naturalized American in 1946. Koopman studied mathematics and physics at the University of Utrecht

before gaining an economics doctorate from Leiden in 1936. In 1940 he went to Princeton University in America as a researcher. During the war, together with the mathematician George Dantzig, he developed the theory of linear porgramm-ing. At the same time, Kantorovich in Russia was independently formulating the same theory. In 1975 Koopmans and Kantorovich shared the Nobel Prize for Economics for their contributions to the theory of optimum allocation of resources.' Koopmans has in particular helped to develop the discipline of econometrics. Most of his work has been in this area where economic theory, mathematics and statistics are combined together to permit understanding of the quantitative

relationships between economic variables.

Kuznets, Simon S (1901-) Russian-born economist who emigrated to America in 1922. Kuznets attended Columbia University where, in 1926, he was awarded his doctorate. After working in various capacities as a govern-ment economist, he was appointed Professor of Economics first at Pennsylvania, then to John Hopkins and, finally in 1960, to Harvard, where he

1700   1710   1720   1730   1740

○ 1701 War of Spanish succession begins   ● 1717 Value of English golden guinea fixed at 21 shillings

                ○ 1739 Persian Army takes Delhi

        ○ 1710 Porcelain factory at Meissen (Saxony) founded   ○ 1740 Frederick II ("the Great"

       ● 1716 First budget in Russia   ○ 1745 Jacobit

      ○ 1715 Louis XIV dies

       ● 1718 First bank notes in England

            ● 1729 B. de Mandeville: The Fable of the Bees or Private Vices, Pu

     ○ 1713 Peace of Utrecht ends War of Spanish Succession

○ 1700 Great Northern War between Sweden, Denmark and Russia begins

       ● 1720 South Sea Bubble (speculation craze) bursts

       ● 1724 Paris Bourse opens

    ● 1716 First provincial banks in England

held the chair until retiring in 1971. In that year he was awarded the Nobel Prize for Economics. Kuznets emphasised the empirical nature of economic research, systemized national income accounting and has been credited with coining the term and the theory of Gross National Product. His Nobel Prize citation praised him for "the empirically founded interpretation of economic growth which has led to new and deepened insight into the economic and social structure and process of development."

Lange, Oscar (1904-1965) Polish economist, econometrician and politician. Studied in the US, became a naturalized American and taught at the universities of Michigan, Stanford and Chicago. His 1937 Review of Economic Studies article *On the Economic Theory of Socialism* established his academic reputation. He carried out path-finding work in the new discipline of econometrics and was an early advocate of Keynesianism in *Price Flexibility and Full Employment* (1944). He renounced his American citizenship in 1945 to become Polish Ambassador in Washington. In 1947 he returned to Poland to serve as an economist, eventually becoming chairman of the Economic Council. His later work concerned the use of computers and cybernetics to aid economic policy and decision making.

Lenin, Nikolai or Vladimir Illich Ulyanov (1870-1924) Russian revolutionary and statesman who constructed the Soviet Communist state. His pamphlet *What is to be Done?* published in 1902, has been described as the true origin of modern communism. The major work, *Imperialism, the Highest Stage of Capitalism*, completed in 1916, a year before the revolution, sought to explain why certain Marxist prophecies had not taken place. In this book Lenin emphasised the role of financial monopolies and the need for capitalists to maintain their profits by forever conquering new markets. Imperialist wars would only end when the capitalist system ended. Furthermore, industrialized workers had not developed their proper class consciousness and feeling of oppression because the capitalists shared some of the profits from these new markets (the colonies) with them.

Leontief, Wassily (1906-) Russina-born economist, and econometrician, first taught in Germany, then in 1931, joined economist department at Harvard University where he has remained ever since. He was appointed Professor in 1946. His greatest contribution to economic theory is the formulation of input-output models for which he was awarded the Nobel Prize in 1973. These show in matrix form the relationships between different sectors and industries in an economy. With the advent of high-speed computers, input-output tables have grown in size and sophistication. Leontief's book *The Structure of the American Economy 1919-1929*, published in 1941, is a direct descendant of Quesnay's *Tableau Économique*.

Lerner, Abba P (1903-) Russian-born American professor of economics. Educated at the London School of Economics, he taught successively at Roosevelt, Michigan State and, from 1965, California Universities. His early work centred on the nature of monopoly. In his 1933 *Review of Economic Studies* article *The Concept of Monoply Power* Lerner introduced a quantitative measurement of the degree of monopoly. His later work is mainly in the field of welfare economics as in *The Economics of Control* (1944).

List, Friedrich (1789-1846) German economist. After holding a chair in economics at the University of Türingen, fled to America in 1825 and became involved in mining and railways. Subsequently developed views on economic protectionism for underdeveloped economies.

Malthus, Thomas Robert (1766-1834) English clergyman

50	1760	1770	1780	1790	1800

○ 1755 Lisbon Earthquake : 30,000 killed

1750 Thomas Gray, English poet, writes "Elegy"   France becomes a republic 1792 ○

d destroys Mogul power in India   ○ 1763 Peace of Paris ends Seven Years War. Britain gains colonial empire in Canada and India

comes king of Prussia   ○ 1762 Catherine II ("the Great") becomes Empress of Russia   ● 1787 J. Bentham: *Defence of Usury*

○ 1756 Seven Years War begins   Steamboat launched on the Delaware River USA 1787 ●

bellion defeated in Britain   ○ 1764 James Hargreaves invents the spinning jenny

○ 1764 James Watt invents a condenser which leads to his construction of a steam engine

○ 1759 British capture Quebec. First modern canal (Liverpool-Leeds) constructed in England.   ○ 1790 First patent law in USA

● 1753 Vienna stock exchange founded

efits   Combinations Act : British workers are not allowed to combine 1799 ●

● 1751 F. Galiani: *Della Moneta*   ○ 1764 J. Winckelman: *History of Ancient Art*

● 1776 A. Smith: *Wealth of Nations*

● 1752 D. Hume: *Political Discourses*   ● 1765 Frederick the Great founds the Bank of Prussia   ● 1787 Dollar currency introduced in the USA

● 1766 Anne Robert Jaques Turgot: *Reflections sur la Formation et la Distribution des Richesses*

1758 F. Quesnay: *Tableau Economique*   Louis XVI guillotined : Britain goes to war against France 1793 ○

Eli Whitney invents the cotton gin in US which leads to to the rapid growth of cotton export from the southern states of N America 1793 ○

● 1773 Americans protest against tea duty : "Boston Tea-party"

Bank of North America established in Philadelphia USA 1782 ●

French Revolution begins : Bastille stormed 1789 ○

Nicolas Cugnot's steam road carriage 1769 ○○ 1770 James Cook lands in Botany Bay, NSW

● 1755 R. Cantillon: *Essai sur la Nature du Commerce en Général*   ○ 1775 Skirmish at Lexington begins American War of Independence

Peace of Versailles : Britain recognizes American Independence 1783 ○

● 1770 Begining of the Industrial Revolution

First clearing house in England (Lombard Street, London) 1775 ●   ○ 1776 American Declaration of Independence

○ 1769 Richard Arkwright's spinning machine

Cable making machine invented 1792 ○

First steam rolling mill in England 1790 ○

and author. Ever since Malthus, economics has been referred to as the 'dismal science.' The Malthusian argument that gave rise to unhappy label was propounded in *An Essay on the Principle of Population* published in 1798. In this, he argues that population unchecked grows in a geometric progression while the means of subsistence increases only at an arithmetic rate. The result is inevitable poverty. Subsidies for the poor only increase the population and hence their misery. The only long term escape from deprivation for the masses is later marriage and fewer children.

Mandeville, Bernard de (1670-1733) Born in Holland, Mandeville worked in London as a doctor. He is remembered for his satirical poem *The Fable of the Bees: or Private Vices,* *Public Benefits* originally published under a different title in 1705. Mandeville points out that private greed and the pursuit of luxury results in general good whereas virtue and a sober life has dreadful results. Adam Smith did not approve of the '*Fable*.'

Marshall, Alfred (1842-1924) Influential English academic economist. After a mathematical training at Cambridge, Marshall turned to economics and, from 1885 to 1908 when he retired, was Professor of Political Ecomomy at his old university. His chief work is the classic *Principles of Economics* published in 1890, and still a standard textbook. Marshall used his mathematical back-ground to refine micro-economics; he clarified the concepts of value, utility and consumers surplus and introduced the now widely used con-cept of elasticity. A giant in the develop-ment of modern economic theory in his own right, Marshall also encouraged Keynes to study the subject.

Marx, Karl (1818-1883) German philosopher economist and father of communism, Marx was awarded his doctorate by the University of Jena in 1841. His political activites entailed a nomadic existence on the Continent of Europe until, in 1849, he settled in London where he remained for the rest of his life. The *Communist Manifesto*, written with his friend Engeis in 1848, summarizes his social and political philosophies. After years of scholarly research, much of it in the British Museum Reading Room, the first volume of *Das Kapital* was published in 1867. Engels edited the further two volumes which were issued posthumously in 1885 and 1894. In this mammoth work Marx propounds his economic inter-pretation of history and the theory of class struggle. Capitalism is described as simply a form of social order that contains its own inherent contradic-tions. The labour theory of value, the exploitaition and alienation of the worker, a falling rate of profit ensure an inevitable crisis, leading to revolution and eventually to the socialist state.

McNamara, Robert S (1916-   ) American businessman and public servant. McNamara studied at the universities of Calfornia and Harvard, later becoming Associate Professor of Business Administration at Harvard from 1940 to 1943. After a dis-tinguished business career, he served as US Secretary of Defence for seven years from 1961. In April 1968, he was appointed President of the World Bank.

Meade, James Edward (1907-   ) British economist. Educated at Oxford and Cambridge, Meade served as chief economist at the League of Nations from 1938 to 1940. During and after the war he held high posts in Government service. He has taught at London and Oxford and was Professor of Political Economy at Cambridge from 1957-1968. Professor Meade's greatest con-tribution has been to the theory of inter-national trade. For his

The Glossaries

1800   1810   1820   1830   1840

○ 1802 *Charlotte Dundas*, first practical steamship, built   ○ 1830 Revolutions in France and Belgium   ○ 18

● 1813 Last gold guinea coins issued in England

● 1801 Bank of France founded   ● 1813 East India Company's trade monopoly in India abolished, but its monopoly in China continues   ● 18

● 1821 London Cooperative Society founded   ○ 1838 Anti-corn law league establish

○ 1800 Alessandro Volta invents electricity   ○ 1814 George Stephenson constructs the first effective steam locomotive   ● 1839 Charles Goodyear vulcanis

○ 1815 Corn law passed in England   ● 1833 End of East India Company's monopoly of Chi

● 1819 Florida purchased by USA from Spain

● 1816 Protective tariff in USA   ○ 1830 Steam cars in the streets of London

● 1828 Tariff of Abominations passed by US congress, curtailing impo

● 1803 Louisiana Purchase : US buys large tract of land from France   ● 1837 Financial and economic panic

● 1817 D. Ricardo: *Principles of Political Economy and Taxation*   ○ 1846 Aboliti

● 1805 Break between Britain and USA over trade   ○ 1830 Railway line Manchester–Liverpool, England

○ 1810 Krupp works open at Essen (Germany)   ○ 1836 Boers make Great Trek in South Afri

● 1820 Rich deposits of platinum discovered in the Russian Urals   ● 1843 Export

○ 1805 Battle of Trafalgar : Nelson destroys French and Spanish navies   ○ 1829 Greece secures independence from Turkey   ○ 18

● 1807 Slave trade abolished in British Empire   ● 1825 Rapid growth of trade unions in Britain   ○ 1840 Penny postage establish

● 1811 Austria bankrupt   ○ 1820 First iron steamship launched   ○ 1833 Prussia establishes Zollverein (Customs Union

● 1807 US embargo against Britain and France   ● 1825 Spanish colonies in Latin America gain independence   ● 1847 Go

○ 1812 Napoleon invades and retreats from Russia   ○ 1838 N. W. Senior: *Outline of t*

● 1816 Economic crisis caused large scale emigration from England to Canada and USA   ○ 1845–9 Iri

○ 1811 "Luddites" destroy industrial machines in North England   ● 1843 First iss

○ 1812 Blenkinson's railway locomotive hauls coal waggons at a colliery near Leeds, England

○ 1814 Allies invade France : Napoleon abdicates   ○ 1840 2,816 miles of railro

● 1803 J. B. Say: *Traite d'Economie Politique* (develops his 'law of markets' which says that there can be no overproduction of goods)   ● 1844 Ba

○ 1815 Napoleon returns from exile, defeated at Waterloo   ● 1841 F. List: *National Syste*

● 1837 First private banks in South Afri

---

pioneering work in this area he shared the 1977 Nobel Prize with the Swedish Professor Bertil Ohlin. Meade's best known publication is The Theory of International Economic Policy published in two volumes in 1951 and 1955; others include *Planning and the Price Mechanism* (1948) and *The Structure and Reform of Direct Taxation* (1977).

Menger, Carl (1840-1921) Founder of the Austrian School and Professor of Economics at Vienna from 1873-1903. Menger's work was concerned with methodology, monetary theory and the theory of value. It is for the last of these that he is principally famous. One of the first marginal utility theorists, along with Jevons and Walras, Menger has greatly

influenced the development of economic science. In his book *Grunsätze der Volkswirtschaftslehre*, published in 1871, he analyses the basic problem of human wants and their satisfaction. His solution uses the concept of subjective value and marginal analysis.

Mill, John Stuart (1806-1873) English economist, philosopher and social

reformer. The son of the intellectual James Mill, and friend and disciple of Ricardo, John Stuart Mill was extraordinarily erudite. Having commenced his mastery of Greek at the age of three, he turned to Latin, mathematics, logic and economics. Having reached man's estate, he became a Member of Parliament and wrote prolifically on philosophy, logic and politics as well as economics. In his classic work *On Liberty* (1859), he states his philosophy of the supremacy of individual liberty. His major economic work *Principles of Political Economy* (1848) rapidly became the leading text for the study of the subject. The last of the great classical economists, Mill consistently emphasised policy recommendations arising from his analysis.

Mises, Ludwig von (1881-1973) Austrian-born economist. Taught at the University of Vienna until the Nazis came to power. He became a naturalized US citizen in 1946 and taught at New York University from 1945 until his retirement in 1969. Mises did some important early work in monetary theory, but is best known for his criticism of socialist planning and his hostile attitude to government intervention in the economy.

His greatest work, *Human Action* published in 1949, covers the entire spectrum of economics.

Mitchell, Wesley Clair (1874-1948) American economist. Educated at the University of Chicago, where he was influenced by Veblen, he later taught at Chicago, Calfornia and Columbia universities. He was one of the first researchers to use statistical techniques in the investigation of economic phenomena, in particular the determination of the level of business activity. His researches gave an impetus to quantitative work in many branches of economics. His first important publication was *Business Cycles* (1913) and this field continued to be his primary interest. *Measuring Business*

Cycles written with A F Burns, was published in 1946.

Morgenstern, Oskar (1902-) Austrian-born economist. Morgenstern first studied and then taught at the University of Vienna. In 1938 he left Austria and went to Princeton University where he joined the mathematician John von Neumann. Together, they wrote the brilliantly original *Theory of Games and Economic Behaviour* (1947).

Mun, Thomas (1571-1641) English merchant and writer on economics. Director of the East India Company whose trading activities he defended in his book *A Discourse of Trade from England into the East Indies* (1621). In this early explanation of the gains from international trade he

50   1860   1870   1880   1890   1900

O 1870   Franco-Prussian War begins : Paris besieged. Germany unified

volutions in France, Germany, Italy and Central Europe   O1869   Suez Canal opened   K. Wicksell: *Geldzins und Guterpreise* 1898 ●

. Mill: *Principles of Political Economy*   ● 1867   K. Marx: *Das Kapital, Volume I*   J. B. Clark: *Distribution of Wealth* 1899 ●

Manchester, England   O 1857   Indian mutiny against British rule : siege of Delhi   O1878   Karl Benz builds motorized tricycles

ber   ● 1856   Bessemer invents process for large-scale production of steel   O 1889   London dock strike

de   O 1855   First iron Cunard steamer crosses Atlantic   ● 1882   First meeting of London chamber of Commerce

850   Californian and Australian gold discoveries   ● 1874   M. L. Walras: *Elements d'Economie Politique*

1851   Great Exhibition in Hyde Park, London   ●1871   Germany adopts gold standard   ● 1882   Bank of Japan founded

● 1854   Introduction of the florin in UK   ●1873   Germany adopts the mark as unit of currency   ● 1890   Sherman Act

merica (inflated land values, wildcat banking, paper speculation) ●1873   Economic crises in Europe, US and Australia

corn laws in Britain   O 1859   Darwin's *Origin of Species* published   ● 1875   Reichsbank founded in Germany

O   1854   Crimean War begins   O1865   American Civil War ends. Lincoln assassinated . Marconi invents wireless telegraphy 1895 O

ray from British rule   O1860   Italy unified   ●1873   US adopts the gold standard   ●1885   Gold discovered in Transvaal, South Africa

chinery from England legalised O   1861   American Civil War begins   O   1876   Protection for patents in Germany

Marx and F. Engels:*The Communist Manifesto* ●1866   Black Friday on London Stock Exchange   ●1885   American Economic Association formed

Great Britain   ●1861   US government issues paper money   O 1876   A. G. Bell patents the telephone

● 1864   Imperial Government (China) resurrects paper money   ● 1882   Bills of Exchange Act

coveries in California lead to first gold rush   London's first telephone exchange 1879O   ●1884   E. V. Bohm-Bawerk: *Capital and Interest*

● 1857   Financial and economic crisis in Europe, caused by speculation in US railroad shares

ence of Political Economy   T. A. Eddison invents the phonograph 1876O   ● 1879   H. George: *Progress and Poverty*

mine   W. S. Jevons: *Theory of Political Economy* 1871●   O1880   Canned fruits and meats appear in English stores

the London weekly financial paper The Economist   African and Alaskan gold discoveries 1890 ●

A. Marshall: *Principles of Economics* (in which he successfully defines micro-economic theory) 1890 ●

peration in US ; 1,331 miles in England   O 1876   Bell invents telephone   Imperial Bank of China founded 1897 ●

arter Act, England   First oil well sunk in Baku, USSR 1873 O   O 1877   Frozen meat shipped from Argentina to Europe

Political Economy   First issue of the Financial Times, England 1888 ●

1851   Great Exhibition in Hyde Park, London   Spanish-American War begins and ends : Spanish code Cuba 1898   O

---

justified the company's export of gold from Britain by claiming that the overall effect of its actions was to add to the wealth of the country. Mun's book *England's Treasure by Forraign Trade* published after his death, is a clear statement of mercantilist thinking.

Musgrave, Richard Abel (1910-) German-born economist, who emigrated to the US before the Second World War. Educated at Heidelberg and Harvard, Professor Musgrave has served as a consultant for several major organisations including the Federal Reserve, and has taught at Michigan, Princeton and Harvard universities. He has been an influential figure in the area of taxation and public finance. Two important texts

reflecting these interests are *The Theory of Public Finance* (1959) and *Public Finance in Theory and Practice* (1973).

Myrdal, Karl Gunnar (1898-) Swedish economist and social scientist. Myrdal was awarded his doctorate in 1927 from Stockholm University, won a Rockefeller scholarship to the US, and was Professor at Stockholm from 1935 to 1950 and again from 1960. He has worked for the Swedish

government, the United Nations and served as Minister of Trade and Commerce. Myrdal shared, with von Hayek, the 1947 Nobel Prize. The citation stressed his work on 'the interdependence of economic, social and institutional phenomena.' His publications range from *An American Dilemma – the Negro Problem and Modern Democracy* (1944) to *Economic Theory and Under-developed Regions* (1957).

Ohlin, Bertil (1889-) Swedish economist and politician. A brilliant student, Ohlin received his doctorate from Stockholm University in 1919 and was appointed Professor at Copenhagen when only twenty-five. From 1944 until 1967 he led the Swedish Liberal Party. Ohlin

shared the 1977 Nobel Prize with James Meade for 'pathbreaking contributions to the theory of international trade and international capital movements.' His classic work is *Interregional and International Trade* (1933). He is now Emeritus Professor of Economics at Stockholm.

Okun, Arthur (1928-) American economist. Okun taught at Yale University before moving to Washington in 1961. He acted in

various capacities to successive administrations, becoming chairman of the President's Council of Economic Advisers in 1968. His name is associated with the 'law' propounded in his 1962 paper, *Potential GNP, its Measurement and Significance.* Okun's Law states that to avoid the waste of

unemployment an economy must continually expand and relates changes in unemployment to changes in national product.

Paish, Frank W (1898-) British economist. After studying at Cambridge and then working in South Africa, Paish joined the London School of Economics in 1932. He was appointed Professor of Economics in 1949, and made Emeritus Professor in 1965. Much of his written work has been on the problem of inflation and methods of controlling it. The 'Paish Theory' in the sixties argued that wage inflation had to be combatted by unemployment, and that incomes policy should also be used to restrain wage demands.

Pareto, Vilfredo F D (1848-1923) Italian who came to economics after twenty years as an engineer. Pareto's application of mathematical and statistical techniques

Timeline

1900 **1910** **1920** **1930**

Titanic sinks 1912 ○

1914 Bank of England authorised by Government to issue money in excess of statutory limit

● 1907 Epidemic of bank failures in the USA

P. H. Douglas: *Theory of Wages* 1934 ● ● 1935 Bank

● 1909 W. Sombart: *Der Moderne Kapitalismus*

○ 1926 General strike in Britain

● 1908 General Motors Corp. formed, USA ● 1920 National Bureau of Economic Research founded in US

● 1907 London conference ○ 1915 Ford produces one millionth car

● 1933 US goes off

1914 Federal Trade Commission ● 1925 Unemployment Insurance Act in Britain ● 19

● 1903 Henry Ford founds the Ford Motor Company, USA ● 1922 Stockmarket boom starts in America after depression

● 1903 Detroit, USA, becomes the motor capital of the world

UN conference at Geneva leads to signing of GATT (General Agreement

● 1914 Clayton Anti-trust Act, USA

● 1909 W. H. Beveridge: Unemployment – a problem of industry ● 1929 US stock exchange collapses

● 1904 T. H. Veblen: *Theory of Business Enterprise* ● 1924 New reichsmark introduced in Germany Natio

● 1905 Austin Motor Co. founded, England ○ 1916 Food rationed in Germany ● 1926 France returns to the gold standard

J. M. Keynes: *General Theory of Employment, Interest & Money* (turning point in economic thought Keynsian revolution) 1936 ●

○ 1905 Revolution in Russia: "Bloody Sunday" in Petersburg, ● 1924 Bartering returns to Germany, for short period Brit

● 1910 US Postal Savings Bank established ● 1923 Value of German mark drops to rate of four million to one

○1901 Trans-Siberian Railway opened ● 1912 J. A. Schumpeter: *Theory of Economic Development* ● 1929 Wall Street Crash, USA: w

● 1911 I. Fisher: *Purchasing Power of Money* ● 1931 Bankruptcy of Gerr

○ 1903 Wright brothers make first controlled flight, in USA US congress passes Marshall Aid Act, contributing $5.3 bill

● 1910 First labour exchanges open in Britain ○ 1925 Mussolini becomes dictator, Italy ● 1933 World Econo

● 1913 Federal Reserve Act reconstructs US banking and currency system by creating federal banks

First World War begins 1914 ○ ○ 1918 First World War ends ● 1930 Bank for Internatio

● 1912 A. C. Pigou: *Wealth and Welfare* ● 1927 Black Friday in Germany – the econo

● 1914 Currency and Bank Notes Act, repealing Bank Charter Act of 1844, empowers Bank of Engl

Roald Amundsen reaches South Pole 1911 ○ Paris meeting of nations of European Recovery Programme sets up OEEC (Organisation for Europ

● 1907 First British census of production ● 1921 Rapid fall of German mark begins ● 1932 Japan begins its conqu

● 1914 French hoarding of gold, silver and copper coinage leads to Bank of France 5, 10 and 20 fr

---

to his new subject attracted the attention of Walras, whom he succeeded as Professor of Economics at Lausanne in 1892. In the *Cours d'économie Politique* (1896), Pareto uses mathematics to tackle the question of general equilibrium, while the *Manuale di Economia Politica* (1906), is considered the starting point of modern welfare economics. His study of income distribution led to the formulation of what is called Pareto's Law. This states that whatever the political or taxation conditions, income will be distributed in exactly the same way in all countries.

Pigou, Arthur Cecil
(1877-1959) British academic economist. Pigou was a student under Marshall at Cambridge and succeeded him as Professor of Political Economy in 1890, a post he held until retirement in 1944. The leading classical economist of the two decades before the Second World War, he wrote widely and authoritatively on many aspects of his subject, especially macro economics and welfare economics. His book *Economics of Welfare* (1920) is a classic in its field. Far from impressed by Keynes' 'General Theory' he wrote a notably hostile review of it. Pigou's name is always associated with the real balance effect. This states that as prices fall, an individual's real wealth increases. In consequence, he will consume more and hence output will be stimulated.

Phillips, Alban W H
(1914-1975) New Zealand-born economist. Phillips trained initially as an electrical engineer, the legacy of which is apparent in his economic work. He taught at the London School of Economics from 1950 to 1967, being appointed Professor in 1958. In 1967 he joined the Australian National University where he remained until his death. Despite significant work on multiplier-accelerator models, his fame rests mainly on his 1958 paper in *Economica*. In this, he developed what rapidly became known as the 'Phillips' curve.' This demonstrates the supposed trade-off possible between unemployment and inflation. The meaning, or even existence, of such a relationship has been the subject of much debate ever since.

Prebisch, Paul D
(1901-) Argentinian economist. Adviser on economics to the Argentine government and Secretary-General of the United Nations Conference on Trade and Development (UNCTAD). He has argued that the terms of trade shift against primary producers in developing countries and that they should introduce tariffs to protect their infant industries. In development economics this thesis has become known as the 'Singer-Prebisch hypothesis.'

Quesnay, François
(1694-1774) French economist, educated as a surgeon in Paris. Court physician to Louis XV in 1752. Quesnay is principally remembered for his book *Tableau Économique* (1758). The vision and imagination of this work made him by far the most outstanding Physiocrat. In the book, Quesnay divides society into three groups: agricultural workers, proprietors, and the 'sterile manufacturing sector.' The Physiocrats believed that nature was the source of all wealth and that agricultural workers provided society's means of receiving the surplus, or 'produit net' given up by nature. *Tableau Économique* sets out to show how the 'produit net' was distributed among the various classes of society and was the first attempt to look at the workings of the economy as a whole. Its broad approach is similar in some respects to input-output analysis.

Ricardo, David (1772-1823) British economist. At fourteen he entered his father's business, but in 1793 he set up on his own and made a fortune on the Stock Exchange. Ricardo's most important work was *Principles of Political Economy and*

40   1950   1960   1970   1980

nk of England Act 1946●

nada founded   ●1945   Black markets for food, clothing and cigarettes develop throughout Europe   ● 1970   Equal Pay Act UK

ropean Coal and Steel Community founded   1953 ●   Inflation becomes a world wide problem 1969 ●

ld standard   ●1945   £5 notes with metal strips introduced in England   ●   1966   Australia abandons sterling for dollar currency

tional Institute of Economic and Social Research founded in London   ●1959   EFTA (European Free Trade Association) founded

       ●1947   Bank of England nationalised   Highest bank rate in the world, Brazil at 20% 1972 ●

riffs and Trade) 1946   ●● 1947   P. A. Samuelson: *Foundations of Economic Analysis*   ●1963   President Kennedy round negotiations on tariff cuts, USA

     ● 1948   F. A. Hayek: *Individualism and Economic Order*   ●   1968   IMF introduces two-tier Gold system

ct. 29th ; world economic crisis begins (Great Depression)   Largest annual expenditure budgeted USA $304,400 million 1974 ●

onomic Development Corporation (NEDC) created by the British Government   1962 ●   Largest national debt $486,400 million 1974 ●

     ●1947   US Congress passes Taft-Hartley Act ●1958   European Common Market comes into being

    ●   1944   Bretton Woods, USA, conference leads to the establishment of the International Monetary Fund (IMF)

values the pound sterling   1949 ●   ●1950   Kefauver Antimerger Act   IMF introduces special drawing rights 1969●

llar   World wide inflation ; dramatic increases in the cost of fuel, food and materials ; economic growth slows down 1974 ●

onomic crisis   ● 1945   World Bank (International Bank for Reconstruction and Development) founded   ●1973   Fair Trading Act

natbank leads to closure of all German banks   ● 1957   Treaty of Rome   ●1965   Confederation of British Industry created

r European recovery 1947●   ● 1950   T. Scitovsky: *Welfare and Competition*   ●1966   Supermarket retailing expands in Europe and Far East

nference in London   ●1947- Labour Government nationalises coal, iron, steel, gas, electricity, 51 railways

     ● 1943   J. A. Schumpeter: *Capitalism, Socialism and Democracy*   ●1961   OEEC becomes OECD   ●1971   American astronauts land on Moon

ropean Payments Union formed 1950●

ttlements, founded at Basle   ●   1949   Comecon founded in Moscow   ●1962 Kennedy Trade Act

stem collapses   ● 1947   Taft – Hartley Act   ●1954   Currency and Bank Notes Act in Britain   Employment protection Act 1975 UK

issue one pound and ten shilling notes   ● 1952   W. W. Rostow: *The Process of Economic Growth*   ●1968   Two tier system of gold prices introduced UK

onomic Cooperation)   1948 ● ●1948   Monopolies and restrictive practises act in Britain   ●1963   M. Friedman: *Monetary History of the US, 1867-1960*

world markets by undercutting prices   ○1953 Stalin dies   US suspends convertibility of dollar into gold 1971●

tes   ●1948   J. E. Meade: *Planning and the Price Mechanism*   ●1965   British government introduces selective employment tax

---

Taxation (1817). This book deals with all the controversial questions of political economy at the time: value theory, economic growth, rent etc. His other works include *The High Price of Bullion* (1810), *Essay on the Influence of a low price of corn on the Profits of Stock* (1815), *Proposals for an Economical and Secure currency* (1816), *and the Plan for a National Bank* (1824). Ricardo is most famous for his 'Theory of Com-

parative Advantage' and of 'Rent'. The former states that countries will be better off if they specialize in producing goods where they have a comparative advantage. He defines rent on land as being the surplus over the costs of production. Ricardo had a profound influence on his time. His theories provided a rationale for the repeal of the Corn Law in 1846, since he argued that high corn prices could lead to a reduction in economic growth. He also influenced many social thinkers, including Marx, whose labour theory of value is similar in many respects to that of Ricardo.

Richardson, Rt Hon Gore-William Humphreys (1915-) Governor of the Bank of England since 1973, and Member of the Court of the Bank of England since 1967.

Robbins, Lionel Charles (1898-) British economist, educated at University College, London, and the London School of Economics. Taught at Oxford and at the LSE. During the war, he took a post in the Economic Section of the War Cabinet Office. Robbins draws a sharp distinction between economics and political economy and he regards economics as being a 'positive' description

of what occurs in the real world, and political economy as a 'normative' study involving value judgements. Robbins was involved in the economic debates that arose out of the depression of the 30s. At that time, he profoundly disagreed with Keynes, outlining his views in his book *The Great Depression* (1934). However, Robbins was to turn his back on these views, which had a heavy classical bias, and later agreed with Keynes that higher public expenditure was necessary in a depression. Robbins' other works include: *The Economic causes of War* (1939), *The Economic Problem in Peace and War* (1947), *The Theory of Economic Policy in English Classical Political Economy* (1952), and *Robert Torens and the Evolution of Classical Economics* (1958).

Robinson, Joan (1903-) British economist, educated at Girton, Cambridge and taught at Cambridge from 1931 to 1971. In the *Economics of Imperfect Competition* (1933), she pioneered the analysis of monopolistic competition, although E H Chamberlin was independently developing a similar approach at the same time. Her later work has been mainly in the

form of radical criticisms of sections of economic theory. Ideologically, she is against the market system of resource allocation and the institution of private property. Her writings include *Private Enterprise and Public Control* (1945), *An Essay on Marxian Economics* (1942), *The Accumulation of Capital* (1956), *Economic Philosophy* (1963), *Economics: an awkward corner* (1966), *Freedom and Necessity* (1970).

Rostow, Walt Whitman (1916-) American economist and historian, educated at Yale and Oxford. He taught at Cambridge and at the Massachusetts Institute of Technology before becoming special assistant to President Johnson in 1966. His most important writings include *The*

Process of Economic Growth (1962), and *Stages of Economic Growth* (1960). Rostow said that during economic development societies passed through five stages: the traditional society, the pre-conditions for take-off, the take-off, the drive to maturity, and maturity.

Samuelson, Paul Anthony (1915-) American economist, won the Nobel Prize for Economics in 1970. He is best known for his textbook *Economics: An Introductory Analysis*, first published in 1955, and now in its 10th edition. Samuelson has been a Professor of Economics at the Massachusetts Institute of Technology since 1947. The distinguishing feature of his work is his ability to draw together the diverse strands of economic theory to form a cohesive structure, a task to which Samuelson often applies mathematical principles. Samuelson has also made significant contributions to economic analysis by developing the concept of revealed preference, the factor price equalisation theorem, and the accelerator-multiplier model. Samuelson's works include *Foundations of Economic Analysis* (1947), *Readings in Economics* (1955) and *Linear Programming and Economic Analysis* (1958).

Say, Jean Baptiste (1767-1832) French economist who originally intended to pursue a business career. However, reading Smith's *Wealth of Nations* inspired him to take up political economy. He taught at the Conservatoire des Arts et Métiers, and the College de France. His most important works are *Traité d'économique politique* (1803) and *Courts complet d'économie politique practique*. Famous for 'Say's Law' which states that supply creates its own demand. This concept was heavily criticised by Keynes.

Schumpeter, Joseph Mois *(1883–1950)* Austrian economist, educated in Vienna. He taught at Czernowitz, Graz and Bonn. In 1932, he moved to Harvard where he taught until his death. Among Schumpeter's writings are *Theory of Economic Development* (1912), *Business Cycles* (1939), *Capitalism, Socialism and Democracy* (1942), and *History of Economic Analysis* (1954). Schumpeter developed a theory of trade cycles and growth; he argued that 'abnormal' profit was the entrepreneur's reward for innovation. He predicted, however, that the scope for innovation would be declining in the course of capitalist development as competitive market structures were replaced by monopolies. He believed that capitalism would gradually evolve into socialism.

Scitovsky, Tibor *(1910–1999)* Born in Hungary, he was educated at the Universities of Budapest, Cambridge, Paris, and at the LSE. He taught at Stanford, California, Berkeley and Yale. Scitovsky contributed to the theory of prices and welfare economics. His most famous book *Welfare and Competition* synthesises these two aspects of economic analysis. In *Economic Theory and Western European Integration* (1958), he applied welfare economics to the theory of international trade.

Smith, Adam *(1723–90)* Scottish political economist and philosopher. Educated in Glasgow and at Balliol, Oxford, Smith later became Professor of Moral Philosophy at Glasgow University and frequently lectured at Edinburgh. The text of some of these lectures provided the base for his book *The Wealth of Nations*, published in 1776. This remarkable work, which exercised a profound influence on the political thinking of the ensuing century, advocates a simple system of political liberty in which each man should be free to 'pursue his own interest and bring his capital and industry into competition with any other man or group of men.' Turning away from the mercantilism of his own day, Smith proposed that the true wealth of a nation lay with the labour 'that supplies it with all the necessaries and conveniences of life.' In the natural course of things, he felt, the capital of a society should be devoted first to agriculture, then to manufacture and only thirdly to foreign commerce. In its brilliant evocation of the interdependences of economic life, *The Wealth of Nations* laid the foundations of political economy as a discipline in its own right.

Senior, Nassau William *(1790–1864)* British economist, educated at Oxford where he twice held the post of Drummond Professor of Political Economy. Senior's most important book was *Outline of the Science of Political Economy* (1836). He is best remembered for his abstinence theory of interest in which interest is a payment, rewarding the investor for refraining to use his savings unproductively.

Staffa, Piero *(1898–)* Italian economist, educated at the University of Turin. He later became a Fellow of Trinity College, Cambridge, Emeritus Reader in Economics. His article *The Law of Returns under Competitive Conditions* printed in the *Economic Journal* in 1926, provided the groundwork for later theories of imperfect competition. Staffa's other important works are *The works and correspondence of* (1951–5) and *Production of Commodities by means of commodities; Prelude to a critique of Economic Theory* (1960). Staffa has been at the forefront in initiating the recent revival of interest in the work of the classical political economists.

Taussig, Frank William *(1839–1940)* American economist, spent his academic life teaching at Harvard. Between 1917 and 1919 he chaired the US Tariffs Commission. Important books are *Tariff History of the United States* (1888), *Wages and Capital* (1896), *Principles of Economics* (1911), and *International Trade*. His work shows influences from Ricardo and Marshall.

Thünen, Johann Heinrich von (1783-1850). German economist whose theories stemmed from a practical background of farmer and landowner. His main contribution to economics is his work *Der Isolierte Staat in Beziehung Auf Landwirtschaft und Nationalökonomie* (1826-63) in which he analysed factors influencing the profitable locations of industries. His theory of rent is similar to that of David Ricardo. In addition, by means of calculus, he developed a theory of distribution based on marginal productivity.

Tinbergen, Jan (1903-). Dutch economist who shared the 1969 Nobel Prize for Economics with Ragner Frisch. Tinbergen had made outstanding contributions to econometrics. In the 30s, he developed models for demand management useful in avoiding depressions and counteracting the problem of unemployment. More recently Tinbergen has analysed the economic problems of underdeveloped countries. His publications include *Business Cycles in the USA* (1939), *Economic Policy: Principles and Design* (1936), *Shaping the World Economy* (1962) *Development Planning* (1968).

Tobin, James (1918-). American economist. Actively interested in the policy side of economics. In 1961, he founded President Kennedy's Council of Economic Advisers, and later, advised George McGovern on economic matters during his bid for the Presidency in 1972. *New Republic* (1960) and *The New Economics–One Decade Older* convey Tobin's conviction that current social and economic problems are soluble. In addition he has made many important contributions to macro-economic theory; his particular interest is in the 'portfolio balance' theory of the demand for money.

Torrens, Robert (1780-1864). British economist; during the Napoleonic Wars, he served as an officer in the Royal Marines, but rejected this career to become a novelist and Member of Parliament instead. His first work in economics was *The Economist Refuted* (1808). His later works include *Essay on the External Corn Trade* (1815), *Essay on Money and Paper Currency*, *Production of Wealth* (1912) and *Letter to Lord Melbourne* (1837). Torrens was founder of the Political Economy Club and had considerable influence in the development of the Bank of England. He was foremost in promoting the 'currency principle' which was translated into policy in the Bank Act of 1844. Torrens' ideas precisely reflect the doctrines of classical political economy that were current in his age.

Turgot, Anne Robert Jacques (1727-81). French writer on economics. Initially educated for a career in the Church, Turgot was for some time an Abbé at the Sorbonne. Having abandoned this for the Civil Service, he was appointed Administrator of Limoges and later, Secretary of State for the Navy. For a short time, he was also Controller of Finance to the King of France. In his *Reflections sur le formation et distribution des richesses* (1726), he developed an analysis of the law of diminishing returns.

Veblen, Thorstein (1857-1929). American economist of immigrant farming stock who spent most of his academic life at the University of Chicago. Veblen saw economics as being an evolutionary process in which man's survival relied on his ability to adapt his behaviour. The role of economics, he felt, should be that of analysing the ephemeral political and social institutions which, he believed, determined people's behaviour. His two main works are *Theory of the Leisure Class* (1899) and *Theory of Business Enterprise* (1904).

Walras, Marie Esprit Léon (1834-1910). French economist, originally trained as an engineer, and was in turn a journalist, novelist, railway clerk and bank manager. Turning to the academic life, he became Professor of Economics at Lausanne in 1870, which post he held until his retirement. His writings include *Elements d'économie politique pure* (1874-7), *Études d'économie sociale* (1896), and *Études d'économie politique appliquee* (1898). Walras shares the distinction of having initiated the 'Marginalist Revolution' with Menger and Jevons. In *Elements* Walras proposed that relative prices of commodities were determined by the commodities' relative marginal utilities. He also devised a mathematical model designed to show that all prices and quantities are uniquely determined.

Weber, Alfred (1868-1958). German economist. He gained his Ph.D from the University of Berlin, taught economics there and at Prague and Heidelberg. Weber's most important economic work was *Theory of the Location of Industries* (1909). In this book, Weber emphasised the role of production costs, especially those of transportation, in determining where firms are located. During the Nazi regime, Weber's works were distinguished by being forbidden to German readers.

Wicksell, Knut (1851-1926). Swedish economist. Having studied philosophy and mathematics at the University of Uppsala, Wicksell pursued his later enthusiasm for economics to Austria, Germany and England. In 1900, he was appointed Professor at the University of Lund. His most important works are *Über Wert, Kapital und Rente* (1893), *Finanztheoretische Untesuchungen* (1896), *Geldzins und Güterpreise* (1898), and *Lectures in Political Economy* (1901). Wicksell developed a marginal theory of distribution. His theory of interest and the general level of prices had a marked influence on monetary theory.

GLOSSARY OF TERMS

A

Absolute Advantage. In international trade theory, the ability of a country to produce a commodity at absolutely lower cost, measured in terms of factor inputs, than its trading partners. (See

Accelerator. A term used in macro-economics to show how changes in the demand for consumer goods bring about larger changes in the amount of new capital expenditure. The term acceleration is sometimes used instead of accelerator.

Accepting House. Financing institution specialising in accepting (i.e. guaranteeing) bills of exchange. By adding its name to the bill the Accepting House ensures that any third party taking the bill has a reliable name to turn to should the bill be dishonoured.

Account Sales. A document sent by an agent (usually an overseas agent) to his principal, accounting for the way in which he has disposed of the principal's property. The commission is deducted and a draft settlement (or remittance advance note about the transfer of funds) is attached.

Actuary. A mathematician skilled in the calculation of probabilities, and so calculates risks for insurance companies.

Ad Valorem Tax. A tax levied as a fixed percentage of the value of a particular item.

Administered Pricing. A policy, not uncommon in manufacturing industry under conditions of imperfect competition, where price is set by a firm that then sells as much as it can at this price. Administered pricing may be contrasted with competitive conditions, where market forces of supply and demand determine price.

Affluent Society. The title of a book by Professor J.K. Galbraith; the advanced capitalist society is critically examined.

Aggregate Demand. Total effective demand, or total planned expenditure, by all sectors in the economy for consumption, investment, and government goods and services.

Aggregate Supply. The total volume of goods and services offered for sale in the economy.

Allocation. In economics, resource allocation means determining what will be produced, how it will be produced, who will produce it, and for whom it will be produced.

Amalgamation. The union of two or more enterprises to form a new business unit. It has financial implications for investors, employees and creditors.

Anti-trust Laws. A series of laws in the U.S.A. beginning with the Sherman Act of 1890, that defines U.S. government policy towards monopoly.

Appreciation. Increases over an accounting period in the current value of plant, equipment, stocks, financial investments, or other assets.

Arbitrage. Financial dealings which seek to make a profit from the differential pricing of currencies in various world centres. The result of buying in cheap centres and selling in dear centres, is that prices are raised in the former and lowered in the latter. This settles the prices at the same level throughout the world.

Assets. The resources of an organisation used in conducting its affairs.

Liquid assets are those in money form, or readily convertible to money, such as a credit balance in the bank.

Current assets are those which will be converted to cash form in the near future, such as money owed and stock in trade.

Fixed assets are those which are not liquid because they are required for use in the business on a permanent basis, such as premises, plant and equipment, office furniture and motor vehicles.

Intangible assets are those which have no tangible existance, such as goodwill and formation expenses – the costs of forming a company.

Automatic stabilizers. Taxes which automatically increase more rapidly than increases in national income, and thus reduce spending in an economy.

Average cost. See COSTS.

B

Backward Sloping Supply Curve. A supply curve demonstrating that an increase in price over a certain range reduces the quantity offered for sale. The backward sloping supply curve is often suggested as an explanation of the behaviour of labour, where an increase in wage rates to affluent employees reduces their willingness to work. It is especially a feature of unpleasant or dangerous occupations such as mining.

Balance of Payments. A balance struck between the receipts and payments passing between one country and all other countries. Earnings and payments fall into three categories: visible trade (the trade in goods), invisible trade (the trade in services), and capital movements (both official loans and private sector capital movements). Any surplus or deficit on the Balance of Payments requires to be covered by lending to, or borrowing from, overseas. This is called 'Official Financing.'

Balance of Trade The term usually applied to the visible trading transactions in the current account of the balance of payments. The term is sometimes used, however, to refer to the entire current account balance of payments, that is, the balance of both visible and invisible transactions.

Balanced Budget Multiplier. The multiplier effect on national income of increasing the size of goverment's budget by raising government expenditure on goods and services, and Government income from taxation by the same amount.

Bancor. The name given by J. M. Keynes to a proposed international currency which would eventually be the basis for international transactions. The name means 'Banker's Gold.' Although differing slightly from Keynes proposed 'bancor' the S.D.R. unit (Special Drawing Rights unit) is beginning to fill the same role in the economy that Keynes envisaged.

Bank bills. Bills of exchange that have been accepted, or endorsed, by a reputable bank. As such, they are highly reliable and are usually discounted at a competitive rate called the Fine Rate.

Bank charges. Charges made to customers who do not leave substantial balances in their current accounts, to cover operating expenses, clearing cheques etc.

Bank Deposit. Colloquially, any payment into a bank resulting in a credit entry on a customer's account is a deposit. If entered into a current account, it enables the customer to draw cheques against his deposit. If entered in a Deposit Account, the money earns interest, but seven days notice is required for withdrawal.

Bank Draft. A document similar to a bill of exchange (but lacking the true legal status of a bill of exchange), drawn by a bank on behalf of a debtor; the creditor can present the draft to his local branch and receive payment. It lends the authority of the bank to the debtors's payment.

Bank Rate. The term used up to 1971 by the Bank of England for the minimum rate at which the Bank would discount first class Bills of Exchange. Since 1971, this term has been replaced by Minimum Lending Rate (q.v.).

Bank Return. A balance sheet published weekly by the Bank of England, showing the assets and liabilities of the Bank's two departments – the Issue Department and the Banking Department.

Banking Department. One of the two departments of the Bank of England.

Base Rate. Since 1971, each major commercial bank had, from time to time, its base rate (having regard to the supply of, and demand for, money). This is the minimum rate at which loans will be made, but actual charges for loans and overdrafts reflect the credit-worthiness of the borrower.

Bear. Speculator who sells shares because he expects them to fall in price. His intention is to buy them back again when the price has fallen, so that he will regain the same number of shares as before, and make a profit as well.

'Big Four.' The four major United Kingdom commercial banks – Barclays, Lloyds, Midland and National Westminster.

Bi-Lateral Monopoly. A market situation in which there is a single buyer and a single seller of a product.

Bill of Exchange. A Bill of Exchange is 'An unconditional order in writing, addressed by one person to another, signed by the person giving it, requiring the person to whom it is addressed to pay, on demand, or at a fixed or determinable future time, a sum certain in money to, or to the order of, a specified person or to bearer.' (Bills of Exchange Act 1882 s.3). This rather difficult definition means that the drawer (writer), of a bill orders the person to whom it is addressed (the payee), to pay the sum of money (obviously the drawee's debt to the drawer), on a certain date. By placing his name on the bill, the drawee then becomes the 'acceptor' of the bill, and accepts the obligation for honour on the due date. The drawer may now discount the bill with a bank if it is agreeable, thus obtaining his money (less discount), at once, and the bill will be honoured on the due date by payment to the banker.

Bi-metalism. Currency system in which the law defines the monetary unit in terms of two metals (usually gold and silver).

Bond. A fixed interest security.

Breakeven analysis. A business decision-making technique that relates fixed and variable costs to revenue, in order to identify the level of output needed to break even on a project.

Bretton Woods Conference. The important conference

held at Bretton Woods, New Hampshire, in 1944, at which the International Monetary Fund and the World Bank were set up, and the system of 'managed flexibility' of exchange rates was devised.

Built-in Stabilizer. An element in the Government's budget which automatically offsets changes in private incomes in a depression or a boom. Examples include progressive taxation and unemployment insurance contributions and benefits.

Bull. Speculator who buys shares in the expectation that their price will rise, so enabling him to make a profit.

Bullion. Bars or ingots of precious metals, of a known degree of purity.

Business Cycles. The name used to describe the tendency for national income, employment and other aggregates to oscillate in a regular pattern.

C

Call money. Money loaned by banks and other financial institutions to the Discount Houses on the strict understanding that it is repayable 'at call,' i.e. immediately the return is demanded. This sometimes 'forces the Discount Houses into the Central Bank' which must then act as 'lender of last resort.'

Capital. In economics, the word means the stock of producer goods created in previous periods which the current period receives as a factor endowment from the previous era. In finanacial terms, capital is a store of money made available by the owner of a business to purchase its initial assets and meet its working expenses until cash flows are generated by the sale of its outputs,

either of goods or services. See also LIQUID CAPITAL, FIXED CAPITAL, WORKING CAPITAL.

Capital Budgeting. The area of business decision-making that focusses on long-run investment decisions.

Capital flows. Balance of payments flows which are not the result of visible trade, or trade in invisibles (services), but are the result of lending and borrowing by private or official bodies.

Capital Market. The market in which funds for the purchase of goods is borrowed or loaned.

Capital-output Ratio. The ratio of the value of capital in an economy to the value of income (the average capital-output ratio). The incremental capital-output ratio is the ratio between an increase in investment and as associated increase in output.

Capital Stock Adjustment Principal. A theory which relates investment expenditure to changes in stocks of goods, which in turn are influenced by sales. The capital stock adjustment theory is a version of the accelerator theory of investment.

Cartel. A group of firms that acts in combination to exercise monopoly power in a market.

Cash Ratio. A term formerly used to describe the proportion (usually about 8 per cent), of the liabilities, of a bank which were not available for lending to customers. Instead they had to be kept in cash form to meet withdrawals by depositors. Half of the cash ratio was in till money, the other half at the Bank of England to meet 'daily clearings' at the Clearing House.

Central Bank. A national bank, such as

the Bank of England, which acts as the central financial institution for the nation, and fulfils the function of controlling the economy on behalf of the government, through influencing the level of credit available and other matters.

Certificate of Deposit. A certificate stating that a sum of money (either sterling or dollars) has been deposited for a fixed period. If the borrower wishes to regain his money, he does so by selling the Certificate of Deposit, instead of demanding the money back from the bank where it was deposited.

Ceteris Paribus. Literally, 'other things being equal.' This term is used to describe assumptions in an economic argument that examines the impact of one changing influence, assuming that other influences are not changing at the same time.

Cheap Money Policy. Government economic policy of maintaining low interest rates to stimulate the borrowing of money and thus stimulate demand.

Cheque. A bill of exchange drawn on a banker, payable on demand. The drawer, the customer of the bank, calls on the drawee, the branch of his bank, to pay on demand a certain sum to the named payee (or possibly to his order).

Clearing House. A bankers' organisation, at 10 Lombard St., London, where the 'daily clearing' of indebtedness is settled by exchanging credit or debit transfer slips drawn on the Bank of England, for the net indebtedness of each bank with all the other clearing banks.

Cobweb Theorem. The analysis of supply and demand in a market

where a time lag exists between price and quantity supplied. In the cobweb theorem, market price may converge gradually towards equilibrium, oscillate perpetually around it, or diverge increasingly from equilibrium.

Coins. Tokens of a designated value issued by authority, and declared to be 'legal tender'.

Collateral Security. Security lying alongside a debt, which may be realized by the creditor if repayment is not made in the agreed manner.

Command Economy. A political form of organization, wherein decidecisions on resouce allocation are taken by a central authority.

Commercial bank A bank offering the full range of services to ordinary customers, including current acaccounts, deposit accounts, night-safe services, travellers' cheques and so on.

Commercial bills. Bills of exchange drawn by commercial firms, but as yet not supported by the confirmation of a major banking house.

Commodity Inflation. A variety of cost-push inflation in which a spontaneous increase in commodity prices leads to general price increases.

Comparative advantage, principle of. The principle employed in the analysis of foreign trade between countries, according to which a country gains from trade by specialising in the goods in which it possesses the greatest advantage relative to other commodities, or the least disadvantage relative to other commodities.

Comparative costs. see COMPARATIVE ADVANTAGE.

Complements. Goods which are demanded in combination with other goods. If two goods, A and B, are comple-

ments, a fall in the price of A will lead to an increase in the demand for B.

Compounding. Calculation for a final amount of money after adding the originally invested sum to the compound interest gained over the years.

Compound Interest. Interest which is calculated not only on the originally invested sum of money, but on the interest earned in preprevious years as well.

Concentration Ratio. The share of total sales of an industry that is in the hands of a specified number of the largest firms.

Confirmed letter of credit. A letter of credit (q.v.) which has been confirmed by a major bank. Through this, the bank accepts the obligation of honouring the amount stated to be payable for export goods when proof of export (the shipping documents), is made available.

Consolidated Fund. That part of the United Kindom Government's accounts which is subject to permanent legislation. It includes the National Debt, the Civil List, etc. Other expenditure is 'supply' expenditure, and has to be agreed annually in the Finance Act.

Constant Returns to Scale. If all the factors of production are increased in a given proportion, and output increases in the same proportion, there are said to be constant returns to scale.

Consumer Sovereignty The situation when resources are allocated in response to consumer preferences.

Consumer Surplus. A measure of the excess of satisfaction obtained by a consumer if he buys a commodity at a price that is below the price he would be prepared to pay.

Consumption Function. The functional relationship between planned expenditure on consumption and income. The average and marginal propensities to consume, are specifiied by the form of the consumption function. The average propensity to consume is defined as total consumption expenditure divided by income. The marginal propensity to consume is defined as the change in consumption expenditure divided by the change in income that gave rise to it.

Convertibility. Currencies are said to be convertible when they can be freely exchanged for other currencies.

Cost-Benefit Analysis (CBA). A systematic comparison between the cost of carrying out a service or activity, and the vaue of that service or activity, quantified as far as possible, with all costs and benefits (direct and indirect, financial and social) being taken into account. This requires the analyst to decide on monetary values for such things as the death of a child on the public highway, or the loss of the use of an open space.

Cost-push theory of inflation. Connects inflation with excessive wage demands by unions, or price demands by raw materials suppliers.

Costs. The more common types of cost are listed below:
Alternative Cost see OPPORTUNITY COST.
Average cost. Total cost divided by the number of units produced.
Fixed costs. Costs which do not vary with output, but depend on the passage of time (such as rent, rates and other overheads).
Historical cost. The original cost to an organization of purchasing an asset.

Marginal cost. *The amount of any given volume of output by which aggregate costs are changed, if the volume of output is increased by one unit.*
Opportunity cost. *The maximum amount which could be obtained at any given point of time if assets or resources were to be sold, hired or put to the most valuable alternative use which would be practicable. It is the cost experienced when we surrender one opportunity for another.*
Overhead costs. *see* FIXED COSTS.
Prime costs. *The initial costs incurred in starting up production to pay for factors which are actually embodied in the product i.e. raw materials and wages. Often called variable costs, since they vary with output.*
Private costs. *The costs borne by a private firm when producing its output of goods or services.*
Replacement costs. *The current cost of replacing an existing asset.*
Social costs. *The costs borne by the community in general as a result of the private activities of firms.*
Standard costs. *A predetermined cost which is calculated from management's standards of efficient operation. When compared with actual costs it throws up 'variances' which detect inefficiecy, or changes in prices which must be passed on to the customer if possible.*

Cross Elasticity of Demand. *A measure of the responsiveness of the demand for one commodity to a change in the price of another.*

Cum Div. *"With Dividend". This is the way shares are normally sold, with any dividend due to them included in the price. Twenty-one days before dividend day, the shares are announced to be 'ex div' – which means that* anyone buying them will not be paid the next dividend; it will instead be paid to the seller. An 'ex div' price is therefore lower.*
'Currency Basket'. *A unit of account which is based not upon a national currency such as dollars or pounds, but on a trade-weighted basket of currencies. Two in common use today are the EUA (European Unit of Account), and the SDR (Special Drawing Rights) unit. The EUA is made up of the nine currencies used in the EEC, while the SDR is make up of 16 important world currencies. By designating contracts in units of account, the value of the contract is less subject to fluctuations than if designated in a national currency. For example, one EUA only contains £0.08 sterling. If the pound declines in value, the EUA only declines by ·08 of the pound's decline – but as other currencies rise, in fact it declines even less than ·08; it might even increase in value.*
Current Assets. See ASSETS.

Customs Union. *An economic union between countries where all members reduce tariffs on trade between themselves, and adopt a common external tariff between the union and the rest of the world.*

D

Dear Money (Tight Money). *Government policy of maintaining interest rates at a high level to curb total expenditure in the economy.*

Debenture. *A fixed-interest bond issued by firms empowered to do so by their Articles of Association, as a security for a loan. A fixed debenture is secured against named fixed assets, a floating debenture floats over* the stock (current assets), and only crystallizes into control of the asset if the terms of the debenture are not honoured.*

Decreasing Returns to Scale. *If all factors of production are increased in a given proportion, and output increases by a smaller proportion, there are said to be decreasing returns to scale.*

Deficit Financing. *Planned excess of expenditure over revenue by governments in order to stimulate economic activity.*

Del credere. *The phrase means, 'in the belief that'. A 'del credere' agent sells goods for his principal in the belief that the buyers are solvent. As such, he is prepared – for a small commission – to carry the risk of bad debts. The principal has no worries. about non-payment if he agrees to allow the commission to be deducted from the sum due to him for the goods.*

Demand Curve. *A curve on a graph which depicts the quantities of a commodity which would be demanded at each of a range of prices over a given period of time. Changes in the price of a commodity lead to movements along the demand curve. Changes in any of the ceteris paribus (q.v.) assumptions may lead to shifts in the demand curve.*

Demand Schedule. *A table containing information used in the construction of a demand curve.*

Demand Management. *A term for fiscal and monetary policies used to influence aggregate demand in an economy.*

Demand-pull theory of inflation. *A theory that attributes inflation to an excessive aggre-* gate demand caused by full employment.*

Deposit account. *An account in a commercial bank which earns interest because the money will not be withdrawn without notice. A cheque book is not issued with a deposit account.*

Depreciation. *The amount by which a capital asset declines in value over a given period of time, either because of physical deterioration or obsolescence. In the national income accounts, depreciation is usually referred to as "capital consumption." The term is also used to describe the gradual decline in the value of a 'floating' currency.*

Devaluation. *A sudden decline in the value of currency under the Bretton Woods System. The United Kingdom devalued twice, in 1948 and 1967.*

Differential opportunity see ARBITRAGE.

Diminishing Marginal Utility, "Law" of. *A proposition which states that the satisfaction to be derived from possessing successive extra units of a commodity tends to fall. In other words, you can have too much of a good thing.*

Diminishing Returns, "Law" of. *A proposition which relates to the returns, or output, obtained from the use of factors of production in varying proportions. If, for exaple, there are a fixed number of machines in a factory and a steadily increasing number of workers, the point comes when the addition of one more worker causes a decrease in production. The fixed factor, in other words gives rise to diminishing returns from the variable factor.*

Direct Taxes. *Taxes which are levied on individuals (usually on incomes, but sometimes* on wealth), and paid directly to the tax authorities.*

Discount House. *A business house specialising in 'bill broking'. Bill-broking is a process of borrowing money, at an agreed rate of interest, from those who have surplus funds and lending it to those in need of funds at a higher rate of interest. The phrase 'short-term money' is oten used, for much of the money borrowed is 'at call' or 'short notice'.*

Discounting. *A method of comparing the value of receipts or outlays made at different points in time, by applying an agreed discount rate.*

Discounted Cash Flow (DCF). *A method for estimating the value of capital expenditure by discounting the flows of costs and earnings, associated with capital expenditure, to obtain their net present value.*

Discount Market. *The real of discount houses whose business is conducted through binding oral contracts, made largely over the telephone.*

Discount rate. *The interest rate charged by the Federal Reserve Banks in the United States for loans., that is, the rate at which they will re-discount 'eligible paper'.*

Discretionary Stabilizers. *Changes in Government taxation or expenditure, which form part of fiscal plicy. These are not automatic stabilizers, but require positive action to put into effect.*

Discriminating Monopoly. *The term used to describe a monopolist who is able to charge different prices for the same commodity or service to different purchasers.*

Diseconomies of Scale. *Said to be experienced whenever long-run average cost* increases as output increases.*

Disequilibrium. *A state of affairs in the market or in the economy, where economic forces tend towards a change. If there is disequilibrium in te market for a single commodity, for instance, then supply and demand are not equal. Commonly used in describing balance of payments difficulties.*

Disposable Income. *Personal income, minus income tax and contributions to National Insurance.*

Dividend. *Part of a company's profits which are available for distribution to the shareholders.*

Dollar bloc. *Countries which have tied their currencies to the dolar and carry out a large portion of their foreign trade with the United States.*

Dollar Certificate of Deposit see CERTIFICATE OF DEPOSIT.

Dollar premium. *A premium payable by United Kingdom residents for using foreign currencies for investment purposes. These currencies originated chiefly from the sale or redemption of foreign currency securities, and, as they are in short supply, the seller of such currencies is able to command a premium.*

Dumping. *Sale of goods on a foreign market at a price below the one that is being charged for similar goods on the home market.*

Duopoly. *A market situation with only two sellers. A special case of oligolopoly (q.v.).*

E

Econometrics. *The study of the problems of quantifying economic relationships.*

Economic Rent. *The return received by a factor of production which is in excess of its trans-*

fer earnings or opportunity costs.

Economies of Scale. The productivity of a business when all factors are increased in the same poportion. Economies of scale may be constant, increasing or decreasing.

Effective Demand. Effective demand in economics means wants that are backed by the will to purchase a commodity or service.

Elasticity. The economist's way of measuring the responsiveness of a dependent variable to a change in an independent variable. (e.g. elasticity of demand, elasticity of supply, elasticity of substitution).

Elasticity of Demand, (Price). The economist's measure of the responsiveness of demand to changes in price.

Elasticy of Substitution. Economists use this term to denote the degree of ease or difficulty with which factors of production may be substituted for each other.

Elasticity of Supply. The measure used by economists to describe the responsiveness of quantity in a market to changes in price. The co-efficient of elasticity of supply is the proportionate change in quantity supplied, divided by the proportionate change in price.

Embargo. Suspension of trading, usually a block on the export of a particular commodity.

Equilibrium. The state of affairs in which the economic forces that tend to change conditions, are in blanace. Equilibrium in the market, obtains when supply is equal to demand, and market prices satisfy both consumers andproducers.

Equity. The 'risk capital' of a private enterprise firm, which is entitled, with its shareholders, to an equal share in the profits made, once the prefer-

ence share dividends have been paid.

Ergonomics. The study of the effect of the working environment on the worker and his productive capacity.

Eurodollar deposits. Dollar deposits held in European banks and overseas branches of American banks.

Ex Ante. A synonym for 'planned' or 'intended'. Thus, ex ante savings implies the quantity of savings which are planned by consumers. Ex ante concepts are often contrasted with ex post.

Ex. Div. see CUM. DIV.

Ex Post. A synonym for 'actual' or 'realised'. Thus, ex post savins are actual savings realised in an economy. They are the total savings which the economy will have been observed to have made, looking back after the end of a particular period. The term 'ex post' is used in contrast with the term 'ex ante'.

Excess Demand. The situation that normally obtains in the market for a commodity if price is below equilibrium level.

Excess Supply. The situation that normally obtains in a market, if the price of a commodity is above equilibrium level.

Exchange control. A system of control, operated by the central bank of a country, to supervise transactions requiring the conversion of its own currency to foreign currencies – generally with a view to avoiding Balance of Payments problems.

Exchange rates. The price at which one currency is exchanged with another. Usually expressed to four decimal places – e.g. £1= $1.8655.

Expected Rate of Return. The annual net revenue that a firm expects to obtain by making an investment, usually expressed as a

percentage of the sum invested.

External Diseconomies. Negative external economies.

External Economies. Spillover effects in production or consumption. External economies in production are reductions in cost which accrue to firms as a result of expenditure by other organisations. External economies in consumption are benefits that accrue to consumers as a result of expenditure by other consumers.

F

Factor Cost. The method of valuing the output of the economy in the national income accounts, in terms of the incomes accruing to factors of production.

Factors of Production The resources which are available to an economy to produce goods and services. Factors of production are traditionally classified into land, labour, capital and enterprise.

Fiduciary issue. An issue of notes over and above the gold available to back them, on the assumption that some notes were at any given moment out of circulation, probably in private hands. Today, the note issue is not tied to gold and all important monetary systems are relinquishing any link with gold.

Fiscal Drag. Automatic growth of government revenue due to the rise of tax revenue in periods of inflation, as incomes increase.

Fiscal Policy. Budgetary measures introduced by government to influence the level of aggregate demand through taxation and expenditure.

Fixed Costs see COSTS.

Fixed exchange rate. A system of exchange rates used under the Bretton Woods System,

(q.v.),1944–71, in which exchange rates were expressed against the dollar and could fluctuate no more than 1 per cent either side of the agreed parity. Later, for a short period, the margin was widened to 2¼ per cent either side of the parity, but this was abandoned as currencies floated in the early '70s.

Fixed Inputs. Inputs whose quantities cannot be varied in response to short-run changes in output.

Flexible exchange rates. Floating exchange rates. They are exchange rates determined by demand and supply, rather than those fixed by international agreement.

Foreign Exchange Market. Market in which foreign currency is bought and sold by authorised bankers.

Foreign exchange reserves. The reserves available to a nation to finance any dis-equilibrium in its balance of payments.

Founder's Shares. Shares issued to the founder of a firm on his relinquishing control, as part settlement of the purchase price offered by the take-over company.

Free trade. International transactions unrestricted by quotas, tariffs, or direct controls.

Free Trade Area. A type of economic union between countries in which members reduce tariffs and other barriers to trade between themselves, while maintaining their individual external tariffs with the rest of the world.

Frictional unemployment. Short-term unemployment caused by movements of workers between jobs.

Fully paid-up capital. Captial of a company which has subscribed the full nominal value of the shares issued.

Today, nearly all shares are issued 'payable in full on application.'.

Funding. Conversion of government short term debt into long term debts.

'Future' Dealings. Dealings in the commodity and financial markets to fix a firm price now, for materials or currency that will be made available at a later date.

G

Gain From Trade. The conclusion of the doctrine of comparative advantage is that there will be a gain from international trade, (increase in economic welfare), if countries specialise in the goods in which they have the greatest comparative advantage or the least comparative disadvantage. The gain may be shared between the countries, and the extent to which this occurs will depend upon the terms of trade.

General Agreement on Tariffs and Trade. An agreement negotiated after the Bretton Woods Conference (q.v.), and still effective where nations surrender tariffs and other controls on trade in a re-reciprocal way. The 'Kennedy Round' and the 'Tokyo Round' of negotiations are often referred to.

Griffen Goods. Goods that do not obey the law of demand which states that less is purchased as prices rise. A familiar example is bread, whose consumption increases as prices go up. This paradox was first observed by the economist Sir Robert Griffen (1837–1910).

Gilt edged securities. Securities issued by the United Kingdom Government. The name derives from the original securities which were recorded on expensive hand-made paper with gilded edges.

Gini Coefficient. A

measure of inequality in the distribution of income, capital, etc. The value of the co-efficient varies between zero and unity; the higher the co-efficient the greater the degree, of inequality. It measures the disparity between the Lorenz curve (q.v.), and the line of equal distribution.

Gold Standard. An international monetary system established before the First World War, in which the quantity of paper money issued was linked to gold reserves, except for a tiny fiduciary issue (q.v.). The system also effectively fixed the rate of exchange between currencies which were on the gold standard, within the gold import and export points, beyond which it became cheaper to transfer gold across national boundaries to settle international indebtedness, rather than buying foreign currency.

Gresham's Law. A law, wrongly attributed to Sir Thomas Gresham, financial adviser to Queen Elizabeth I, which holds that 'bad money drives out good'. The theory is that, if debased coins are issued of a higher nominal value than their intrinsic value as metal, the holders of older coins will melt them down and exchange them for more than the same value of debased coins.

Gross Domestic Product. The value of all the goods and services produced within a country over a period of time.

Gross Fixed Capital Formation. The value of a country's investment before allowing for depreciation over a given period, excluding investment in stocks and working capital

Gross National Product. The total value of the goods and services available for consumption or investment by the residents of a

197

country over a given period of time. The gross domestic product, plus net income from abroad, is equal to the gross national product. The term 'gross' is used as a preface to product in order to distinguish it from net product (q.v.). The difference between gross and net is the depreciation, or capital consumption, estimated to take place over the period.

H

Hedging. Action taken by an individual to seek protection against possible adverse effects due to price changes in the future.

Hire Purchase. A system for purchasing durable domestic consumer goods, or business assets, by paying a deposit and an agreed number of instalments. The ownership of the goods does not pass until the final instalment is paid to the buyer

Historical cost see COSTS.

Horizontal Integration. Amalgamation between firms engaged at the same stage of production of a commodity or service.

Hot Money. Financial funds which are moved from one country to another to take advantage of more favourable interest rates, or of an anticipated revaluation of the foreign currency.

Human capital. The capitalized value of the earning capacty of individuals, which may be increased by education and training.

Hyper-Inflation. A state of affairs in which the pace of inflation in an economy has accelerated to the point where it is virtually out of control. The rapid decline in the purchasing power of money in situations of hyper-inflation leads to collapse of confidence, and it is usually necessary to establish a new unit of currency.

I

Identity. A statement of equality between two sets of variables which is always true for all values of the variables. For example, $Y-C=S$ is an identity (not an equation). Since S is defined as Y minus C, then the two sides of the identity must always be equal. Identities should be distinguished from equations, which are statements of the relationship between sets of variables; these are true only for certain values of the variables. For example, $C=50+\frac{3}{4}$ $\frac{3}{4}Y$ is an equation, not an identity.

Imperfect Competition. The term applied to a variety of market situations when one or more of the conditions necessary for perfect competition are absent. The term imperfect competition, however, is sometimes applied in a more narrow sense to describe market situations where a small number of sellers are each producing a similar product, as a means of differentiating this kind of competition from monopolistic, monopoly, obligopoly, monopsony (q.v.), and other non-perfect competitive market.

Incidence of Taxation. The persons or institutions on whom the burden of paying a tax falls. One measure of the incidence of a specific tax on a commodity is the extent to which its market price rises in comparison with the tax. This is, however, only a first approximation when establishing the true incidence of a tax.

Income Effect. The effect of a change in price on the demand for a commodity, which is due to the change in a consumer's real income consequent upon the price change – always assuming that relative prices are held constant. The income effect

and the substitution effect together make up the price effect.

Income Elasticity of Demand. The co-efficient of responsiveness of demand for a commodity to changes in income. The co-efficient is numerically expressed as the proportionate change in quantity demanded, divided by the proportionate change in income.

Incomes Policy. A policy designed to control inflation by controlling rents, wages, interest and profits. By this means, the demand on the economy may be kept within the limits of growth estimated for the ensuing period – often, a year.

Increasing Returns. More correctly, increasing returns to scale. This refers to the situation when an equal proportionate increase in all factors of production within a firm gives rise to a more than proportionate increase in output.

Index number. Measurement of changes in the price level over time.

Indexation. Measures taken to link incomes and assets to changes in the price level.

Indifference Curve. A curve plotted on a graph, the axes of which represent physical quantities of two commodites. Each indifference curve on the graph joins points which represent all combinations of two goods between which the consumer's real income remains constant. The slope of an indifference curve at any point represents the marginal rate of substitution between the two commodities.

Indifference Map. A graphical representation of a consumer's scale of preferences, using a number of indifference curves, each of which represents a dif-

ferent total level of satisfaction.

Indirect Taxes. Taxes on goods and services that are collected indirectly from purchasers – e.g. expenditure tax, purchase tax, excise tax, value added tax.

Inelastic Demand. A tem applied to the demand for a commodity where the elasticity co-efficient is less than unity.

Inelastic supply. A term used in the same sense as 'elastic demand' when referring to supply.

Inferior goods. In the economic sense, these are goods for which demand falls as consumers' incomes rise.

Inflation. The state of affairs in an economy, at the macro-economic level, when there is a tendency for the general price level to rise. Inflation may be open, when prices actually rise; or suppressed, when prices are only prevented from rising by government control.

Inflationary Gap. A term used in Keynsian economics to describe the excess of aggregate planned expenditure over income during periods of full employment.

Injections. The opposite of withdrawals. Injections is a term used in macro-economics to describe flows of expenditure on goods and services.

Input-Output Analysis. A description of the inter-relationships between different sectors in an economy. Input-output analysis is based upon a matrix or table, which sets out the purchases and sales by each sector to and from every other sector. Each input co-efficient so calculated, indicates the input requirements for an industry from every other industry, after taking account of all indirect inter-

relationships between sectors.

Insolvency. A situation where liabilities are greater than the liquid assets available, or likely to become available, before payment is due.

Integration see VERTICAL INTEGRATION and HORIZONTAL INTEGRATION.

Interest. The reward paid for financial investments, or for choosing to abstain from consumption.

Intermediate Goods. Goods which are both the ouputs of one sector of the community, and the inputs of another sector.

International Bank for Reconstruction and Development (IBRD). The 'World Bank' set up after the Bretton Woods Conference, (q.v.), to channel money into investment projects throughout the world, but particularly in the developing countries.

International Liquidity. The   of International money (gold), reserve currencies and special drawing rights) available for the finance of international transactions.

International Monetary Fund. The international body set up at the Bretton Woods Conference, (q.v.), to provide an inexhaustable fund of reserves, which are available to support the currency of any member country coming under speculative pressure.

Inventories. An American synonym for 'stocks'.

Investment. The term investment has a special meaning in economics, separate from that in general, financial usage. Here, investment implies expenditure of a capital kind on assets such as machinery, buildings, houses etc. It also includes changes in stocks.

Investment Trust. A company that invests its funds in a wide range of firms and industries.

Invisible Trade. Trade in services, such as banking, insurance, travel and tourism, shipping etc.

Isoquant. A curve drawn on a graph, the axes of which represent physical quantities of inputs, such as labour and capital. An isoquant represents the locus of points, each of which describes the same quantity of output produced by different combinations of inpus. The slope of an isoquant represents the marginal rate of factor substitution. A set of isoquants for the production of a given commodity is, in effect, the production function for that commodity, since it shows the various factor combinations that can be used to produce all quantities of the commodity.

Irrevocable letter of Credit. A letter of credit (q.v.) which cannot be cancelled without the permission of the exporter, in whose benefit it was issued.

J

Jobber. One of the two specialist classes of dealer on the London Stock Exchange. Jobbers act as wholesalers of shares, buying and selling according to the needs of stockbrokers (q.v.) who are acting on behalf of private investors.

K

'Kennedy Round'. A round of negotiations inspired by the late President Kennedy which increased free trade under the G.A.T.T. (General Agreement on Tariffs and Trade) system (q.v.).

L

Letter of Credit. A document in international trade which notifies an exporter that funds have been made available at a named bank to a named amount. The exporter may obtain release of the funds by complying with the letter of credit, which usually requires him to submit to the bank proof of the shipping of specified goods, which have been packed, insured and inspected in the manner specified in the letter of credit. The usual letter of credit is expressed as 'irrevocable', and it may also be 'confirmed' by a merchant banker in the exporter's own country.

Liabilities. Amounts owed by an individual, company, organisaion or government to external creditors and to the proprietors who provided the original capital.

Linear programming. A technique for solving allocation problems – the assigning of limited resources to a number of activities in order to achieve maximum effectiveness.

Liquid Assets see ASSETS.

Liquidity. The ease with which assets can be exchanged for money.

Liquidity Preference. The idea, developed by Keynes, that persons and institutions prefer to hold a portion of their assets in liquid form, that is, in cash, or a form readily convertible into cash.

Liquidity Trap. The expression used to describe a feature of the Keynsian economic system. Keynes argued that when the rate of interest is very low, the speculative demand for money becomes infinitely elastic. Liquidity preference increases sharply due to the expectation that interest rates will rise, and the price of bonds will therefore fall. In this case, no increase in the quantity of money can further depress the rate of interest. The liquidity

trap is therefore associated with the idea of under-employment equilibrium.

Liquid Ratio. Liquid assets (comprising cash in hand, credit balances at the Central Bank and money at call and short notice), as forming a percentage of the total assets of a bank.

Loanable Funds. A term used to describe the market in which the rate of interest may be determined.

Lorenz Curve. A curve used to depict the distribution of income, capital etc. The Lorenz curve for income distribution is drawn on a graph, the axes of which measure the cumulative percentage of the numbers of income recipients, and the cumulative percentage of total income received by any given percentage of income recipients.

Lump-Sum Taxes. A term that describes per capita taxes that do not vary with income.

M

Macro-Economics. The area of economic theory that concentrates on the total level of national income, employment, the general level of prices, and other aggregates.

Marginal Cost. The difference in total cost arising from the production of an additional unit of output.

Marginal Efficiency of Capital. The expected annual net returns from undertaking an additional unit of investment by a firm. The marginal efficiency of capital is the term used by Keynes to describe what is known in compound interest analysis as the internal rate of return – that is, the rate of discount which makes the present value of a series of future income streams equal to the cost of a unit of capital invest-

ment. The main difference between the marginal efficiency of capital, and the internal rate of return as stressed by Keynes, is that the former is only an expected yield, rather than an accounting one.

Marginal Firm. A firm which is on the margin of continuing in production. A marginal firm makes only 'normal' profit.

Marginal Physical Product. The addition to total product of a factor of production obtained by the employment of an additional unit of that factor, together with the fixed factors.

Marginal Product, Value of. The addition to total product of a firm due to the employment of an additional unit of a variable factor of production (i.e. marginal physical product, q.v.), multiplied by the price at which the output is sold. Under conditions of perfect competition, the value of the marginal product is equal to the marginal revenue product, because marginal revenue is equal to price.

Marginal Propensity to Consume. The change in total consumption expenditure in an economy, relative to the change in total income with which it is associated.

Marginal Propensity to Import. The change in expenditure on imports divided by the change in income with which it is associated.

Marginal Propensity to Invest. The change in investment expenditure divided by the change in national income with which it is associated.

Marginal Propensity to Save. The change in total saving associated with a change in total income in an economy.

Marginal Rate of Substitution. The amount of one commodity that must be given to a consumer in order to com-

pensate him for the loss of one unit of another commodity, while keeping his real income constant.

Marginal Revenue. The change in total revenue accruing to a firm from the sale of an additional unit of product.

Marginal Revenue Product. The addition to total revenue resulting from the sale of the extra output attributable to the employment of an additional factor of production. Marginal revenue product is marginal physical product multiplied by the marginal revenue from its sale.

Marginal Social Product. A term to describe the increase in total product accruing to the community of a unit increase in expenditure by an individual. Marginal social product should be contrasted with marginal private product, which refers to the addition to total product accruing to a private individual as a result of his expenditure on a unit of resources. The difference between marginal private product, and marginal social product, may be explained in terms of external economies and diseconomies.

Marginal Tax Rate. The net increase in taxes paid, or decrease in transfers received, by a family for each unit of currency increase in the family's earned income.

Marginal Utility. The change in total utility enjoyed by a consumer as a result of an additional unit increase in consumption of a commodity.

Market. The term used in economics to describe a state of affairs where buyers and sellers are in touch with each other to fix prices.

Maturity date. The date on which the principal value of a bond,

loan, or savings certificate, will be repaid to the lender.

Mercantilist policies. Governmental measure aimed at maintaining an excess of exports over imports.

Micro-Economics. The area of economics where attention is concentrated on the allocation of resources and the movement of relative prices, rather than on aggregate economic behaviour. (See Macro Economics.)

Minimum Lending Rate. Term introduced in Britain in 1971, to describe the interest rate at which the Bank of England is prepared to lend to the banking system; prior to 1971 this interest rate was called the bank rate.

Minimum Reserve Ratio. The ratio which banks in the United Kingdom must maintain between eligible reserve assets and eligible liabilities. This was fixed at 12½ per cent in 1971. It means that one eighth of all funds must be kept in cash or other liquid assets to meet possible withdrawals by customers.

Mixed Economy. An economy in which commercial interests and the state combine to regulate economic affairs.

Model. A set of economic assumptions about behavioural relationships in an economy, within which it is possible to deduce the results of certain economic events. Occasionally, the word 'model' is used in economics to describe a hypothesis of the factor or factors that determine one particular aspect of economic behaviour.

Monetarists. Economists who believe that movements in the money supply are the primary causes of 'booms' and 'recessions' in business activity. To

control the economy they advocate firm control of the money supply.

Monetary Policy. Policy measures operated by governments, mainly through the central banks, to influence the level of aggregate demand through changes in the quantity of money and/or the level of interest rates.

Money. Any liquid asset. A financial asset which is declared 'legal tender' for the settlement of debts.

Money at Call and Short Notice. Assets of commercial banks which consist of loans made on very short term to financial institutions such as discount houses, who guarantee to repay it at call, or within a few days. Such assets are allowed to count as eligible reserve assets for the Minimum Reserve Ratio (q.v.).

Money illusion. Description of people's behaviour when treating money values as if they represented real values.

Money supply. The 'money' available in the economy. Various definitions exist, of which the following are the most important: M1 Notes, coins and current account (cheque account) moneys. M3 As in M1, plus deposit accounts, in home and overseas currencies. Sterling M3 As in M3, but omitting the overseas currencies on deposit.

D.C.E. (Domestic Credit Expansion) The I.M.F.'s favourite measure of money supply. It measures the change in money supply in the year, but only as it affects domestic credit. It makes it very difficult to mislead the I.M.F. when this measure is used.

Monopolistic Competition. *A market situation in which a large number of sellers market a similar product under different brand names.*

Monopoly. *A market situation in which a single firm controls the entire output of an industry, whose product has no close substitutes.*

Monopoly Power. *A seller's power to raise the price of a product without losing his customers, because his product is both unique, and in high demand.*

Monopsony. *A market situation in which there is only a single buyer for a particular product.*

Multinational Corporation. *Firm producing goods in a number of countries.*

Multiplier. *A term used in macro economics to describe the co-efficient by which a change in autonomous expenditure must be multiplied in order to find the change in total income. More often used is the term, 'investment multiplier,' which defines the change in income divided by the change in investment expenditure.*

N

National debt. *The total outstanding borrowings of a government, which may be owed to the private sector, central banks, or lenders from overseas.*

National Income. *The money value of all goods and services produced in an economy during a given period plus the net income received from exports.*

National Product. *The national income.*

Natural Monopoly. *A firm which enjoys a monopolistic position because its marginal costs of production cover the entire range of output as limited by* demand. *The presence of high fixed capital costs of production is generally responsible for the existence of a natural monopoly.*

'Near' Money (Quasi Money). *Assets that are not liquid, but can be used for settlements of debts, for example, a bill of exchange (q.v.).*

Negative (Reverse) Income Tax. *A system in which people with particularly low incomes would automatically receive a payment from the government.*

Negotiable certificates of deposit see *CERTIFICATES OF DEPOSIT.*

Net investment. *Gross private investment, minus expenditure to cover replacement costs of worn out machinery or obsolete plant.*

Net National Product. *The national product or income, after making allowance for capital consumption and depreciation of national assets.*

Net present value. *The present value of outlays less income, calculated by discounting at a given rate of interest.*

Net Worth. *The value of a business according to the balance sheet. That is, the total value minus external liabilities.*

Nominal Value. *In Stock Exchange terms, the face value of a share, which may be greater or less than its market price.*

Non-recourse finance. *Finance arranged by a finance company or merchant bank on such terms that, if the debtor does not pay, the financier has no recourse to the client who received the money, and will have to seek indemnity from a third party.*

Normal Goods. *The demand for such goods remains constant as incomes rise. The term* 'inferior goods,' (q.v.), is *used in contrast.*

Normal Profit. *The minimum rate of profit that a firm must earn in order to continue its operations in a particular industry.*

Normative Economics. *Propositions made with regard to economic policy which cannot, in principle, be settled by appeal to the facts. Normative statements involve the making of moral value judgements in such matters as unemployment or inflation. These are usually judgements contrasted with statements of positive economics.*

O

Oligopoly. *A market situation in which there are a small number of firms, each of which is large enough to influence market price by changing its output. The analysis of oligopolistic situations involves taking the reactions of each firm to the policies of its rivals into account.*

Open Market Operations. *A technique of monetary policy involving the purchase or sale of government securities by the central bank on the open market, in order to control the stock of money in circulation. Purchases of securities by the bank involve increases in the quantity of money, which goes into the current accounts of customers, so raising the amount of money in circulation. On the other hand, sales of securities by the bank reduces the supply of money.*

Opportunity Cost. *The cost of doing something as measured by the loss of the opportunity to follow an alternative course of action.*

Optimum. *A term used to describe the best possible situation from an economic point of* view. *The optimum factor combination is the combination of factors of production that minimise the cost of producing a given output, while optimum output is the output that maximises profit. Optimum allocation of resources describes the best distribution of resources to ensure the maximisation of economic welfare.*

P

Par Value. *Nominal price at which shares or securities are issued.*

Paradox of Value. *The apparent paradox of the price of necessities – such as water – being lower than the price of luxuries – say, diamonds. The paradox is suggested by price being used as a measure of value for utility. Price, however, measures value only at the margin. The total utility of water may indeed be greater than the total utility of diamonds; but the marginal utility of water may be less than that of diamonds.*

Pareto Optimum. *A situation that exists when no single member of the economy can move to a preferred position without making someone else worse off – a theory first advanced by the Italian economist, V. F. D. Pareto (1848-1923).*

Payback Period. *The time it takes an investment to generate sufficient net income to repay the additional capital and other outlay involved.*

Pay-off Matrix. *A table or matrix used in the theory of games, and the analysis of oligopoly. The results of the adoption of all possible combinations of strategies by all participants in the game (oligopolists) are included in tabular form.*

Pegging. *System whereby changes in an* exchange rate are not taking place at once, but are spread instead over a number of months.*

Perfect Competition. *A set of assumptions describing a market in which no firm has any influence over market price. Such a situation can follow more than one set of assumptions, the most common of which is the existence of a large number of firms selling a similar product. Free entry and exit to and from the industry, and perfect knowledge of prices ruling in all parts of the market, are assumptions which are sometimes included in the model of a perfect competition. They imply that the representative firm is making only normal profit, and that only a single price can obtain in the market.*

Perfect Market. *A market situation where perfect competition is assumed to exist.*

Perfectly Elastic Demand. *When the elasticity of demand for a commodity is infinite. that is, when a small change in price causes an infinitely large increase or decrease in demand, then that demand is said to be perfectly elastic. The demand curve facing an individual firm under perfect competition would be perfectly elastic.*

Perfectly Elastic Supply. *The situation which obtains when a small change in the price of a product calls for an infinitely large increase or decrease in supply. Perfectly elastic supply curves are horizontal straight lines which indicate that firms have constant costs of production.*

Permanent Income Hypothesis. *A theory attributed to Friedman and others, that changes in aggregate consumption expendi-* ture can be explained by changes in the permanent income that individuals receive.*

Phillips' Curve. *A curve on a graph which shows the relationship between the rate of change of prices and wages, and the level of unemployment.*

Ploughing Back. *Retention of profits to finance expansion.*

Poll tax. *A tax levied per head of the population irrespective of income. Since everyone pays the same, it falls most heavily upon the very poor.*

Portfolio. *Collection of securities owned by a person or financial institution.*

Positive Economics. *Statements in economics which do not involve value judgments but may, in principle, be tested against the facts.*

Precautionary Demand for Money. *The desire to hold a proportion of assets in cash form as a precaution against unforeseen circumstances.*

Premium on Shares. *Payment above the nominal (par) value of shares, by those wishing to obtain a shareholding.*

Present Value. *The equivalent value today of a future sum of money, as calculated by the discount formula.*

Price Discrimination. *A situation in which different prices charged for the same commodity, do not reflect supply cost differences.*

Price/earnings Ratio. *The ratio of the price paid for a share in the profits of a firm, after paying Corporation Tax and Preference Share dividend. It informs the investor of the true return on his investment, though it may not all be returned to him as dividend. The amount returned depends on the policy of* the directors. Any extra will be kept in reserve, and used as capital appreciation.

Producers' Surplus. A synonym for economic rent, as applied to a firm, rather than as a factor of production.

Product Differentiation. Action taken by a manufacturer to create goodwill for his product by giving it a unique image in the minds of the consumers.

Production Function. A description of the alternative ways in which the output of a particular commodity by a firm can be produced; the relationship between inputs and outputs which are often expressed in mathematical form.

Production Possibility Frontier. A curve showing the possible combinations of goods that can be produced by an economy with a given endowment of factors of production, given full and efficient utilisation of all such factors.

Profit. The reward of enterprise. The difference between total costs and total revenues of an organisation.

Profit-Push Inflation. A variety of cost-push inflation in which a spontaneous increase in profit margins leads to price increases.

Progressive Tax. A tax that takes a progressively large percentage of income from people whose incomes are high.

Protectionism. A policy of shielding domestic industries from foreign competition.

Public Goods. Commodities consumed collectively by the community as a whole, and impossible to withhold from a single individual; national defence, for example.

Purchasing power parity theory. A theory that holds that the rate of exchange between

currencies will be such as to enable the purchasing power of the money to remain the same.

Q
Quantity Theory of Money. A theory which relates the quantity of money to the general price level. A simple form of the theory can be expressed in the equation MV=TP where M stands for the quantity of money, V for the velocity of circulation, T for the total number of transactions, and P for the average general price level. If T and V are constant, the price level varies directly with the quantity of money.

Quasi-rent. A factor of production, such as a machine, which earns economic rent in the short run only, is said to receive quasi-rent.

Quotation. The price range fixed daily by the Stock Exchange within which dealers are prepared to trade shares. Such quotations are published daily in the press.

R
Real Cost. A synonym for opportunity cost.

Real Income. Income changes in money terms over time as a result of two forces; changes in price level and changes in volume of output. The latter is termed real income, and changes in income due to price movements may be removed statistically by use of price index numbers, to leave a residual estimate of real income.

Real Values. Measurements of economic values that include adjustments for changes in prices between one year and another.

Redemption. Repayment of a loan or other liability.

Reflation. An expan-

sion of aggregate demand after a period of high unemployment or decelerating inflation.

Re-funding. An exchange in which new government securities are offered to owners of maturing government securities.

Regressive Tax. A tax that takes a larger proportion of income from people whose income is low.

Resale Price Maintenance (RPM). A practice whereby sellers of a product are precluded from varying the price at which they can resell.

Reserve currency. A currency which organisations and governments are prepared to hold as part of their foreign exchange reserves, and which can be used to finance international transactions.

Returns to Scale. The relation between output and input factors in a firm when all factors of production can be varied, and the proportion in which they are used is held constant. Returns to scale may be increasing, constant or decreasing, depending upon whether output rises more than, proportional to, or less than proportionately to, increases in factor inputs.

Revaluation. A rise in the price of currency expressed in terms of other currencies.

Revealed Preference. The notion that a consumer reveals his preference for particular goods, or combination of goods, in the market by purchasing them. Should any change in price or income occur, it can be expected that the changes of demand he makes will be in accordance with the preferences which he has revealed through purchase.

Revenue Reserve. A reserve made up of past profits which have been retained in the business, but not used to increase capital assets. They may therefore be available, perhaps as an investment portfolio, for use as dividends in a future year when profits may have dropped.

Rights Issue. An issue of shares, as of right, to existing shareholders. This capitalises reserves of profit retained in the business which have been used in development by creating fixed assets. They are therefore not available for dividends in the future (see REVENUE RESERVES) but have become permanent capital.

S
Satisficing. An alternative assumption to that of profit maximisation for a firm, according to which the business goal is the achievement of a minimum satisfactory level of profit.

Savings. Any income that is not spent on consumption is, by definition, saved.

Seigniorage. The profit that a country makes on its currency. It is the difference between the nominal value of the currency and its cost production.

Self financing. A policy of financing future growth of a business by using the profits made, instead of distributing them to shareholders. This means that external debts and overdrafts can be avoided, but dividends must be reduced to a lower level than would otherwise be possible.

Social Cost. Those costs which are imposed upon society as a whole, as a result of expenditure on goods and services by a person or institution. Social costs, as conventionally defined, include the

costs which accrue to the person or institution making the expenditure, as well as the additional costs not reflected in the accounts which accrue to the rest of the community.

Social Welfare function. A function showing the relative preference of society as a whole for various combinations of resource allocations and income distributions. The welfare ordering of such combinations involves the making of value judgements.

Special Deposits. One of the weapons of monetary policy in the armoury of the Bank of England. The Bank may require the commercial banks to deposit sums of money in a special account at the Bank of England, usually in proportion to their total deposits. Such deposits are blocked and cannot be used as a base for credit expansion. Additions to, or subtractions from, special deposits may be used as part of a policy for deflation or reflation.

Special Drawing Rights. A currency basket (q.v.), unit of account sponsored by the International Monetary Fund which is based on the 16 most important world currencies. It is used in international trade, and by the Fund, as a basic unit for calculating and managing reserves for the settlement of international indebtedness.

Speculation. Interference in a market to achieve profits. Speculation is not necessarily bad – on the contrary, it is the only way the general public can be sure that the market operates efficiently. If the speculator were not present, to buy when others are selling and sell when others are buying, it would not always be possible for

those with disposable assets to sell them, nor, for those with money available, to buy them.

Speculative Demand for Money. A part of liquidity preference. The tendency of certain financial speculators to hold, or not to hold, their financial assets in the form of cash, rather than bonds, depending on whether they expect the rate of interest to fall. If the rate of interest is expected to fall, the capital value of fixed interest bonds will automatically rise, and the speculative demand for money will be low, since speculators prefer to hold bonds rather than money.

Stag. A speculator who applies for shares with a view to re-selling any shares allotted to him, after the date of issue, at a profit.

Stocks and Flows. A stock is a variable measured at a specific point in time (e.g. a balance sheet item); a flow is a variable which can only be measured in relation to a period of time (e.g. income).

Structural Unemployment. Unemployment resulting from long term changes in demand or technology, in an economy.

Structuralist theory of inflation. Connects inflation with economic growth, combined with supply inelasticities (usually of food and imports).

Substitution Effect. That part of the effect on quantity of a commodity demanded, due to a change in price which can be ascribed solely to the change in relative prices, assuming that real income is held constant. The income effect, and the substitution effect, of a change in price together make up the price effect.

Super-normal Profits. Profits greater than normal, accrued by a firm that is not a marginal firm in an industry.

Supply Curve. A graphical representation of the quantities that sellers are prepared to offer for the sale of a commodity over each of a range of prices during a particular period of time.

Supply price. The market price necessary to call forth a given quantity of output.

Supply Schedule. A tabular representation of material that shows the relationship between quantities, which sellers are prepared to offer for sale, at each of the range of prices on which a supply curve may be used.

Surplus, economic. A term occasionally used as a synonym for economic rent, (q.v.).

Swap arrangements. Government arrangements to obtain foreign currencies on call through the Bank for International Settlements.

T

Tariff. A tax levied on imported goods.

Tenders. A system of offering shares and other securities that enables the buyer to make a bid for the security. Thus, a person more anxious than others to obtain an allotment, will offer a higher price, so enabling the organisation to benefit from a premium on shares, or from a more favourable rate of interest on loans (see Treasury Bills),

Terms of Trade. The ratio of the change in the price of exports to the price of imports, over a given period of

time.

Time Deposits. Interest-bearing bank deposits. These include savings deposits, savings certificates , and certificates of deposit.

Time Preference, Rate of. An expression that denotes the rate at which an individual is prepared to forego present consumption, in return for consumption in the future.

Total Revenue. Price multiplied by number of units sold.

Trade Cycles. Changes in the level of economic activity – alternating phases of rising and falling business activity.

Trade-Off. A term used almost synonymously with opportunity costs,(see COSTS) to indicate the cost of pursuing a particular economic policy in terms of the benefits which accrue from it.

Transactions costs. The costs of shifting from one type of asset to another, or to money.

Transactions demand for Money. The desire by persons and institutions to hold a part of their assets in the form of cash, in order to pay

transactions.
their current

Transfer earnings. The difference between the earnings of a Factor of Production in its current occupation, and the earnings it could obtain in its next most profitable activity.

Transfer payments. Payments made by

government to individuals or institutions which do not directly involve the State in any use of scarce

Transformation Curve. A line or curve on a graph, the axes of which represent physical quantities of two goods or services, and depicting all the efficient combinations of goods that the economy can produce. Also known as a Production Possibility curve, or as an opportunity cost curve. The slope of the transformation curve at any point, measures the ratio of the marginal costs of production of the two goods.

Transmission Mechanism. The way in which monetary policy exerts an impact on an economy.

Treasury bills. These are offered every Friday by the U.K. Treasury to investors prepared to lend money on short term. The tenor of the bill is 91 days, and the investor tenders the price he is prepared to pay per cent. Thus, a tender for 98.15 on a £10,000 bill means that the investor will lend the Treasury £9,815 for 3 months, receiving £10,000 on maturity – an interest gain of 7 54 per cent.

Two-part Tariff. A form of discriminatory pricing policy adopted, in particular, by some public utilities in order to cover fixed costs, and at the same time to charge marginal costs for additional units of its products.

Two Tier System
Description of the market for US gold operated after 1968, with an official (controlled) gold price for transactions between governments and a market (free) price for all other gold transactions.

U

U-Shaped Cost Curve. The graphical representation of the tendency for average costs of production to decline up to a point, and then to increase.

Under-employment Equilibrium. A level of national income in a Keynesian model, which is at an equilibrium level in the sense that there are no economic forces tending to change it, but at which there is less than full employment. An explanation of the persistence of under-employment equilibrium is related to the liquidity trap (q.v.).

Unemployment rate. The percentage of the labour force not in employment.

Unit of account. See Currency Basket.

Unit Trusts. An organisation that raises money from small investors, and invests these funds in a large number of securities with the aim of reducing the risk for the small investors, who thus get the benefit of a balanced portfolio of shares.

Utility. The economist's term for the pleasure and satisfaction we get from the consumption of material goods and services.

V

Value Added. The total revenue of a firm, less the value of inputs of materials and services purchased from other firms.

Value Added Tax. A system of tax raised upon the total sales of a firm (output tax) but which is reduced by the tax paid on the purchases of goods and services (input tax). The effect is that the trader collects tax on his 'value added', for which he is accountable to the revenue authorities.

Variable Inputs. Those inputs whose quantities are varied with short-run changes of output.

Veil of Money. Description of thinking in money terms, rather than in term of real values. Also used to describe the way in which the money system obscures what is happening in the exchange between groups of surplus values created in their productive activities.

Velocity of Circulation. The average number of times that a unit of money changes hands over a given period of time.

Vertical Integration. Mergers between firms, one of which is a supplier or customer of the other.

W

Wage Drift. The tendency of wages to drift upwards from planned levels, because of the difference between the progress, over time, of wage rates and that of net weekly earnings.

Wage drift may be attributed, in particular, to overtime earnings and to the departure by individual firms from nationally agreed wage rates.

Wage-Push Inflation. A variety of cost-push inflation, in which a spontaneous increase in nominal wage rates leads to price increases.

Welfare Economics. Branch of economics concerned with the study of the 'efficiency' of an economic system.

Wholesale Price Index. A price index based on a sample of goods purchased in large quantities in transactions between firms.

Window Dressing. The pre-World War II practice of the joint stock banks to make up their weekly accounts on different days of the week, to give the impression that the assets (especially cash) of each bank were higher than was actually the case.

Withdrawals. The opposite of injections, (q.v.). A term in macro economics used to describe reductions from the flows of expenditure other than those on consumption. Savings, imports and direct taxation are withdrawals.

World Bank. See International Bank.

Y

Yield. Income from securities (shares, bonds, etc.) expressed as a percentage of their current market price.

INDEX

Index

ACKNOWLEDGMENTS

Page 8 Camera Press; **12** Pitt Rivers Museum; **13** Chase Manhattan Archives, Pitt Rivers Museum; **14** British Museum, Chase Manhattan Archives; **15** British Museum, Chase Manhattan Archives; **16–17** Chase Manhattan Archives; **18** Mansell Collection; **19** Mary Evans; **21** Chase Manhattan; **22** Pitt Rivers Museum, Keystone; **23** Popperfoto; **24** Alastair Campbell; **25** Chase Manhattan Archives, Alastair Campbell; **26–27** Institute of Bankers; **28** Walter Rawlings, British Museum; **29** Anne-Marie Erhlich, Kobal; **30–31** Popperfoto; **32** Anglo-American Corporation of South Africa; **33** Camera Press; **34** Walter Rawlings; **35** David Mallott; **36** ZEFA, David Williamson; **37** ZEFA, Popperfoto; **38** Camera Press; **39** Press Association; **40** ZEFA, Roger Pring/QED; **41** Roger Pring/QED; **42** Roger Pring, Camera Press; **43** Margaret Murray, Popperfoto; **44** David Williamson; **45** Tony Stone; **46** Walter Rawlings; **49** Kirkaldy Museum, Popperfoto; **52–53** Picturepoint; **55** Popperfoto; **56** Alan Hutchison; **57** Keystone, Syndication International; **58** Mansell Collection; **61** American Picture Library; **62** Alan Hutchison; **63** Mander and Mitchenson Theatre Collection; **64** Bildarchiv; **65** Mansell Collection; **66** UML Ltd.; **67** Mansell Collection; **68** Mansell Collection; **72** Novosti; **73** Society for Cultural Relations with USSR; **74** Kramarz; **77** Picturepoint; **79** Richard and Sally Greenhill, Picturepoint; **80** Margaret Murray; **84** David Williamson; **85** Alastair Campbell/QED; **86** Bavaria Verlag; **88** Richard and Sally Greenhill; **89** J. Allan Cash; **90** David Mallott/QED; **92** Alastair Campbell/QED; **94** Alan Hutchison; **95** Alan Hutchison, Walter Rawlings, J. Allan Cash; **96–99** Alan Hutchison; **100** Roger Pring; **102** Margaret Murray, K. Pradel, Camera Press; **103** Walter Rawlings, Clive Sawyer, Roger Pring/QED; **104** Studio Benser; **105** Paolo Koch, Popperfoto; **106** Jon Wyand; **107** Picturepoint; **108–109** Jon Wyand; **110** Popperfoto; **113** Keystone; **114** The Bank of England; **116** Alan Hutchison, Picturepoint; **118** Anne-Marie Erhlich; **120** Peter Grunert; **122–123** Richard and Sally Greenhill; **125** Robert Harding Associates; **128** Hulton Picture Library; **131** New Statesman and Nation; **132** The Bettmann Archives, American History Picture Library; **133** Mansell Collection, Anne-Marie Erhlich, Photo Research International; **134** Popperfoto, Tennessee Valley Authority; **135** Keystone; **136** Popperfoto; **138** ZEFA, Mander and Mitchenson Theatre Collection, Popperfoto, Hans Tasiemka; **140–141** Mansell Collection; **143** Photo Research International; **144** Anne-Marie Erhlich, Mary Evans Picture Library, Keystone; **146** Servizio Editoriale Fotografico; **148** Popperfoto; **149** Hulton Picture Library; **150–151** Keystone; **155** International Monetary Fund; **158** Keystone; **160** Chris Osborne; **161** J. Allan Cash, Keystone, Popperfoto; **162** ZEFA; **164** Rosmarie Pierer; **165** Camera Press; **166** Barnaby's **167** Picturepoint; **168** Popperfoto; **170** Picturepoint, Robert Harding Associates; **172** ZEFA